D1601151

Crusade
Against Radicalism

KENNIKAT PRESS

NATIONAL UNIVERSITY PUBLICATIONS

SERIES IN AMERICAN STUDIES

General Editor
JAMES P. SHENTON
Professor of History, Columbia University

Julian F. Jaffe

Crusade
Against Radicalism

NEW YORK DURING THE RED SCARE,
1914-1924

National University Publications

KENNIKAT PRESS

Port Washington, N.Y./London/1972

Library of Congress Catalog Card No.: 75-189556
ISBN: 0-8046-9026-X

Manufactured in the United States of America

Published by
Kennikat Press, Inc.
Port Washington, N.Y./London

To Miriam and Bill

PREFACE

The events described in this history deal with a period which most Americans would prefer to forget. The era was hardly one of consensus; rather, it was a time of confrontation and strife, marked by changing values, as the nation attempted to recover from wounds inflicted by the World War and to adjust to the years of peace.

Searching my memory, I am hard pressed to account for the fascination which this period holds for me. Perhaps my interest began in the 1950's when, as a young college student, a favorite professor was dismissed from his position for alleged radical affiliations. The college administrators did not consider the fact that he was an excellent teacher and that his membership in the group in question had been severed years before. The case went to the courts and after many years of appeal the professor's right to employment was vindicated.

The incident sparked my interest in the Red Scare and while this book describes a time earlier than that involving my former teacher, the similarity between the two is striking.

Surprisingly, standard textbooks and even popular literature have paid little attention to the Red Scare which followed World War I. Fortunately, a number of serious scholars, among them Robert K. Murray and Stanley Coben, have written works which have analyzed these events from a national viewpoint. Here, no attempt is made to repeat their scholarship. Instead, this book seeks to develop perspective on the scare as it unfolded in a single but significant, industrial state. In this way important elements can be discussed in greater detail than would be possible in a more broadly based study.

While I am solely responsible for all of the facts and interpretations presented here, I would like to acknowledge the assistance of a number of people who helped in its preparation. These include Mrs. Dorothy Swanson, curator of the Tamiment Institute Library, New York; Donald S. Mosholder and Mark G. Eckhoff at the National Archives, Washington, and other librarians at the Library of Congress, New York Public Library, Library of the Bar Association of New York, Municipal Archives and Records Center, and the New York University Library.

Grateful acknowledgment is also made to the faculty of the Graduate History Department, New York University, especially to Professors Vincent P. Carosso, Henry Bamford Parkes, Albert U. Romasco, Bayrd Still, and Irwin Unger, and to Cornell Jaray, of Kennikat Press. Also to my typists, Mrs. Frances Cohen and Miss Augusta Jane Keating, my wife, Miriam, and my son, Bill, both of whom were extremely helpful and patient while the manuscript was being completed.

J.F.J.

New York, 1972.

CONTENTS

Crusade
Against Radicalism

INTRODUCTION

During the years 1919–1920 the American people went through a political experience known as the Red Scare. At this time all left wing political activity was highly suspect and was regarded by many as opposed to the best interests of the United States. Many leftists were jailed after a series of spectacular raids on their headquarters. Others were deported from the country.[1]

The Red Scare was largely the result of wartime developments. The federal government set the pace and demanded absolute loyalty from all segments of the population. Many private agencies, the National Security League, the American Defense Society, and the American Protective League, cooperated with the government and enlisted thousands of Americans as unofficial agents and "spy catchers" to help guard against subversion. They put pressure on the American people to accept a high degree of political conformity. At the same time they waged a campaign against political radicals, pacifists, and those liberals whose opinions fell short of their standards of patriotism. They were most concerned with those holding antiwar views, but their interest soon broadened to include radical opinions only peripherally related to the issue of the war. Governments at the state and local levels cooperated in the suppression of antiwar opinion and thus helped to contribute to the postwar hysteria.

While many groups were affected by the wartime demand for loyalty, the political radicals offered the most prominent target. Their constant propaganda against preparedness, and later, against America's entrance into the war seemed to many the equivalent of treason. After the war they were regarded with even greater suspicion.

Who were these political radicals? By the year 1914 two organizations, the Socialist party and the Industrial Workers of the

1

World, dominated the American left. Of the two the Socialist party was larger and more important. It was an evolutionary, Marxist political party whose leaders hoped to achieve socialism through education and political activity. Since its founding in 1901 the Socialist party had campaigned vigorously to increase its membership, elect its people to office, and to "convert" the American people to socialism. By 1912 it had increased its national vote to nine hundred thousand and had achieved considerable electoral success. Throughout the nation, there were fifty-six Socialist mayors, over three hundred aldermen, a number of state legislators, and one congressman. The American people tolerated the Socialist party, at least until 1917.

The First World War halted the forward movement of the Socialist party. This began in 1914, when the Socialists spoke out against the war as a struggle between the capitalist powers. Soon after America entered the fighting the party met in emergency convention at St. Louis where, despite the opposition of a small pro-war group, it adopted a declaration which denounced American intervention and pledged "continuous, active, and public opposition to the war through demonstrations, mass petitions, and all other means within our power." This St. Louis declaration split the party. Many leaders and a good part of the membership abandoned its ranks and gave their support to Woodrow Wilson. Other Socialists remained in the party but challenged the official antiwar stand.

Led by the superpatriots, the press, and many politicians, the public became angered at the Socialists' apparent lack of patriotism. Soon, mobs of citizens and soldiers were raiding Socialist meetings and subjecting its speakers to physical assaults. Some Socialists were jailed by the federal government for violating the Conscription Act and, later, for their opposition to the Espionage and Sedition Acts. In addition, radical publications were barred from the mails.

The Industrial Workers of the World, the second most important radical organization (also called 'Wobblies"), was a loosely knit group of anarcho-syndicalists who had made some inroads in organizing miners, lumber men, and those employed in the textile industry. Their appeal was greatest among the most alienated workers. They carried out a number of spectacular strikes and preached a doctrine of revolutionary activism as the immediate solution to economic difficulties. But their rhetoric was always greater than their accomplishments and at no time were they a serious threat to the institutions of the country.

Like the Socialists, the Wobblies opposed the war as an instrument of "capitalist oppression" and campaigned against it. Because of their activities in certain mines and lumber camps they were accused of obstructing the war effort and subjected to the severest penalties. Their headquarters and halls were raided while some Wobblies were publicly whipped, tarred and feathered. These raids were either carried out by mobs or were officially sponsored by state and local governments. The campaign against the IWW culminated in a nationwide raid in September 1917 in which most of their top leaders were sent to jail.

Of course the Socialists and the IWW were not alone in expressing antiwar sentiments. They were joined by a varied assortment of pacifists, liberals and some clergymen. These groups were in opposition for different reasons, but as the war progressed the public made little attempt to distinguish between them. Stirred up by rightest elements, many began to believe that any opposition was disloyal regardless of its motivation. Soon, the net widened to encompass immigrants and aliens, who were also suspected of harboring disloyal feelings. These memories lingered after the war, setting the stage for a second and far more important Red Scare.

Peace came to America in November 1918. The people greeted the Armistice with relief and hoped to return to a period of normalcy. This would come, but not before a series of economic and political disturbances intervened to make this desire more a dream than a reality. Inflation was the first and most persistent of the postwar problems and, incidentally, the cause of considerable discontent. By late 1919 the purchasing power of the dollar was shrinking. The cost of most items, including food, clothing, and furniture, was rising. For the average family the cost of living was about double what it had been five years before. The hardest hit were public employees, laborers, white collar workers, and those living on fixed incomes. The chief result of the inflation was that it set off a whole series of labor disturbances which kept the nation in a state of anxiety.

All told there were 3,600 strikes in 1919, involving more than four million workers.[2] Among the most important were those in the coal fields, the steel industry and the garment trades. While low wages and poor working conditions were usually the issues in dispute, the strikes reflected deeper and more far-reaching ambitions on the part of the working man. These had their origins during the formative years of the American Federation of Labor; they were reinforced during the war when, in return for labor's cooperation in preventing strikes, the Federation was elevated to a position of importance in the Wilson administration. Along with management, the AFL became a partner of the government in organizing for war.

To the labor movement, the new partnership represented the culmination of years of organizing and the fruit of the progressive movement through which they had secured such needed reforms as the Clayton and Adamson Acts. When the war ended, the unions intended to maintain their newly-acquired position and to surpass it if possible. They had no intention of returning to a second-class status in their relationships with the industrial giants. At the same time, the AFL was under pressure from its rank-and-file to combat the dangerous spiral of inflation which threatened to wipe out its wartime gains.

Management, too, emerged from the war with a set of demands. For many employers a return to "normalcy" meant a return to the privileged position they had previously enjoyed. While they were willing to grant modest wage increases they had no intention of recognizing the labor movement as an equal partner. Their attitude was summarized by Robert K. Murray: "Capitalizing on postwar confusion and reaction, [the industrialists] fought with every means at [their] disposal to undermine organized labor's position and stamp out economic liberalism wherever it existed."[3] Employers equated the open shop with the "American Way" and began to regard the more militant labor leaders as "radical agitators" who intended to transform the economic system along collectivist lines.

Obviously not all industrialists shared this extreme view. For many employers the relationship with the more conservative unions was harmonious. Many industrialists had a high regard for Samuel Gompers because he had successfully defeated radical attempts to take over the leadership of the Federation. But there were a small number of unions and union leaders who had left wing affiliations, and this lent credence to the allegation that the entire labor movement was tinged with radicalism.

The Republican Congress was also partly responsible for the problems faced by the nation in the postwar period. It made no serious attempt to arbitrate the strained relations between capital and labor, and spent more time defeating the League of Nations and investigating the "Bolshevik threat" than trying to cure the nation's economic ills.

Still another development of concern to the American people and contributing to the growing antiradicalism was the forward thrust of Russian Bolshevism. Since the successful revolution carried out by Lenin and Trotsky in November 1917, many Americans had followed Soviet developments with dismay. They saw that communism was gaining adherents and making impressive gains in Eastern Europe, especially in Germany and Hungary. In March 1919, the Third International, or Comintern, was organized; its avowed purpose was to stimulate a worldwide proletarian revolution.

With news of labor disturbances filling the headlines, with Bolshevism making progress in Europe, and with the memories of the antiwar stand of the Left still fresh in their memories, many people listened to predictions that America itself was ripe for revolution. This fear was whipped to hysterical proportions by the press, by some politicians seeking higher office, and by some segments of the conservative business community. Soon others joined them, and the Red Scare of the postwar period was on. The nation embarked on a frightening episode of trying to enforce patriotism through conformity of opinion.

While these factors were most important in precipitating the Red Scare, a full understanding of the problem requires the addition of a number of other ingredients. To historian John Higham, the Red Scare was, in part, an attempt to fill a psychological void created by the ending of the war.[4] Despite its hardships the struggle did provide psychic gratifications for many Americans. In the common resistance to a foreign foe, this nation of immigrants discovered a new sense of unity which tended to disappear once peace was established. Consequently, the public cast about for a new scapegoat; this it found in the "radical agitator" who served as a replacement for the hated "Hun." The agitator provided a new outlet for national energies and permitted the nation to feel unified once again.

Changing immigration patterns must also be considered. Until the war stopped the flow, immigrants had been coming to these shores in ever increasing numbers. This "new immigration" of the twentieth century drew heavily from Southern and Eastern

Europe. To many, the new arrivals seemed less capable of assimilation into the mainstream of American life. They huddled in large ethnic ghettoes where they lived in poverty, recreating the patterns of life left behind in the Old World. Few of the older Americans welcomed the new arrivals. They were held responsible for all that was wrong with America, from corrupt political machines to urban decay. Congress soon responded to pressures for control of immigration with the literacy test and the Dillingham Report which probed all aspects of the problem.

The "new immigration" contributed to the Red Scare by helping to create the stereotype of the immigrant as an economic radical. This view which had been developing throughout the latter part of the nineteenth century gained strength when President McKinley was assassinated by a Polish-American, Leon Czolgosz. It was reinforced by the success of the IWW in organizing immigrant workers and, later, by the numerous foreign language federations created by the Socialist party. Because both major radical groups had adopted antiwar positions, many Americans were only too willing to believe that most immigrants were intrinsically radical and potentially violent.

The postwar Red Scare was also encouraged by nativist feelings harbored by many Americans. Nativism, or fear of foreigners, began early in the nineteenth century. It gained stature as a result of the "new immigration" when the newcomer was perceived as an economic threat as well as a carrier of radical ideas. All social classes were affected by these antiforeign attitudes. Those on the lowest economic rung felt that the immigrants would take away their jobs. The middle classes shared the belief that the immigrants were a threat to established Protestant, Anglo-Saxon traditions, while the upper classes feared any growth of Socialist ideas thought to be common among the foreign-born and used the immigrants, to some extent, as whipping boys to absorb a good deal of public frustration. Even the labor movement shared the xenophobic feelings of the masses and opposed further immigration as a danger to job security. As a result of all of these factors, the American people were highly susceptible to the antiradical crusade.

The events of the national Red Scare are familiar and only a few facts are necessary to indicate the general trend. For example, at a Victory Loan pageant in the District of Columbia, a man was shot to death by an enraged sailor for refusing to rise during the playing of the "Star Spangled Banner." In Hammond, Indiana, a jury took two minutes to decide to acquit the assassin of an alien who had yelled, "To hell with the United States." Early in 1920 a clothing salesman in Waterbury, Connecticut, was sentenced to six months in jail for having remarked to a customer that Lenin was the "brainiest" or "one of the brainiest" of the world's political leaders.

Incidents such as these were not daily occurrences throughout the United States. They came at various times but seemed to proliferate during periods of stress, such as the annual May Day celebration. The government also played a part which included the famous Palmer raids on radical headquarters, and the deportations of many aliens.

But it is not national events that are the main concern here. Instead, this study seeks to explore those aspects of the Red Scare which took place within the state of New York. It covers a ten year period from 1914 to 1924. After a preliminary discussion of radical groups in New York, the study continues with an analysis of antiradical activities during wartime. Subsequent chapters deal with the postwar period and include a discussion of developments on the municipal and state levels, as well as those aspects of the national picture which relate specifically to New York.

This study raises a number of interesting historical questions. In what way was the Red Scare in New York similar or dissimilar to the national movement? How were state and local governments involved? Were the political leaders of the day actually leading the antiradical crusade, or were they merely responding to pressure exerted upon them?

Why was the hysteria extended into the schools? What role was played by the Lusk Committee and by the Judiciary Committee of the state legislature in the expulsion of its Socialist members? How did the radicals fare in the courts? Finally, why did the Red Scare decline suddenly in most places but last longer in New York? This study seeks to provide answers to these questions.

NOTES

1. For a definitive treatment of the Red Scare nationally, see Robert K. Murray, *The Red Scare: A Study in National Hysteria, 1919–1920* (Minneapolis, 1955).
2. *Ibid.,* p. 9.
3. *Ibid.*
4. John Higham, *Strangers in the Land: Patterns of American Nativism: 1860–1925* (New Brunswick, N.J., 1955), p. 222.

Chapter One

RADICAL MOVEMENTS IN NEW YORK ON THE EVE OF THE RED SCARE

By 1914, two organizations, the Socialist party and the industrial Workers of the World, had emerged as the most important radical groups in the country. In addition, leftists were also found in the smaller left wing organizations: the Socialist Labor party, the radical trade unions, and fraternal organizations like the Workmen's Circle. The groups varied in structure and philosophy. Here, we will analyze those which were most important in New York and answer the following question: Were they a threat to the people of the state at this time?

The Socialist Party

Of all the left wing groups in New York on the eve of the Red Scare, the Socialist party was by far the best organized and most significant. It was founded in 1901 by joining together a wide assortment of protestors. Included were some of the followers of Eugene V. Debs, then head of the Social Democratic party, a group of dissidents recently split off from the Socialist Labor party, and a number of Populists. There were also some ministers, trade unionists, and teachers. The various groups distrusted each other, but their differences were resolved at a convention at Indianapolis. By the time it was over, the Socialist party of America had been born.

The new Socialist party was headed by Eugene V. Debs, a labor leader of national reputation; Debs remained at the helm until his death in 1926. For many years he had participated in politics as a Democrat and a Populist. Due to the influence of Victor L. Berger, Debs became interested in Socialism, but his final conversion did not come until he began serving a six-month jail sentence for his part in the American Railway Strike of 1894.

The aims and objectives of the new Socialist party were spelled out at the founding convention. With only a few changes these goals remained intact down through the years. They are found in the constitution of the party which begins:

> The Socialist Party of the United States is the political expression of the workers of the country, and part of the International working class movement.
>
> The fundamental aim of the Socialist Party is to bring about the social ownership and democratic control of all necessary means of production, to eliminate profit, rent, and interest and make it impossible for any to share the product without sharing the burden of labor; to change our class society into a society of equals, in which the interest of one is the interest of all.

In its platform the Socialists called for public ownership of utilities, transportation and communication. It included demands for reduced working hours, increased wages, social insurance and equal political rights for men and women. There was a plank supporting the initiative, referendum and recall. Also the convention explicitly favored the trade union movement, but took no position on the important issue of industrial as opposed to craft unions. The platform merely stated that the "formation of every trade union no matter how small or how conservative it may be, will strengthen the power of the wage and working class." This pronouncement, while not of immediate importance, led to several schisms within the party. The first took place in 1905 when the Industrial Workers of the World was formed, largely for the purpose of promoting industrial unionism.

Structurally, the Socialist party was highly decentralized. In contrast to the socialist parties of Europe, or to the tightly knit structure of the later Communist party, the American Socialist party was a federation of separate state bodies, each capable of doing pretty much as it pleased, with little or no direction from the national committee. Eugene V. Debs was the titular leader of the national party but his control was only nominal. During the height of the Red Scare, Debs was in jail thus rendering him incapable of leading the party even if he had wanted to. Furthermore, there was no party discipline, nor was there any established body of thought, declared or defended by the party as such. There were, instead, a variety of often conflicting ideas expressed through a huge number of party declarations, books, pamphlets, speeches. All of this was generally overlooked during the Red Scare when the party was held responsible for every statement uttered in its name, and for the actions of all of its supporters.

At least one consequence of this decentralization was that the Socialist party permitted its state organizations to concentrate closely on grass roots problems. Thus in New York, the party was concerned with issues arising among the workers in the urban slums while in the West the primary issues were those of miners and farmers. This diversity also led to the development of two wings of the party. The "right wingers" were found in Wisconsin, Pennsylvania and New York. The "left wing" tended to dominate in Ohio, Indiana, Michigan and west of the Mississippi. At the heart of this factionalism was a difference of opinion between those who thought socialism would come about gradually, and those who felt it would come about by revolution. Right wing spokesmen like Hillquit and John Spargo believed that liberal economic reforms were desirable while the left thought that such laws, which served to ameliorate the condition of the working class, only postponed the revolution. The right wingers, or "evolutionists" as they were called, also rejected the idea of an immediate, violent revolution. Instead they foresaw a step-by-step progression toward socialism through worker education and success at the ballot boxes.

Apart from ideology, the state organizations of the party tended to adopt similar structures. The New York Socialist Party was no exception. At the head of each state organization was the central committee to which all the branches sent delegates. In New York the central committee met every Saturday night in Labor Temple on East Eighty-fourth Street. These meetings were usually spirited; they lasted well into the morning, and delegates thrashed out the smallest points of party doctrine and tactics. The party prided itself on its democracy and would not have it any other way. But to outsiders it seemed as if the Socialists were all talk and no action.

In the Socialist parties of the Far and Middle West, leadership was generally drawn from the working class, the trade unions and the farmers. In the East, and especially in New York, intellectuals dominated the leadership. This was probably due to the fact that New York, at that time and even today, attracted a large number of such people. Of these intellectuals, three groups predominated: lawyers, writers, and teachers. Among the lawyers were Morris

Hillquit, Louis B. Boudin, and Meyer London, several times a Socialist member of Congress. Among the writers were William James Ghent, an able journalist and historian; Gustavus Myers, the famous author of the *History of the Great American Fortunes;* and Ernest Poole, the author of a number of proletarian novels. Other writers and journalists of distinction were Howard Brubaker, Floyd Dell, Max Eastman, Robert Hunter, Charles Edward Russell, and William English Walling. Among the teachers were Jessie Wallace Hugham, a holder of a Ph.D. from Columbia University, and a public school teacher in the city; and Algernon Lee, the Iowa-born and Minnesota-raised head of the Rand School of Social Science.

At times there appeared to be a certain amount of tension between the intellectual leadership and the rank and file, largely composed of workers from the New York City slums. The membership protested that the leaders were converting the party into an agency of radical, middle class reform. This brought a reply from the top that without this intellectual, largely middle class leadership, the Socialist party would soon become the "sport" and "plaything" of its economic masters. "Intelligence should be rewarded," said William J. Ghent, "with the responsibility of leadership," no matter what anybody might say. At least until 1919, when the left wing of the Socialists withdrew to form the Communist party, this elitist leadership was never seriously challenged.

Of all the leaders of the New York Socialists, Morris Hillquit was easily the most outstanding. He functioned not only as a dynamic spokesman but as a distinguished Marxist theoretician as well.[1] Born in Riga in 1869, Hillquit came to the United States when he was sixteen years old. Soon after his arrival, he joined the Socialist Labor party, then under the leadership of Daniel De Leon. He attended New York University Law School and after graduating threw himself into Socialist activities. He soon found himself in conflict with the egocentric De Leon who felt that Hillquit was a threat to his personal leadership. The conflict came to a head in the late 1890s when at the Rochester convention, Hillquit formed the "Kangaroo Wing" of Socialist Labor party. It was this group which bolted the parent organization and joined with the Debs group to form the Socialist party of America.

During his career Hillquit tried to give shape and form to the American Socialist movement. A major idea was his prediction that the American Socialist state would be a democratic, federal republic, divided into its then existing forty-eight states. Power would be shared between the federal government and the states, with the central government responsible for those matters which were national in scope. Congress would continue to be divided into houses, but the jurisdiction of each house would be different. The House of Representatives would concern itself with questions of a "political" nature; it would control foreign policy, defense, education, insurance, and the fine arts. The Senate would be responsible for "economic" affairs, such as post offices, railroads, mines, public works, and trusts. Hillquit foresaw a government that would be far less centralized than it had become even in those days, with added powers given to states and municipalities.

There was little that was revolutionary in all of this. This should not be surprising for the New York Socialists were basically progressive reformers. Still, they managed to retain many of the characteristics of earlier European Socialist movements. They constantly used terms such as "dialectical materialism" and "proletariat"; however, when they used the term "revolution" they were talking about a revolution achieved through the ballot box. This facility with Marxist concepts gave a slightly foreign flavor to the New York Socialists, which contributed to the belief that the Socialist Party could not be regarded as an American political party. During the Red Scare this was seized upon and used with telling results.

Below the intellectuals stood the many thousands of loyal party members who filled out its ranks. This group was drawn mainly from the large, predominantly Jewish, wave of immigrants from Eastern Europe that came around the turn of the century. Many of the younger members of this group had received an education in Europe but were forced by economic adversity to take unskilled jobs in the garment industry. Here they found sweatshop conditions prevailing and quickly decided that their best solution was in unions and socialism.

Of the two, the unions appeared to be the most practical. Within a short time after their arrival the needle trades workers had succeeded in setting up strong industrial type unions in the clothing fields as well as among the fur and millinery workers. It was among these workers that the Socialist party found its greatest support. Even the union leadership tended to preach socialism and aided the party financially.

To the garment worker, the Socialist party was as important as his Socialist-dominated trade union. Indeed, the two were often indistinguishble. This preoccupation with socialism is easily explained. For the worker, the party provided a meeting place where he could join his friends for conversation and fellowship. He was intellectually stimulated by its public speakers and its press. Then, too, the party provided the one place where the immigrant Jewish worker could meet other Americans of varying backgrounds on conditions of complete equality. By voting for Socialist candidates, he increased his sense of political participation. Finally, the party offered to the immigrant a messianic vision of a better world in which his poverty would be ended and all men would be brothers. This vision, while somewhat naive by modern standards, did much to sustain him and give meaning to his life.[2] The subversion of American institutions by means of a bloody revolution was rarely, if ever, one of his intentions.

All of these motives were well understood by the leadership of the New York Socialists, who carefully adjusted the party structure to enroll as many immigrants as possible. It was for this reason that the foreign language federations were formed. The first came in 1908; in the years that followed the number of federations was rapidly increased. Their growing importance can be seen in the fact that in 1912 they made up less than 12 percent of the total national membership, while by 1919 they composed over 53 percent. Although no membership figures exist for the foreign language federations in New York, they were probably similar to the national percentages.

While the immigrant workers made up the bulk of the party membership, their ranks were augmented by many native-born Americans. In this smaller group were teachers, students, ministers and white collar workers of various kinds. They were sometimes cited by the leadership as proof that the Socialist party was becoming Americanized and would soon triumph because of its ability to widen its electoral base. Even the non-Socialist press welcomed these "parlor Socialists," as they were sometimes called, hoping they would moderate the Party's politics and direct it on a course of progressive reform instead of socialism.

When all of these people were added up, the total Party membership was still quite small. The New York locals received thousands of applications for membership every year, but recruits dropped out as fast as they came in. For example, in 1914 there were 10,717 members in New York State out of a national total of eighty thousand.[3]

Nevertheless, to the general public the Socialist party always seemed to be making a greater impact than its numbers would suggest. This was due, in no small measure, to its ability to spread its propaganda through a bewildering number of periodicals, supplemented by street speakers and workers' classes. The party surveyed its own press in two different years and found, in the first survey, that there were 5 English and 8 non-English dailies, 262 English and 36 non-English weeklies, and 10 English and 2 non-English monthlies.

In New York, the leading paper in English was the *New York Call*. Yet with its circulation of 15,000, the *Call* found itself in constant financial difficulties. Its Socialist editorial policy repelled advertisements from the conservative business community, and subscriptions were never sufficient to pay the bills. Nevertheless, the Party felt that to allow the *Call* to die would be a disaster; to prevent this it carried on an almost endless number of fund raisings. Charles Edward Russell recalled: "Men and women gave money to the *Call* they could not afford to give, denied themselves every luxury, and worked overtime so that the publication might go on."[4] But these efforts were not enough, and the paper finally folded in 1923.

Among the New York monthlies, some mention needs to be made of *The Masses*. This journal was first published in 1911. By 1913, Max Eastman had taken over as editor, and the magazine hit its stride. The paper described itself as "an illustrated magazine of art, literature, politics, and science devoted to the interests of the working people." It was a Socialist magazine generally expressing a point of view to the left of the party. Its articles, editorials, and especially its cartoons, by such noted cartoonists as Art Young, were always provocative, and to many seemed to add a little fun to the often dreary task of being a Socialist. Over the years *The Masses* attracted a remarkable number of fine writers. Among the better known were Sherwood Anderson, Konrad Bercovici, Floyd Dell, Arturo Giovanitti, Walter Lippmann, Jack London, John Reed, Upton Sinclair, Lincoln Steffens, Louis Untermeyer and Mary Heaton Vorse.

Of the foreign language papers, the *Jewish Daily Forward* played a distinctive role in the New York Socialist movement. In contrast to the *Call*'s financial difficulties, the *Forward*, with a circulation of two hundred and fifty thousand, was a money maker. There were, however, no profits. Through the years the *Forward* used its surplus to make large contributions to the party.

At least part of the success of the *Forward* can be attributed to its editor, Abraham Cahan. From the time he first took over the top editorial post, Cahan dedicated himself to an objective presentation of the news. The editorial and feature sections followed the Socialist line, but in the news columns Cahan insisted upon perfect objectivity. As he explained it: "There is no need for Socialists to distort news. The case against capitalism is quite strong as it is."

Still another reason for the success of the *Forward* was its ability to translate socialism into terms that were meaningful to its Jewish readers. Socialist propaganda was dispensed by *De Proletarischer Magid* (the proletarian preacher), and the lessons were called the *Red Sedre* (the weekly portion of the Torah). In addition, the *Forward* never missed an opportunity for helping the immigrant adjust himself to American life. The paper was full of self-help hints and stories describing the life of its readers in the slums.

Apart from the printed word, the Socialist party used the street meeting with great effectiveness in spreading its message. These became so numerous that the New York leadership found it necessary to draw up a list of instructions to its speakers. A few of these were:

> Do not advocate or oppose any religious belief; make clear that the party does not align itself with one type of union against another. Do not class all capitalists as thieves, blacklegs, and scoundrels, etc. Remember that it is the system that creates capitalists. Do not attack or abuse the police unnecessarily for they are members of the working class, and we should have their good will.

Equally important in the Socialist party propaganda apparatus was formal instruction through schools. The Rand School on Fifteenth Street in New York functioned as a workers' university; it attempted to bridge the gap between the intellectual leadership of the party and its rank and file. The school was founded in 1906 with an endowment from the will of Mrs. Carrie D. Rand, the wealthy mother-in-law of the Iowa Christian Socialist, George

D. Herron. In the building (which is still standing), the Rand School offered courses in public speaking, English grammar, composition, Socialist theory and history, American history, and stenography. Charles A. Beard, the noted historian, was associated with the school for a number of years, as were David S. Muzzey, the historian, and Franklin H. Giddings, the sociologist. Some of the Socialist staff members were William H. Ghent, Algernon Lee, and August Claessens, an assemblyman.

For those of college age, there was the Intercollegiate Socialist Society founded in New York in 1905 for the purpose of "promoting an intelligent interest in Socialism among college men and women." The idea for the Society was first conceived by Upton Sinclair, then twenty-seven years old and a struggling writer, and George Strobell, a jewelry manufacturer and devoted Socialist. The organizational meeting was held on the top floor of Peck's Restaurant on Fulton Street. Morris Hillquit later recalled this meeting with some pleasure: "It was an enthusiastic gathering attended by many persons unattached to the Socialist movement." Among those present were Clarence Darrow, the famous civil rights lawyer; J. G. Phelps Stokes, the millionaire Socialist; and William English Walling. Jack London, the writer, was chosen as its first president with Upton Sincair as vice-president.

After a slow start, the Intercollegiate Socialist Society began to make rapid progress in recruiting members. By 1917, it reported chapters in some seventy colleges and universities throughout the country, and about a dozen organized alumni groups. The Society sent out large quantities of Socialist literature and operated a speaker's bureau which sent Socialists like John Spargo, Rose Pastor Stokes, and Harry Laidler to scores of campuses across the land.

Even those below college age were not overlooked. To teach socialism to the young, the party set up a number of Socialist Sunday schools, mostly in New York, but in a few other cities as well. The Sunday school concept grew out of a complaint by comrades in the New York locals that the public school system "glorified the competitive idea," rendering their children "prejudiced against Socialism." They conceived of the Socialist schools not as replacements for the public schools but as a corrective device which would teach "the value of the Socialist spirit and cooperative effort."

The party leadership never quite accepted the idea of a separate school system, and, despite an enrollment of more than one thousand pupils, the schools were only marginally successful. They suffered from a lack of qualified teachers, and from the difficulty of devising a curriculum appropriate for the young. By the 1920s the Sunday school movement was largely abandoned.

Still another device for attracting the young was the Young People's Socialist League. By 1916 the League had set up over 150 circles throughout the country with more than four thousand members. Close communication was maintained by the Socialist party with the League whose national secretary also served as the director of the Young People's section of the party's national office. League members assisted in devising propaganda and in educational work; they raised funds and prepared for leadership in the party when they reached manhood.

Aside from its educational work and its efforts at spreading propaganda, a major Socialist pastime was running for office. The party knew that few of its candidates would be elected, but the electoral contests offered excellent opportunities for publicity. Then, too, the party hoped that by steady and persistent effort among the voters, the stature of the party would be improved. The results of this effort can be measured in the election statistics. In the national elections the Socialist party increased its vote from about one hundred thousand in 1901, when it was organized, to about nine hundred thousand in 1912. This year, 1912, was a high point in Socialist electoral success; it was not equaled until 1920, when Eugene V. Debs, the party's perennial candidate for President, received slightly more votes. These figures, however, conceal an important point concerning the party's strength. Before 1912, Socialist strength was concentrated largely in the agrarian and mining areas of the West and Southwest. In the next few years, this support decreased while the strength of the party increased greatly in the Northeast, especially in New York. This trend was observed as early as 1911 when a study was made of the election returns, ranking the states as to the number of communities in which Socialists were elected. In 1911, New York ranked thirty-third on a list of thirty-three states. After 1911, New York ranked twenty-third on the same list. Other statistics tell the same story. By 1920, New York contributed more than one-fifth of Debs' total vote, although in previous campaigns, New York never provided more than 10 percent of the total Socialist vote.[5] The New York vote increased in these

years in both absolute and relative terms. The great increase in
Socialist strength was due largely to the influx of European, and
especially Jewish, immigrants into the Empire City. These new
immigrants sustained the Party at least until 1932, when the
return of progressivism in the form of the New Deal resulted in
its decline.

The shift of voting strength to the eastern urban areas is borne
out by an analysis of state and local elections held in New York
during these years. There would be little point in discussing every
election campaign, but some detail is necessary in order to increase our understanding of the Red Scare. In 1906, for example,
Morris Hillquit ran as a candidate from the Ninth Congressional
District, at that time comprising most of the Lower East Side.
In a letter accepting the nomination, Hillquit gave this vivid
picture of the district and its inhabitants:

> The Ninth Congressional District is the home of the tene-
> ments, pushcarts, paupers, and tuberculosis. It is the experi-
> mental laboratory for the sentimental settlement worker, the
> horrible example of the pious moralist, and the chosen prey of
> the smug philanthropist. Geographically, it is located in the
> slums; industrially it belongs to the sweat shop system; polit-
> ically it is a dependency of Tammany Hall.[6]

According to Hillquit, the campaign of 1906 kindled an "in-
describable fire of enthusiasm" on the East Side. Besides the
Republican and Democratic candidates, William Randolph Hearst,
the publisher, ran as an independent. In spite of the competition,
the Socialists felt that they had a good chance of winning. A few
trade unions organized demonstrations in the form of street
parades. The women of the district, not yet entitled to vote,
banded together to help bring out a large vote. Young boys and
girls were enlisted in a Juvenile Workers League, while doctors,
dentists and lawyers formed a Professional League in support of
the Socialist ticket. Even Maxim Gorky, the Russian writer then
visiting the United States, made speeches for Hillquit and the
other Socialist party candidates. The Socialists lost, but did not
do badly—Hillquit came in second in a field of four candidates.

That same year the Socialist party campaigned actively
throughout the state. To Henry Slobodkin, the Socialist candidate
for Attorney General, the meetings of the party rivaled "any of
those held by the old parties." No stone was left unturned. From

state headquarters, the party sent out over two million pieces of literature, as well as enormous quantities of mail circulated by local committees. More than one hundred speakers traveled throughout the state; while hundreds more were active in New York City. But again, this effort was not sufficient and all of their candidates went down to defeat.

In the New York City mayoralty election of 1909 the Socialists ran Edward F. Cassidy, a perennial Socialist candidate; he did poorly, with his vote running well behind that of Debs in the presidential election of 1908. Neither Cassidy nor the party was discouraged. Said Cassidy: "Our movement is not one to be fanned with a temporary triumph by a political Moses. It is founded on science and a knowledge of society." One reason for the poor showing was the ability of Hearst, again running as an independent, to cut into the Socialist vote. Many of the voters liked his liberal ideas, but in characteristic fashion the *Call* deplored his "pseudo-radicalism."

By 1910 the Socialists were making notable progress in Milwaukee, where Victor Berger became the first Socialist ever to be elected to the House of Representatives. The *Call* was jubilant: "The election of Berger breaks the spell that has hitherto kept the doors of Congress hermetically sealed to the representatives of the working class, to the apostles of Socialism."[7] While this was an overstatement, it was true that Emil Seidel, the party's candidate for mayor, won by a plurality of 7,000 votes. Also victorious were their candidates for city attorney, comptroller, two civil judges, and twenty-one aldermen out of a total of thirty-five.

In the New York elections of 1910, the party was less successful. Charles Edward Russell ran for governor; Hillquit was nominated for the associate justice of the Court of Appeals. Other candidates for state office represented the cities of Syracuse, Schenectady, Buffalo, and Rochester, as well as New York City. Russell mounted a vigorous campaign but soon found that outside of New York City and a few urban areas upstate, he could generate little interest. For instance, in one small town, he delivered an address in a fire station. Seats were provided but nobody came to occupy them. Only a few people stood at the back and listened to him in "sullen silence."

While Russell lost this election, the party was heartened by large numbers of Socialist votes in many upstate communities. There were significant gains in Schenectady, Buffalo, Rochester,

Auburn, Jonesville, Johnstown, Gloversville, and Troy. To the
Call, this was a "fine, healthy gain" which "filled the local comrades with enthusiasm."[8]

Within the city of New York, the Socialist party put Meyer
London's name on the ballot. Again the campaign was vigorous,
but London was beaten by the Democratic party regular, coming
in second in a field of three candidates. He met his defeat with
defiance: "The East Side is learning to organize. It has taken the
Jewish workingmen a number of years to form substantial trade
unions. I have no doubt that he [*sic*] will also learn to organize
effectively in the political field."[9]

London's prediction was not quite correct. The first Socialist
victory in New York came, not in the city, but upstate, when the
voters of Schenectady turned out almost the entire city administration to bring in a Socialist mayor, Dr. George R. Lunn, and
eight Socialist aldermen out of a total of thirteen. "In New York
State," said the *Call,* "the ice has been broken, broken pretty
thoroughly. . . . If the good work is kept up, not only will the
ice be broken, but the back of capitalism will be broken and
speedily."[10]

Schenectady was a strange town to see such a significant Socialist victory. Most of the workers were employed by the General
Electric Company which maintained a laboratory and factory
there. The workers were generally skilled and some were organized into craft unions.

There are two possible explanations of this victory. The first
was the excellent leadership provided by Dr. Lunn, an Iowa-born,
ordained Presbyterian minister. For a time Lunn served as the
associate pastor of a Brooklyn church. Then he moved to Schenectady where he was caught up, like so many other Protestant
ministers of the day, in the cause of municipal reform. This led
to his membership in the Socialist party because of his belief that
it offered the best opportunity to secure meaningful changes.

Additional leadership in Schenectady was provided by Charles
P. Steinmetz, for many years a consulting scientist to the General
Electric Company, and a leader in the field of electricity. Steinmetz had been forced to emigrate from his native Germany
because of his affiliation with the Socialist movement. He came
to the United States in 1889, found employment with General
Electric, and continued to pursue his Socialist interests in his
spare time.

A second factor explaining the Socialist victory was the dissatisfaction of the people of Schenectady with municipal government and the high cost of living. This was noted by G. E. Emmins, the general manager of the General Electric Company's Schenectady plant, who said: "There has long been a feeling in Schenectady that the Republicans and the Democrats were playing together. Certain people charged that there had been a good deal of graft, and many believed these charges." The chairman of the Democratic county committee agreed: "There is no doubt that a lot of voters were sore at both parties, and wanted to give them both a good scare."

On the other hand, the Socialists spent little time in analyzing the election. Instead, they made immediate preparations for a transfer of power. To lend a hand, Morris Hillquit came up from New York and helped set up an informal cabinet composed of the principal city officers. The new cabinet then proceeded to pass on all appointments and measures of importance. They decided that appointments were not to be restricted to party members, but were to be made on the basis of merit. For example, the commissioner of public works, an important post in the city government and a source of much corruption, was recruited from another city. Then Mayor Lunn appointed as his secretary a young Harvard graduate, Walter Lippmann. This talented man had organized the first Socialist club at Harvard; he was later to leave the Socialist party and make his mark as a journalist of world renown.

The record compiled by the Lunn administration was not a bad one. A number of reforms were carried out: the building of parks, increased school construction, an improved sewage system, and the establishment of a city dental clinic. These were generally welcomed and went through unchallenged. Lunn found greater opposition when he tried to "socialize" some public utilities. For instance, in an attempt to reduce the cost of ice, an important refrigerant in those days, the city "harvested" several tons which it sold at twenty-five cents per one hundred pounds, well below the market price of forty cents. Next, the city went into the coal business, selling coal below the going rate. Both of these attempts at municipal socialism, as well as an attempt to set up a city-owned grocery store, were halted by injunction. The court stated that it was not proper for a city government, even a Socialist one, to compete with private enterprise in this way.

Divisions within the party itself were soon to result in even greater difficulties for the Schenectady Socialists. This came to a head when some of the leaders, who had viewed the election results as a mandate for radical change, demanded that the mayor introduce socialism immediately. They found that Lunn had neither the power nor the intention of doing this. This led some leaders to suspect that Lunn was using the party as a stepping-stone for his own political advancement. To prevent Lunn from building up a new machine, the leaders tried to force him to submit all municipal appointments, even those on the police force, to the party local for approval. This action drove a wedge between the mayor and the party, and from that time on there was increasing hostility between the two. Lunn was not officially expelled from the party until 1915, but by then he had already aligned himself with the Democrats. As a member of this party, he served as mayor, congressman, lieutenant governor, and public service commissioner.

In 1911, when George Lunn was first elected mayor, the *Call* had predicted that New York City would not "lag behind." The city must follow, it said, for everywhere "things are ripe for revolution."[11] As we shall see, New York City was "ripe" but the rest of America apparently was not. For after 1912, the entire Socialist movement, with the exception of New York and a few other eastern urban centers, began to suffer a permanent malaise.[12]

There are a number of reasons explaining the decline of the Socialist movement after 1912. A rapid decrease in membership took place when the party adopted an amendment to its constitution calling for the expulsion of any member advocating sabotage or violence. In the wake of this amendment the party lost fifty thousand members since those Socialists who were also members of the IWW either left or were expelled. Another cause of decline can be seen in the rigidity of rules imposed upon Socialist officeholders. Some Socialists, like George R. Lunn, found these to be too restricting and in the desire to "get things done" decided not to be bound by them once they got into office. Perhaps the most important reason was the increasing ability of government to solve the country's economic problems. On the national level, the reforms instituted by the Wilson administration: the Federal Reserve Act, the Federal Farm Loan Bank System, and the Clayton Act, tended to dull the cutting edge of Socialist criticism. These progressive measures, as well as the charismatic personality of Wilson, drew off the progressive and many of the Socialist votes. Then, too, there were the structural weaknesses of the Socialist party. As a collection of state parties, each concerned with local and regional issues, the party could never attract enough of a national following.

As a result, after a record of nine hundred thousand votes for Debs in 1912, the Socialist vote began to decline. The same trend was observed in New York, when Herbert Merrill from Albany, the lone Socialist member of the state legislature, lost his seat to Arthur P. Squire, a party regular. A year later, in an election called by *The New York Times* "the most exciting in the history of the city," George R. Lunn, the Socialist mayor of Schenectady, was defeated by a Fusion candidate representing three parties.[13] The *Times,* incidentally, headlined the story, "Schenectady is Redeemed."

Only in New York City were the Socialists able to secure significant election victories. Success came first in 1914, when Meyer London went to Congress as the representative of Manhattan's Lower East Side.

The new congressman was not new to politics. London was a Russian immigrant who arrived in America at the age of twenty. He attended New York University's Law School, ran unsuccessfully for the state assembly, and helped Debs and Hillquit found the Socialist party. For many years he played a role in the International Ladies Garment Workers Union, and in the Furriers Union; he was active in the garment strike of 1910 which resulted in a victory against the sweatshop then common in the industry. London's first try for Congress was in 1910. In 1912, he ran again. This time he came in second, less than three hundred votes behind the winner, Henry M. Goldfogle, a Tammany machine politician. In an unproven charge, the *Call* explained his defeat candidly: "Tammany gorillas and strong-armed men intimidated the watchers and frightened our timid voters." The Socialist party charged further that their poll watchers were literally thrown out of the polling places.[14]

London's victory in 1914 came as a surprise to the major political parties in the city. He was reelected many times despite their best efforts to unseat him. In his desire to attract non-Socialist votes, London compromised his position on many issues. On some, however, he would not; he is perhaps best remembered as the only member of Congress to oppose the wartime Espionage Act.

The wartime election of 1917 sent a surge of hope through the ranks of the New York Socialists. At the same time, it helped to precipitate the Red Scare. The election took place some seven months after the United States first declared war on Germany. The big Socialist vote was largely a result of the party's opposition to the war. One analysis of the returns revealed that the party received 21.7 percent of the total, while in previous elections it had never received more than 5.1 percent. This was sufficient to send ten assemblymen to Albany, seven Socialists to the board of aldermen, and to give Jacob Panken, a Socialist attorney, a ten-year term as a municipal court judge. Hillquit ran for mayor on an antiwar platform but, despite the heavy vote in his favor, lost to John F. Hylan, a former Democratic judge and the choice of Tammany Hall.

Press and public reaction to the campaign was outspoken. Theodore Roosevelt, a man never at a loss for words, denounced Hillquit as "cowardly," "pacifist," and "pro-German." Actually, none of these charges was true. Reflecting the growing intolerance with the Left, the *Journal of Commerce,* a leading business paper, asserted that only "harm came from Hillquit, who by his mixture of socialism and pacifism brought together all of the unpatriotic and disloyal elements." The *Burlington* (Vermont) *Free Press* commented that the large Socialist vote "served an excellent purpose, especially in Germany," while the *Boston Post* found the election of Hylan, a well-meaning but uninspiring candidate, to be "far less deplorable than the election of Hillquit would have been." To the *St. Louis Globe Democrat,* Hillquit's large vote was, simply, "a disgrace."[15]

Hillquit's own assessment of the campaign covered a wide range: from gratitude that the Socialists had done so well, to a prediction that this election would establish the Socialist party as "an important and permanent factor in the politics of the city." Even the anarchists and the IWW, at odds with the Socialists since their expulsion from the party in 1912, took pleasure in the number of Socialists elected to office. Emma Goldman, a well-known anarchist, commented: "[Hillquit's] campaign meetings were the first gatherings of the kind, I have ever attended without being sickened by their inanity."[16]

The Industrial Workers of the World

A second radical group in New York to fall victim to the full weight of the Red Scare was the Industrial Workers of the World.

The IWW was founded in Chicago in 1905 by a varied group of labor leaders, journalists, and Socialists; the founders included Daniel De Leon, Eugene V. Debs, and William D. Haywood, a labor organizer from the West. These men, all of whom called themselves Marxists, were convinced that the labor unions of America were powerless to secure any real benefits for the workers. They proceeded to set up the IWW in order to reestablish the labor movement on a new Socialist basis in the form of an all-encompassing industrial union. These goals were to be achieved by militant struggle in both the economic and political spheres with the end result being the final abolition of the capitalist system.

The philosophical basis of the new organization was discussed in the constitution. Its preamble began:

> The working class and the employing class have nothing in common. There can be no peace so long as hunger and want are found among the millions of working people, and the few who make up the employing class have all the good things of life.
>
> Between these two classes a struggle must go on until the workers of the world organize as a class, take possession of the earth and the machinery of production, and abolish the wage system.

At the time this preamble was written the IWW was mainly socialist in nature. Later on, it dropped its socialist basis, with its strong emphasis on political action, and veered towards syndicalism. This development began in 1908 when the "direct actionists," men like Haywood, Vincent St. John, and William L. Trautmann, swung to the left and adopted the general strike, sabotage, and other such methods as more suitable weapons to achieve their objectives. This alienated the political socialists most of whom pulled out of the IWW in the next few years. In 1912 Haywood and other members of the IWW were expelled from the Socialist party because of their advocacy of violence.

Undeterred, the IWW continued to carry on a nationwide drive for members. It appealed largely to the most downtrodden segments of the American working class: in the mines, the lumber camps and in the textile factories. Its total membership never

amounted to more than fifty thousand at any one time. The very
nature of its constituency accounted for the fact that its membership was transient, with people entering and leaving the organization in great numbers.

In the early years the most successful activities of the IWW
took place in the West; there it organized the workers in mines
and lumber camps. While not abandoning their major efforts
west of the Mississippi, the leaders decided to extend the organizing drive eastward. For this purpose two dedicated IWW
organizers, Joseph Ettor and Elizabeth Gurley Flynn, were sent
out to see what could be done. Within a short time locals were
set up in many eastern cities. In New York small IWW chapters
were established in Buffalo, Jamestown, Little Falls, Rochester,
and Utica. Other locals were set up in New York City, including
one in Brooklyn. These efforts were feeble but by 1910 the
IWW seemed to make a major breakthrough in the East when
it led a successful strike in the shoe industry in Brooklyn,
New York.

The shoe industry was ripe for organization. The workers,
mostly Italian immigrants, worked under poor conditions for
low wages. Joseph Ettor surveyed the scene, and within a short
time had organized about one hundred and fifty men into Local
168 of the IWW. By mid-November the Local had grown to
four hundred and fifty and was supporting a strike in one of
the shoe factories whose members had struck in sympathy with
several workers who had been fired for union activities. Inspired
by the strike then in progress, the workers at the Wickert and
Gardiner Company, one of the largest shoe companies already
organized by the AFL's Boot and Shoe Workers Union, asked
the union to negotiate for an increase in wages. When the union
refused on the grounds that the present contract was still in force,
the workers struck anyway and joined the IWW.

Under IWW leadership the shoe workers fought back against
scabs, police and private detectives hired by the management.
The strike spread to other shoe factories until about three thousand men and women were out of work. The workers began mass
picketing around each of the strike-bound plants and started the
collection of a defense fund to pay strike benefits to the men.
The executive committee of the AFL made no contributions to
the fund, but contributions were received from a number of individual unions with Italian memberships, and from the anarchists

and syndicalists. But the money raised was not sufficient for the needs of the strikers. Then, in February 1911, Frank Buccatori, a shoe worker in a plant which was not on strike, shot and killed his foreman in self-defense after having been attacked by him. In the midst of this crisis the Central Labor Union of Brooklyn, an AFL affiliate, ordered the unions supplying funds to the strikers to stop, warning them that should the Wobblies be successful in this strike they would begin raiding their own unions for members. The strike dragged on; scabs in great numbers were employed as replacements for those workers still on the picket lines. But by the beginning of March 1911 the strikers began to suffer from loss of wages and drifted back to work. The strike collapsed at the end of the month; all of the strikers returned to work without gaining any concessions. Shortly afterwards the IWW locals were dissolved.

The following year IWW efforts were directed at organizing the textile industry. After leading a well-publicized strike at Lawrence, Massachusetts, the IWW scored a victory at Little Falls, New York, a major center of knit goods and underwear. The strike began on October 10, 1912, when one thousand five hundred mill workers, native Americans, Italians, Poles, and Hungarians—seventy percent of them women—walked out of the Phoenix and Gilbert Knitting Mills in protest against a reduction in wages. With average weekly wages of eight to nine dollars for men, five dollars for women, and $3.75 for children, the workers found themselves close to starvation even at the low prices of those days.

Soon after the strike started, the mill workers rallied around three IWW organizers, Benjamin S. Legere, Phillopo Bocchino and Matila Rabinowitz, who came to Little Falls to help out. They organized daily parades past the mills. In one of these a moving chain of pickets, mainly women and girls wearing red sweaters symbolizing the Left, circled round the mill. Mass arrests of pickets followed and gradually all forms of agitation, even open-air meetings and parades, were outlawed.

As the strike wore on it began to pick up additional support from Socialists, liberals, and trade unionists. In mid-October, Dr. George R. Lunn arrived and was arrested while addressing a small group of workers. Later that month all of the IWW speakers and organizers were arrested and jailed. Of this group, two IWW organizers, Legere and Bocchino, were convicted of assault and were not released from jail until July 1914.

Notwithstanding their difficulties, the strikers managed to keep going. State mediators sent by the governor finally ended the strike on January 2, 1913, granting wage increases which ranged from five to eighteen percent. The Utica *Press* noted that the "terms upon which the strikers agreed to go back to work were a substantial increase over what was paid previously."[17]

Following their victory at Little Falls, the IWW became involved in a major industrial dispute at Paterson, New Jersey. The city of Paterson, just across the river from New York, was close enough to involve the New York Wobblies as well. The strike began early in 1913 in the silk mills of the town. These mills employing over twenty thousand workers were located near swamp and marsh lands. According to William D. Haywood, the IWW leader, there wasn't a single park in the workers' quarters for children to play in or "any gardens where mothers could give their babies fresh air." Under the direction of the IWW, the strike closed down all of the mills. At the heart of the dispute were conditions in the plants including a speed-up system through which the employers attempted to increase the number of looms which the silk workers were required to operate. This increased the output of each worker but decreased the number of workers employed. No provision was made for an increase in pay to match the increase in productivity.

Even prior to this strike the IWW was actively organizing in Paterson. When the strike began, they devoted their full resources to it. Elizabeth Gurley Flynn and Carlo Tresca, both IWW organizers, were in charge of day-to-day operations. As in Little Falls, they were assisted by others among whom was Patrick L. Quinlan of the Socialist party. In February 1913 all three were accused by local authorities of being "outside agitators" and were arrested. They were released on heavy bail and, later, rearrested. This time they were indicted for conspiracy to cause an unlawful assemblage of persons as well as "riotously and tumultuously disturbing the peace of New Jersey." They were soon released and continued to agitate for the duration of the strike.

In the meantime the employers were taking measures to break the strike. They decorated their factories and the stores in Paterson with American flags with the implication that the strikers, many of them immigrants, were un-American. This prompted the New York left wing to stage a pageant in Madison Square Garden. Some one thousand two hundred strikers from Paterson crossed the Hudson River and marched en masse to the Garden which had been lighted with electric lights spelling out the initials "IWW."

The strike dragged on for six months. In time the strikers began to weaken. The strike was finally ended after the AFL intervened and secured a settlement on terms not particularly favorable to the workers.

Other Radical Groups

The radical trade unions were also an important part of the New York left. Of these the Amalgamated Clothing Workers and the International Ladies Garment Workers Union were the two largest. It should be remembered that smaller radical unions existed in the other garment trades, but their activities and structure were similar and need not concern us.

The ACW was formed in 1914 under the leadership of Joseph Schlossberg and Sidney Hillman. Initially, the Amalgamated was not affiliated with the AFL. It was an industrial union which included virtually everybody in the industry, from delivery boys to skilled cutters. By 1920, despite considerable friction with the AFL, it had enrolled about one hundred seventy-seven thousand workers.

In ideological terms, the ACW was highly idealistic, even socialistic. The union believed that workers should live in a cooperative society in which production was carried on for the benefit of the whole community rather than for the profit of the few. The union promised workers control of industry and ultimately their final emancipation from the capitalist system.

The idealism and radicalism of the ACW were clearly spelled out in its constitution:

> The economic organization of labor has been called into existence by the capitalist system of production, under which the division between the ruling class and the ruled is based upon the ownership of the means of production. . . .
>
> The industrial and inter-industrial organization, based upon the solid rock of clear knowledge and class consciousness, will put the organized and working class in actual control of the system of production and the working class will then be ready to take possession of it.

While this was a clearly radical statement, two points should be noted about the socialism of the ACW. In the first place, while its constitution does speak of the ultimate triumph of socialism, the more militant tone of the IWW preamble was lacking. Nothing was said of the struggle between the classes which would go on until the workers took "possession" of the means of production. Instead, the socialism of the Amalgamated was more of a morale builder, a help in organizing the unorganized. From its earliest years, the union was basically preoccupied with bread-and-butter issues: wages, hours, working conditions and union recognition. This was emphasized by Joseph Schlossberg who declared that the real radicalism of his union could be found in the work it was doing to establish industrial democracy in the clothing industry and in its ability to train workers to act responsibly as union members.

A second point involves the reason for the very existence of socialism in the clothing unions. It was common at this time to attribute it to the Jewish background of most of its members. This was untrue. While many garment workers came to America well acquainted with the ideas of Marxian socialism, others came imbued with the spirit of competitive enterprise because of their former occupations as merchants and small tradesmen. Their willingness to adopt socialism after their arrival was due to adverse economic circumstances; it varied little from that of other national groups—Poles, Italians, Slovenians, Finns, Lithuanians—employed within the same industry.

Nevertheless, the "socialism" of the ACW was a cause of concern. Most directly affected were the employers who understood that this radicalism was largely of their own making. The great number of small and transitory firms, the keen competition among them, the highly seasonal character of the garment industry, made conditions so unstable that it was bound to provide a stimulus for radical discontent. Their anxiety continued even after the Amalgamated had grown stronger and conditions began to improve. Others charged that the ACW was unAmerican. This accusation was based not only on the union's radical philosophy but also on the fact that many of its members were foreignborn. The charge was resented by the union which pointed out that by 1920 at least three-fourths of its members were American citizens. The leadership asked whether it was more American to have one's children grow up in factories and in ignorance rather than to agitate for a replacement of the system which produced all of this. The ACW also pointed with pride at its attempts to form consumers' cooperatives and a workers' bank as constructive efforts towards reform. Finally, the socialism of the ACW was used as an excuse by the Lusk Committee of the New York state legislature and by certain employers to launch violent attacks on the union during the height of the Red Scare. A more reasoned and tolerant approach would have shown how superficial and transitory this Socialist veneer really was.

The International Ladies Garment Workers Union was the second most important radical union in New York at this time. Like the ACW, the ILGWU was a socialist union with a wide appeal among urban immigrant groups. It was founded in 1900 and unlike the Amalgamated always maintained its affiliation with the AFL. The preamble to its constitution stated that the only way for the workers to get "full value of their product is to organize industrially into a class conscious labor union."

The story of the International is the traditional story of an industrial union: organization, strikes, propaganda, all leading to the writing of a contract, or "protocol" as their first one was called. One observable difference from other unions was the stress that the International put on the need for political representation for the workers "by representatives of the political party whose aim is the abolition of the capitalist system." This explains their early nexus with the Socialists, and later after the early radicalism had been abandoned, with the American Labor and Liberal parties in New York. Still another difference was their interest in worker education, a field in which they were pioneers. The union wanted their members to have a thorough understanding of the labor movement as well as a broad cultural background. To accomplish this, a special education committee was appointed in 1914, and arrangements were made with the Rand School for various courses to be conducted under the joint direction of the union and the school. Two years later, $5,000 was appropriated from the union's treasury for this purpose. The appropriation had been increased to $10,000 by 1918. The cooperation of the New York public schools was secured and "unity centers" established where classes in English, economics, and physical training were carried on. For a time the ILGWU operated a "Worker's University."

The Workmen's Circle was also a part of the socialist movement. This was a fraternal organization supported largely by the Jewish proletariat, with fifty-two thousand members and six hundred branches, mostly in New York. Its founding principles stressed its desire to extend health and welfare benefits to the workers for the purpose of overcoming the unhealthful conditions of modern industry.

Here, too, with the possible exception of carrying out some socialist educational work, and donating fairly large amounts of money to left-wing organizations, the radical contributions of the Workmen's Circle were minimal. On the other hand, its welfare activities were considerable: it paid sick benefits, maintained a sanitorium for tuberculosis (the "proletarian disease"), published a magazine, and in 1917 made arrangements with the New York City Board of Education to use its facilities for courses in American history, the history of the socialist and labor movements, the theory of socialism, botany, civics, and the history of Jewish literature.

Were these radical groups a threat to the people of New York? Could they, either acting individually or together, have carried out a left-wing revolution? Indeed, did they even want to? Were their activities, at least until the outbreak of the war, of such a nature as to justify the later Red Scare?

The answer to all of these questions is "no." Individually, all of the groups were too weak. The IWW, for example, was adept at leading strikes but was unable to develop a syndicalist structure as an alternative to the AFL. Without this base for revolution, the possibilities of a revolution were nil. It is entirely possible that had the Wobblies been stronger, they might have attempted a national "general strike" as a prelude to revolution. But this supposition is mere conjecture for at no time did they even come close to this. With their weak organizational structure, they were never able to organize a mass base strong enough to bring it about.

The possibility of a revolution from the socialist camp was equally remote. The Socialist party was a highly moral and democratic organization. The vast majority of its members were more interested in reforming the economic system than in replacing it. Their sincerity was revealed as early as 1912, when its left, IWW-oriented wing was expelled for its advocacy of force and violence. Later, in 1919, the Socialist party was torn by schism when the remainder of its left wing, inspired by the rise of

Bolshevism, also withdrew, forming the nucleus of two weak Communist parties. This is certainly a self-defeating way to go about the task of "revolution."

Then, too, the revolutionary potential of the Socialist party, even assuming its existence, was weakened by its regional character, its lack of effective national leadership, and its related preoccupation with state and local issues. To this can be added its ability to attract a following from the middle class. With so many reformers, ministers, teachers, students, labor leaders, farmers, humanitarians, and assorted "do gooders" in its ranks, its propensity for revolution was strictly limited.

While it is true that the other radical groups such as the clothing unions and the Workmen's Circle, and even· such liberal organizations as the American Civil Liberties Union, attracted leftists in the early years, none of them had the potential, or even the desire, to participate in a general uprising.

All of this does not eliminate the possibility of cooperation among radical groups; this charge was made repeatedly during the Red Scare. In reality, cooperation was at a minimum. It was quite true that in the early years the Socialist party had many members who were also members of the IWW. They were called "Industrial Socialists" and were mainly concerned with the growing relationship between the party and the AFL. They were also strongly convinced of the usefulness of political action and tried to persuade their fellow Wobblies to be more tolerant of Socialist philosophy. This dual membership also operated in the other direction. Many Wobblies were members of the Socialist party and participated actively in its day-to-day activities. At one time William D. Haywood was even on the National Executive Committee of the party.

This close relationship began to be severed even before 1912, although it was in that year that the break was finalized. The right wing of the Socialist party always opposed the IWW members in its midst because it feared that their presence would alienate the liberal voters. Furthermore, it wanted to concentrate on political reform, and was horrified by talk of a "general strike." The right wing had long since given up the idea of opposition to the conservative policies of the AFL, and thought that the "dual unionism" proposed by the Wobblies would only weaken the labor movement.

As the Socialists began to win elections, the IWW became

apprehensive of the growing strength of the right wing within the party. This apprehension could be sensed when Haywood was nominated to the National Executive Committee of the party in November 1911. In accepting the nomination, Haywood responded with a strong statement against what he termed the hypocritical stand taken by the party on the issue of organized labor. He said that the party could never fulfill its purpose unless it supported industrial unionism as advocated by the IWW.

This conflict precipitated the schism between the IWW and the Socialist party. At first, it merely related to the question of whether the Socialist movement would support syndicalist unions or the craft unions of the AFL. Soon the debate widened to include a more basic question: should the Socialist party permit in its ranks those who advocated "direct action" as justifiable weapons for achieving socialism? The question was debated extensively by the party. Hillquit led the fight against the IWW. He was supported by Debs who recommended that the party place itself on record "against sabotage and every other form of violence and destructiveness suggested by what is known as 'direct action.'" The party responded and, in its convention of 1912, the Reverend W. R. Gaylord, a Socialist minister, introduced an amendment to the constitution providing for the expulsion of any member "opposing political action" or advocating "crime, sabotage or other methods of violence." Victor Berger was one of those who spoke in favor of the amendment. His speech was a wholesale indictment of the IWW: "I do not believe in murder as a means of propaganda. I do not believe in theft as a means of expropriation, nor in a continuous riot as free speech agitation." The amendment was adopted by the convention. Later, the membership voted for it, 13,215 to 4,195. Berger, for one, hailed the vote and called for speedy action so that the party could get rid of anarchists and syndicalists, "and the sooner . . . the better."

This schism was never healed; it split the two major sources of American radicalism then in existence. Nor were the relations between the Socialist party and the AFL made any more harmonious. The decision to expel the IWW-oriented left did not affect the thinking of Samuel Gompers who kept the Socialists at a safe distance. Most assuredly this had not always been so. In the early years there had been a close working relationship between Socialists and labor people. As a struggling labor organization, the AFL accepted help from whatever source it was given. Gompers admitted that he found some of the Socialists to be "high minded and idealistic." But these, he said, were far outnumbered by party members who were less interested in the labor movement than they were in building up a big Socialist vote. Furthermore, Gompers found that most Socialists were unstable in their judgments and intellectually undependable. This was caused by their "inability to recognize facts." So, after the flirtation of the early years, the gap between the right wing and left wing labor leaders widened. Gompers consistently resisted Socialist attempts to take over the leadership of the AFL. The final split came on the issue of the war; Gompers would never accept the Socialist pronouncement that the "ties that bind together the working class were stronger than the ties of country."[18]

It is apparent that the radical left was quite divided on questions of ideology and tactics, to say nothing of its divisions along geographic and even ethnic lines. There was little realistic possibility of a left wing uprising that would have threatened the nation. Yet the significant point was that increasingly large numbers of Americans perceived the left to be far more dangerous than any previous radical group. On strictly historical grounds this feeling is difficult to understand. The Populists, in their day, had elected governors to office. This the Socialists had never done and the Wobblies had no desire to do. Other groups and individuals had challenged conventional thinking by presenting novel economic and social ideas. William Jennings Bryan had literally roared against the money trust and refused to allow the people to be "crucified on a cross of gold." Henry George in his advocacy of single tax theories had attacked real estate interests and was highly controversial. While these earlier reformers were feared as a threat to property interests, they were not subjected to as harsh treatment as the leftists were.

The fundamental difference was that all of these earlier radicals attacked only a clearly defined set of vested interests within the capitalist system. On the other hand, the Socialists and the IWW launched an attack on the system itself. This wholesale attack, reinforced as it was by other factors, namely, the opposition to the war, the rise of Russian communism, the new labor militancy, and the waves of new immigration, enraged the public. Its anger was so great that when the time came it was quite willing to participate in the activities of the Red Scare.

The noted historian, Stanley Coben, has offered still another penetrating explanation. To Coben, the Red Scare was part of a movement to purify American life by eliminating its disturbing elements. It developed as a by-product of the heavy immigration and as a result of stresses and strains caused by the war. Many believed that the American way of life was under attack and might even disappear. They were disturbed by the growth of radical (i.e., foreign) political parties and by the hordes of immigrants flooding the cities. Fears were increased when the leftists joined other groups opposing the war. After the Armistice, the inflation, the great strikes, and the problems of demobilization provided further proof that "un-American" elements were spreading confusion and preventing a return to "normalcy." The Red Scare, then, was a massive act of political surgery which tried to cut out the disruptive elements. By doing so, it was believed that the nation would return to its "Golden Age."[19]

There was also some evidence that by their own actions the radicals themselves were partly responsible for their own difficulties. In his memoirs, William D. Haywood noted the similarity of Section Six, the amendment to the constitution of the Socialist party which expelled the IWW, to the criminal syndicalist laws adopted by many states during and after the war. In his authoritative study of the federal suppression of dissenters, William Preston makes the same point even more strongly. To Preston, the Socialists, by virtue of the passage of Section Six were the first to create an index of permissible belief and action within the larger framework of discontent. After drawing this line, it was only a question of time before others with more rightist views would decide that those to the left of the line were beyond the pale of political consideration.[20] This line of reasoning suggests that it was the Socialists themselves who first opened the door to the possibility that unorthodox opinions could be controlled by repression. It should be kept in mind, however, that while this may have been the effect of Section Six, it was hardly its intention. Furthermore, the repressive forces in American society scarcely needed the leftists to provide inspiration.

NOTES

1. For Hillquit's theoretical works, see *Socialism in Theory and Practice* (New York, 1910), *From Marx to Lenin* (New York, 1921), and

Morris Hillquit and John A. Ryan, *Socialism: Menace or Promise?* (New York, 1920).

2. On the alienation of the immigrant as a cause of radicalism, see Oscar Handlin, *The Uprooted* (Boston, 1951), p. 294.

3. Department of Labor Research, *American Labor Yearbook* (New York, 1916), p. 96.

4. Charles Edward Russell, *Bare Hands and Stone Walls: Some Reflections of A Side Line Reformer* (New York, 1933), p. 203.

5. Nathan Fine, *Labor and Farmer Parties in the United States: 1828–1928* (New York, 1961), p. 224; Daniel Bell, "The Background of Marxian Socialism in the United States," in *Socialism in American Life,* ed. Donald D. Egbert, Stow Persons (Princeton, N.J., 1952), I, p. 309.

6. Morris Hillquit, *Loose Leaves From A Busy Life* (New York, 1934), p. 108.

7. *New York Call,* November 10, 1910, p. 6.

8. *Ibid.,* p. 1.

9. *Ibid.*

10. *Ibid.,* November 8, 1911, p. 6.

11. *Ibid.*

12. For a revisionist view, see James Weinstein, *Decline and Fall of Socialism in America: 1912–1925* (New York, 1967), p. 327. Weinstein argues that the Socialist party grew in "size and prestige" during the First World War. Its decline began in 1919 and not in 1912.

13. *New York Times,* November 5, 1913, p. 1.

14. *New York Call,* November 6, 1912, pp. 1–2.

15. Bell, I, p. 315, quotes T.R.; other opinions, including Hillquit's, appear in *New York Times,* November 7, 1917, p. 4.

16. Emma Goldman, *Living My Life* (New York, 1931), I, p. 636.

17. Quoted in Philip Foner, *History of the Labor Movement in the United States* (New York, 1965), IV, p. 352.

18. Samuel Gompers, *Seventy Years of Life and Labour: An Autobiography* (New York, 1925), pp. 383, 391, 402.

19. Stanley Coben, "A Study in Nativism: The American Red Scare of 1919–20," *Political Science Quarterly,* LXXIX (March 1964), pp. 55–75.

20. William D. Haywood, *Bill Haywood's Book* (New York, 1929), p. 258; William Preston, *Aliens and Dissenters: 1903–1933* (Cambridge, Mass., 1963), p. 50.

Chapter Two

THE RED SCARE
DURING THE WAR: 1914-1918

The earliest manifestations of the Red Scare in New York began as early as 1914. In the immediate prewar years, opposition to the left was fairly mild and was stimulated by its protest against poor economic conditions. The antiradical crusade increased in intensity after the United States entered the First World War. The left opposed the war and the government responded with a series of repressive laws. Soon, large numbers of radicals were being prosecuted. The public held them in contempt and considered their views close to treason. These developments set the stage for the more formidable antiradicalism of the postwar period.

The Protest Against Poor Economic Conditions

The period 1913–1914 was a difficult one for the American people. Beginning in May 1913, pig iron production began to decline. Soon, other industries followed the trend and by year's end a recession was in full swing. The economic crisis reached its peak in the winter months of 1914–1915.

While the downswing hurt business, it was the workers who were most directly affected. Many became unemployed as the recession hit cities throughout the country. At the same time food prices were going up. Charitable societies tried to help out as best they could. The Bowery Mission on Houston Street in New York was crowded daily by the unemployed who tried to get a bit of food to tide them over until good times returned.

Of all the urban centers, New York was hardest hit. According to one survey, there were more than three hundred thousand unemployed men in the city by February 1914. Conditions were the worst since the winter of 1907–1908. The mayor, reformer John Purroy Mitchell, tried to alleviate some of the distress. He advocated a day of rest for those employed in an attempt to spread the work; he implored businessmen to organize an employment bureau. Neither of these suggestions was acted upon. Mitchell was more successful when he established public employment agencies. By the end of March these agencies had helped a total of 3,973 persons get jobs, mostly as snow shovelers, farm hands, and laborers.

Beyond this practically nothing was done by state and local officials to help the unemployed. Even the American Federation of Labor was slow to recognize the magnitude of the problem despite a rising rate of unemployment among its skilled workers. Soon, however, the workers began to take things into their own hands and on February 15, 1914, a large crowd marched in protest to City Hall. After receiving little satisfaction from the mayor, the crowd became angry and, in the opinion of one city official, was close to violence.

Of the many left wing groups in the city, only the Industrial Workers of the World tried to help the unemployed. In late January 1914 a general meeting of all IWW locals took place to discuss the problem. A young anarchist, Frank Tannenbaum, proposed that the IWW lead the city's poor on marches to churches to demand food and shelter. The proposal was adopted and on February 27 Tannenbaum led the first march to Baptist Tabernacle and demanded help. The next night six hundred workers entered Labor Temple, and on March 2 the Fifth Avenue Presbyterian Church was stormed during a service. The clergy responded by offering food and drink.

On each occasion, the press was sympathetic to the appeal for food but hostile to the radical group that had organized the demonstration. By March, however, press opinion began to turn against the marchers. The New York *World,* for example, referred to the workers as a "criminal menace" and warned that unless strenuous measures were used crowds of professional gunmen would join the unemployed and threaten property.[1]

City and labor officials also joined the press in condemning Tannenbaum's activities. One union official questioned the motives of the IWW:

The acts of the IWW are wholly insincere. It is true that at this time of year the building trades are idle, and that thousands of men are out of work. But very many of these men can live on their savings or get assistance from their unions. The reputable laboring man out of work has no sympathy with the IWW movement, and will not take part in its demonstrations.

Other union leaders agreed. One referred to the marchers as "bums and toughs who go shouting through the streets attempting to fool the public." However, this hostility only made Tannenbaum bolder, and on March 4 he led two hundred men to the Roman Catholic Church of St. Alphonsus. While Tannenbaum was holding a discussion with Father Schneider, the rector of the church, about twenty patrolmen arrived and carried them all off to jail. Tannenbaum was charged with "inciting to riot," and was sentenced to a year in jail. Of the others arrested, eight were given lesser sentences while the remainder were released.

With Tannenbaum out of the way, the IWW decided to abandon this technique as a solution to the problem of the unemployed. While agitation did not cease, it took other forms such as meetings and rallies. The police remained vigilant; they did not harass the IWW directly but took steps to insure that owners of public halls would not rent to them.

The Free Speech Campaign

The Free Speech Campaign, a year-long effort in support of the striking miners in Colorado, was the cause of additional agitation throughout the years 1914–1915. It began on September 23, 1913, when about nine hundred miners from the coal fields of southern Colorado went on strike. The struggle was to be marked by increasing violence during its fifteen months' duration. Not only the length of the struggle but the fact that the mines were owned by a company controlled by John D. Rockefeller, Jr. accounted for the nationwide publicity that the strike received.

Rockefeller was not entirely at fault. Within the limits of his knowledge he did what he thought was right. He relied on information supplied by coal executives in the field. Consequently, he blamed the strike on "radical agitators" who had come into a contented community to foment trouble mainly for the purpose of building up their membership.

The coal operator's simplistic explanation missed the point. At the root of the disturbances were conditions in the mining towns. These were graphically described by Rockefeller's biographer:

> The location of the camps [high in the Colorado mountains], the unnatural growth of the communities, soon created a kind of feudal aristocracy in which various companies acted not only as employer but as landlord, merchant, legislator, and indirectly as priest and teacher. This concentration of power led to serious negligence and abuse on the part of company officials. There was no adequate contract between employer and employee, no machinery for the adjustment of grievances, indeed no appreciation of the significant place of labor in cooperative enterprise.[2]

As a result the United Mine Workers closed down all of the mines and presented a series of demands on hours, wages, union recognition, and the right to trade in other than company stores. The union also asked for the right of the workers to elect their own check weightmen (to verify the amount of coal they had mined) and the enforcement of long neglected state labor laws. The management's position was summed up by C. M. Bowers, chairman of the board of the Colorado Fuel and Iron Company, the largest firm in the industry and the one in which Rockefeller was a major stockholder, who said that the striking miners and their leaders were "disreputable agitators, socialists, and anarchists." In a letter to Rockefeller, Bowers wrote:

> When men such as these together with cheap college professors and still cheaper writers in the muck-raking magazines, supplemented by a lot of milk and water preachers with little or no religion and less common sense are permitted to assault the businessmen who have built up the great industries and have done more to make this country what it is than all the other agencies combined, it is time that vigorous measures are taken to put a stop to these vicious teachings which are being sown throughout the country.[3]

With positions hardened on both sides, the strike turned to violence. On October 17, 1913, some strikers in a tent colony exchanged fire with camp deputy sheriffs. At one point in the battle the deputies ran an armoured car through the tents and fired at least one machine gun, killing several men. Later, a pitched battle took place between the strikers and a group of thirty-five militiamen, called into prevent violence. Nobody was sure who fired the first shot but after several hours of fighting, the militiamen set fire to the tent colony, killing several workers. The next morning it was discovered that eleven children and two women had suffocated in the bottom of a cave where they had sought refuge to avoid the gunfire. The "Ludlow Massacre," as it came to be called, triggered a series of violent acts by the strikers. Mines were attacked and burned, buildings were looted, and the entire state seemed close to anarchy. Further violence was finally prevented when President Woodrow Wilson, at the request of the governor of Colorado, sent federal troops to the scene.

The nationwide reaction to the Ludlow Massacre was intense. In New York, it took the form of the Free Speech Movement which demanded justice for the striking miners. Public demonstrations began almost at once. On May 1, 1914, the IWW took the lead by picketing Rockefeller's New York home. Meanwhile, Upton Sinclair, a free speech activist, led a parade of liberals, anarchists, and Socialists down Broadway to the Standard Oil Building to Rockefeller's office. At one point, Alexander Berkman, a nationally known anarchist, was heard to shout: "Kill Rockefeller. Shoot him down like a dirty dog." Another protester managed to make her way upstairs and was finally stopped outside of Rockefeller's office. She demanded that he stop "the murderers of Colorado," and threatened to shoot the industrialist before she was hauled off to jail.

Protesters, this time silent ones, resumed their vigil at Rockefeller's residence. Many arrests were made on May 8, and at least one person was clubbed. Three days later, the socialist minister, Bouck White, the pastor of the Church of the Social Revolution, led ten of his followers to the Calvary Baptist Church where the Rockefeller family maintained membership. The Reverend White challenged the minister to a debate on the Colorado Mine Strike while ushers seized the intruders and held them until the police came. All were found guilty at their trials. The Reverend White drew the longest sentence of six months in jail.

Later, the leaders of the Free Speech Campaign left New York to continue their efforts in a few neighboring communities. In Paterson, New Jersey, they encountered fierce opposition from the city fathers. Alexander Berkman replied to this harassment with uncontrolled rage: "We are going to defy Rockefeller, the mayor, and the city magistrate and will carry on our agitation and hold meetings no matter who is opposed to us or what machinery is used against us."

Berkman's threat was not an empty one, for on May 31 bands of Free Speech protesters, led by the IWW, began to arrive for open-air meetings at Rockefeller's home in Tarrytown, New York. Here they were met by local police who arrested each militant as he began to speak. Nonetheless, the protesters continued to arrive in great numbers. There was more scuffling between them and the police. One activist shouted at a policeman: "If I had a gun I'd shoot you dead where you stand." Berkman tried to speak but the police kept shoving him off the rostrum. Finally the police answered with force and a number of people were hit with nightsticks.

By mid-June tempers were cooled somewhat when Mrs. Charles J. Gould, a local resident and suffragette, offered Upton Sinclair, Leonard Abbott, and other Free Speech leaders the use of the private theater on her estate for airing their grievances. This did little to pacify the more radical IWW members who were soon back parading through the Tarrytown streets. They were met by townspeople who threw rotten eggs and vegetables at the speakers; the police were called in to restore order. *The New York Times* called for "strict law enforcement" while the *New York Call* suggested that the disorders must have been aggravated by "His Oily Majesty" (Rockefeller) and would not be settled until the people and not the capitalists owned the coal mines.[4]

A related incident occurred in July when a bomb exploded prematurely in the New York apartment of Arthur Carron, a twenty-nine-year-old civil engineer and Free Speech activist. The police claimed they had uncovered a plot by the IWW to kill Rockefeller. This had miscarried when the bomb went off. The basis for this charge was a remark made by Carron to some of his friends to the effect that dynamite might well be an effective weapon to use against the industrialist. One newspaper editorial placed the blame squarely on the shoulders of the radical left. "We cannot honestly regret the loss of the men and women who must all have been guiltily cognizant of its manufacture and the purposes for which it was designed."[5]

The next day, the anarchists and the IWW led by Alexander

Berkman planned to parade the bodies of their fallen comrades
through the streets. When the Health Department prohibited
this, they decided instead to hold a memorial meeting at Union
Square and accused the police of interfering with their right of
free speech and assembly. Mayor Mitchell was sensitive to the
charge that free speech was being abridged during his administration. He said that everybody, even the anarchists, had the right
to assemble and speak peacefully.

On the day of the funeral about twenty thousand people gathered in Union Square where the ashes of Carron and the other
anarchists were exhibited. These were placed in an urn made in
the form of a clenched fist rising from the depths. This was then
placed in the office of *Mother Earth,* an anarchist paper edited
by Emma Goldman, where it was decorated with wreaths and
red and black banners. Thousands passed through the offices to
see the urn. At no time did the police interfere with any of these
activities.

In October there was more commotion when another bomb
went off in the nave of St. Patrick's Cathedral on Fifth Avenue.
Again, without proof, some police officers blamed the anarchists
and the IWW while others attributed it to the work of "cranks."
And in November 1914 fears were again heightened with a bomb
was found beneath the seat of a city magistrate, Judge A. L.
Campbell, just as he was about to ascend the bench. Speculation
was rife that leftists were somehow responsible when it was recalled that it was this judge who had sentenced Alexander Berkman and Bouck White to jail. The police were not taking any
chances and additional men were assigned to keep watch on all
IWW headquarters and to keep a stenographic record of their
meetings.

The IWW, incensed with this constant official scrutiny, protested in no uncertain terms. Some even charged that the police
themselves might have planted the bombs for the purpose of
implicating their organization. James Larkin, a former Dublin
labor leader now actively working with the IWW, was more can-
did. He asked: "Why shouldn't you throw bombs? In Europe, the
highest honor a man can attain is to blow up as many people as
possible. Why should you apologize if they charge you with
throwing bombs? They'll blame it on you anyway."

No official investigation of the IWW was undertaken during
this period. However, its continuous agitation created the image
of the Wobblies as lawless rebels. Consequently, the public began

to regard them with hostility. But the provocation was insufficient to implicate other radical groups or to unleash a major Red Scare. It took a world war to do this.

Radical Opposition to the War

The outbreak of the World War forced the international Socialist movement to face the consequences of its own ideology. For years the Socialists had preached that wars were caused by competing capitalist systems. When the fighting began, they set aside their ideology and came to the defense of their nation. In Germany, France and England, Socialists united behind their governments and voted to support the war.

Since the United States was not yet a belligerent, the American Socialists were not faced with this choice. They were free to denounce the war in the strongest terms and even called upon President Wilson to help arrange a negotiated peace. In December, 1915, the Socialist party by a vote of 11,041 to 742 ordered the expulsion of any Socialist official voting for preparedness.

To many Americans, this opposition seemed the equivalent of sympathy for the Central Powers. One writer, expressing the popular attitudes of the day, pointed out that "at no time did [the S.P.] utter a word of protest against the invasion of neutral Belgium, or against the frightful exactions levied upon the Belgian people by the German army." In addition, he felt that the left was unconcerned about alleged "German violations of international law."[6]

In New York, the Socialist leaders echoed their party's opposition to the war. Almost immediately a number of mass meetings were held throughout the city requesting the Wilson administration to rescind its proclamation of neutrality and take more active steps to stop the fighting. A typical meeting was held August 5, 1914, at Union Square. It was attended by a cross section of people from the Socialist party, its foreign language federations, the IWW, and the radical trade unions. Their spokesman was Ludwig Lore, a radical editor, who said: "The Socialists and workers of this country have it within their power at this critical moment to avert what will be the greatest calamity the world has ever known. I mean the continuation of the European war." Similar meetings were held during the summer at the Rand School and at various labor halls throughout the city.

Many antiwar meetings were informal in nature. Union Square

was frequently used during these years not only by radical, anti-war groups but by many speakers preaching a variety of doctrines. At times there were different points of view expressed from different soapboxes. Arrests were made occasionally but only when the speaker allowed the meeting to get out of hand. Indeed, during this early period there was little interference with antiwar activities. The New York Police Commissioner said: "I do not see how . . . a peace meeting in Union Square is in any way objectionable." This laissez-faire attitude was to change drastically once America entered the war.

In late September the New York Socialists held their first official meeting since the war began. The meeting was important and reflected the fact that the party was not united on its antiwar stand. The featured speaker was a left wing cabinet minister from Belgium who tried to explain why the European Socialists had supported the war. Next, Abraham Cahan, the editor of the *Jewish Daily Forward,* praised Woodrow Wilson and suggested that the Socialist party should support his policy of neutrality. Morris Hillquit reiterated the official party position saying that only the Socialists stood in opposition to the race for armaments, colonialism, and war.

Despite these divisions within the party, antiwar opposition was the party's key issue in the November election. The party campaigned under the slogan "a vote for the Socialists is a vote against the war." On the state level the Socialists backed Gustave A. Strebel for governor, Stephen J. Mahoney for lieutenant governor, and Charles Edward Russell for senator. Only one Socialist candidate, Meyer London, was elected.

Thus far, there was little or no response from the public to the Socialist party's antiwar attitude. The reason for this was that while the United States remained at peace, the opinions of the party, as nonconventional as they were, did not collide *in a fundamental way* with those held by the majority of Americans. The party's opposition to capitalism was nothing new; it had been expounding this doctrine since its first convention, and, judging by the election returns, very few people were listening. Its war opposition was equally ineffectual; many pacifists and religious leaders had also preached this with no observable results. The Socialists ran into greater difficulties when the United States entered the war. It was then that the Red Scare of the war years began.

The declaration of war of April 6, 1917, produced no immediate change in the position of the Socialist party. It merely stood on its antiwar declaration of 1914. Some, like Leon Trotsky, a resident of New York at this time, urged the party to adopt a more radical program. With the help of Louis Fraina, a left wing journalist, Trotsky drafted a document recommending resistance to recruiting and the fomenting of strikes. Trotsky suggested further that the war be turned into a civil war between classes. Fortunately for the party this document received little publicity outside of party circles. Had it been more widely circulated, the consequences might have been disastrous.

The party's official position was formulated at St. Louis, three days after President Wilson requested a declaration of war. The St. Louis Declaration began: "The Socialist Party of the United States in the present grave crisis, solemnly reaffirms its allegiance to the principles of internationalism and working class solidarity the world over, and proclaims its unalterable opposition to the war just declared by the government of the United States."

This declaration split the party down the center. Its results might have been predicted, for even before the meeting many Socialists had already resigned from the party and made public explanations of why they could not oppose the war. Later more retired. Upton Sinclair and John Spargo, the journalist, left it voluntarily. Charles Edward Russell was expelled. A. M. Simons, a left wing historian, denounced the convention as scuttled by "German nationalistic jingoes and anarchistic impossibilities." But the major party leaders, Debs, Berger, and Hillquit, remained in the party and faithfully supported its antiwar declaration.

The declaration set off a flurry of activity among party members. The publisher of *Pearson's Magazine,* a radical journal, wrote to Woodrow Wilson assuring him that "a number of us scattered over the United States have entered upon a determined campaign to change the policy and the attitude of the Socialist Party." A Socialist candidate for a local office in Chicago, Nellie H. Baldwin, also wrote to the President informing him that in her opinion "ninety-five per cent of the membership of the Socialist Party is perfectly trustworthy and with you in your determination that we shall stay in the war until it is won right." Many other Socialists held the same opinion. Had the American people been more aware of the divergence of views in Socialist ranks, the effects of the later Red Scare might well have been more contained.

Then, too, the Socialist party was not the only radical group

opposing the war. Opposition came from the IWW as well. While
its objections were not official, so many of its leaders made antiwar
statements that it was generally assumed that these represented
the views of the entire membership. Further protests came from
many progressives, pacifists, and idealists among whom were
Robert M. LaFollette and George W. Norris, both senators of
distinction. Said Senator Norris: "We are going into the war upon
the command of gold." In the confusion of the postwar Red Scare
this liberal opinion was overlooked when it was assumed that
only the radicals had failed to support the war effort.

As the war continued, the left refused to moderate its antiwar
statements. If anything, they increased in intensity. From the
floor of Congress, Meyer London maintained that the "greatest
service this Congress can render humanity is to vote against the
war." London added that the United States was really fighting
against four million German Social Democrats who were "as
interested in getting rid of the Kaiser as we are."

As one might have predicted, talk of this kind irritated the
American people. Some were further upset by the constant criticism leveled at the American Federation of Labor for its prowar
stand. Leading the attack were the New York-based, leftist clothing unions. When Samuel Gompers, for example, called a conference of union presidents to Washington to reaffirm labor's support, *Advance,* the newspaper of the Amalgamated, charged that
he had no right to speak for the labor movement on this subject.
Gompers was also censured for his no-strike pledge. "Think of it,"
said *Advance,* "because the nation is engaged in a war against a
foreign enemy, the private employer is to be permitted to exercise
his powers of oppression over the workers to his heart's content."[7]

This persistent criticism intensified fears of the left. While big
business was not beyond reproach, the public felt that class warfare should be abandoned at least for the duration of hostilities.
And the left refused to do this.

At the same time, as feelings against the left rose, so too did
hostilities towards immigrants. For decades their hyphenated status and assumed split loyalties had always rendered them suspect.
Now, with the country at war, unquestioning loyalty was demanded from them. This point was eloquently expressed by one
New Yorker, Theodore Roosevelt:

> There is no room for the hyphen in our citizenship. . . . He
> who is not with us is against us and should be treated as an

enemy alien. . . . We have room in this country for but one flag.
. . . We have room for but one language. . . . The German-
American alliance, the Sinn Feiners, the East Side Russian
revolutionary organizations . . . and the I.W.W. are anti-
American to the core. . . . Our bitter experience should teach
us for a generation to crush under our heel any movement
that smacks in the slightest of playing the German game.[8]

It must be admitted that this statement was not characteristic of
Roosevelt. On the contrary he was a sensitive man who had
demonstrated his real concern for the immigrant on many occasions. This outburst reflected his exaggerated patriotism during a
time of national crisis. But it also revealed Roosevelt's belief that
disloyalty was associated more with hyphenated Americans than
with those of native stock. While it is true that some immigrants
were radicals and opposed the war, it was equally true that many
native-born Americans did so too. Such statements, however, re-
enforced the stereotype of immigrant radicalism which appeared
and reappeared during the Red Scare.

Criticism of the war, with its implied threat of subversion, also
had its effect on the federal government. Even before America's
entry, steps were taken to tighten internal security and ward off
any possible interference with the war effort. The attorney general
ordered all federal attorneys to maintain "constant vigilance"
and requested urban police chiefs to keep known pacifists and
German sympathizers under observation. The secretary of war
posted a thin line of troops at strategic spots near immigrant
populations and industrial centers. The worst was anticipated but
when war was declared nothing happened.

Initially, the attorney general asked loyal Americans to become
"volunteer detectives" and to report instances of disloyalty and
subversion. The results were even greater than expected. Thousands of complaints were brought in but many proved to be
worthless. In addition, many patriotic associations were formed
to help police the nation. The best known was the American
Protective League, organized in 1916 with the sanction of the
Department of Justice. Its members, all private citizens, helped
check claims for draft exemptions, assisted in bond drives, and
helped distribute ration books. More significantly, they also became involved in loyalty investigations.

The president of the Metropolitan Trust Company headed the
local chapter of the APL. It performed the same functions as other

branches. However, it tended to find a greater evidence of disloyalty among those who had labor connections or belonged to minority groups.

From time to time, the New York local was accused of highhanded methods and even of occasional brutality. These instances were unrelated to the national policy of the organization but reflected simply the excessive patriotism of certain of its members. The *New York Call* maintained that the APL was disrupting Socialist meetings and keeping its members under surveillance.[9] Stronger criticism came from the left wing of the party which declared that the APL and other patriotic organizations were "inaugurating a reign of terror in this country similar to the Black Hundreds in Russia."

To provide the manpower necessary for carrying on the war, Congress passed the Conscription Act on May 18, 1917. This established a wartime draft whose legality rested upon the constitutional provision empowering Congress to raise and support an army and upon the war powers of the president. The constitutionality of the draft was unanimously upheld by the Supreme Court in January 1918.

As expected, the left opposed the conscription law. All these groups—the Socialists, anarchists, and the IWW—agreed that any law which required people to fight was bad. In New York, the Socialists in the assembly tried to delay the passage of a resolution which endorsed the draft. Abraham L. Shiplacoff led the fight against the resolution. His remarks were immediately challenged by Assemblyman McCue who accused the Socialists of a lack of patriotism. McCue added that if Shiplacoff held these views he should resign immediately from the legislature and give up his citizenship papers. Immediately after, Shiplacoff took the floor and delivered an impassioned speech defending his patriotism. In the course of the speech he exclaimed: "I and those I represent are better Americans than Mr. McCue. He is an American by accident of birth. I am an American by choice and desire." And so it went, but, while this appeared to be an isolated incident, it does provide insight into what was later to become a confrontation of major proportions.

Meanwhile, the debate on conscription continued throughout the state. In May, one of the largest anticonscription rallies took place at the Harlem River Casino. The meeting was well attended by many left wingers. The police were also present but no arrests were made. Emma Goldman and Alexander Berkman spoke for the anarchists, Louis Fraina for the Socialists, while the IWW was represented by Harry Weissberger, Leonora O'Reilly, and Carlo Tresca. All denounced the draft and urged young men not to register for it. The meeting called for a "general strike" as a protest against the war and appealed to the American workers to follow the Russian example in forming workingmen's committees to run the country.

About one hundred soldiers attended the meeting. They came dressed in their uniforms with the express purpose of disrupting the proceedings. They heckled the speakers and at one point one of the soldiers rose and demanded the floor. The audience objected strenuously and there were requests that the soldiers be forcefully ejected from the hall. Emma Goldman remained calm. She appealed to the crowd to let the soldier speak:

> We have come here to protest against the coercion and to demand the right to think and act in accordance with our consciences. We should recognize the right of our opponents to speak, and we should listen quietly and grant him the same respect we demand for ourselves. The young man no doubt believes in the justice of his cause as we do in ours, and he has pledged his life for it. I suggest therefore that we all rise in appreciation of his evident sincerity, and that we hear him out in silence.

The audience rose in unison. The soldier started to speak in a quavering voice that barely carried beyond the platform. He stammered something about "German money" which was an insinuation that the enemy had financed the anticonscription cause, talked vaguely about "traitors," became confused, and then came to a sudden stop. Turning to his comrades, he cried: "Oh hell, let's get out of here." The soldiers filed out waving little American flags accompanied by the laughter and the applause of the radicals.

This rally was followed by another held on May 31 at Madison Square Garden. It was sponsored by a pacifist group, the First American Committee for Democracy and Peace Terms. Again the radicals showed up in great numbers. A number of arrests were made when a group stood outside the Garden and distributed antiwar leaflets. Two of those arrested were Morris Becker and Louis Kramer who were accused of violating the

Conscription Act by urging young men not to register for the draft. Kramer was fined $10,000 and sentenced to two years at Atlanta penitentiary. Becker was given 20 months at Atlanta. The Supreme Court sustained the convictions.[10]

Still another anticonscription rally was held in June at the Hunt's Point Palace in the Bronx. This time hundreds of policemen were present and twelve armed soldiers were sent by the Justice Department to maintain order. A large number of soldiers and sailors also came to heckle the speakers. The two principal speakers were to have been Alexander Berkman and Emma Goldman, but when Berkman started to speak the crowd showed signs of erupting into chaos. As usual Emma Goldman saved the day. She rushed to the center of the stage and roared: "Friends, friends. . . . The soldiers and sailors have been sent to cause trouble and the police are in league with them. If we lose our heads there will be bloodshed and it will be our blood they will shed. . . . We must refuse to be provoked by it. . . . Therefore I declare this meeting closed." There was no evidence that the police were conspiring with the troops, but had Miss Goldman not taken this wise step there would indeed have been violence.

In the weeks that followed, raids, arrests, and prosecutions became more frequent. Those arrested were charged with violations of the Selective Service Act. As the New York left was actively opposing the war, the accused were more often than not members of this group. One of the leading cases involved Emma Goldman and Alexander Berkman. In the light of their importance to the radical movement and their later deportation from the country, their convictions at this time were significant.

At first Miss Goldman intended to disregard the indictment and offer no defense. She felt that it was impossible for an anarchist to get a fair trial in an American court. She discussed her plan with a number of her radical friends. They informed her that she was making a grave mistake. John Reed, a Socialist and, later, a founder of the Communist Labor party, told her to fight as hard as she could. Max Eastman suggested that she hire a good lawyer so that she might stay out of jail and help carry on the struggle against the war.

The trial began on June 27, in the federal courthouse at Foley Square. Judge Julius M. Mayer was on the bench. As he had already sent Kramer and Becker to jail, it appeared unlikely that either defendant would be acquitted. The case for the government was ably presented by the United States district attorney, Harold A. Content. Berkman and Goldman were defended by their old friend, Harry Weissberger.

The prosecution tried to prove that the defendants through their writings and speeches had urged young men not to register for the draft. As evidence it presented the anarchist newspapers, *The Blast* and *Mother Earth,* which they edited, and a transcript of a speech delivered by Miss Goldman at the Harlem River Casino. In the course of this speech, Miss Goldman had said: "We believe in violence, and we will use violence."

The defense insisted that nowhere in their writings did the defendants urge resistance to the draft, but were merely preaching against the war. Witnesses were called to prove that neither of the accused had ever advocated violence by word or deed. In Berkman's case this was more difficult to prove as he had already served a long jail sentence for the attempted assassination of the millionaire industrialist, Henry C. Frick.

The jury listened to the evidence and returned a verdict of guilty. Both defendants were given the maximum sentence of two years in prison with a fine of $10,000. The result was not unexpected. Said Berkman: "We have been convicted because we are anarchists, and the proceeding has been very unjust." Miss Goldman asked that the sentencing be postponed for a few days so that she could take care of some personal business. When this request was refused by Judge Mayer, Miss Goldman exclaimed: "I want to thank you for your leniency and kindness in refusing us a stay of two days, a stay you would have accorded the most heinous criminal." The Judge turned white with anger but did not reply.[11]

One can well appreciate how distressed the radicals must have felt after reading about these trials. There was no doubt that a large number of such cases involved their members since they were in the forefront of the antiwar movement. However, they were not alone. Many other convictions were handed down for violation of the Conscription Act. Among these was the case of Roger Baldwin, the pacifist head of the National Civil Liberties Bureau (later called The American Civil Liberties Union), who refused to register for the draft and was charged with a personal violation of the law. In other cases, the accused were charged with inciting others to become lawbreakers. For example, Louis

Fraina was found guilty of preaching that the war was not in the interests of the working class.

Prosecutions under the Conscription Act declined after June 15, 1917, when the Espionage Act was passed. The new law gave the necessary powers to the federal government to protect itself against any interference with the war effort. It provided for imprisonment of up to twenty years and large fines for persons wilfully helping the enemy, inciting rebellion in the armed forces or attempting to obstruct recruiting or the operation of the draft. Another section established postal censorship when it banned treasonable or seditious material from the mails.

At least one influential New Yorker hoped that the government would go no further after the passage of the Espionage Act. In September Charles Evans Hughes, a leading member of the New York bar, assured the members of the Bar Association meeting at Saratoga that Congress now had sufficient powers to protect the country from internal subversion. Congress thought differently; in October it passed the Trading-with-the-Enemy Act which empowered the president to censor all international communications and gave sweeping powers to the postmaster general over the foreign language press in the United States.

Even greater powers were added by the Sedition Act which was signed by the president in May 1918. This law had been requested by the Justice Department for the purpose of expediting prosecutions under the Espionage Act. In juridical terms, the courts were giving a narrow interpretation to the word "obstruct" in the phrase which read, "obstruct the recruiting and enlistment service." To remove the difference in interpretation, the Justice Department recommended to Congress that the section be amended by including "attempts" as well as actual obstructions of the draft. Public pressures also played a part. Under the Espionage Act, the attorney general lacked the power to stop "casual or impulsive disloyal utterances." The attorney general explained:

> These individual utterances . . . occurring with considerable frequency throughout the country naturally irritated and angered the communities in which they occurred, resulting sometimes in . . . lawlessness and violence and everywhere in dissatisfaction with the adequacy of federal law to reach such cases.

The new legislation plugged the loopholes and pacified the public.

The Sedition Act was to have important consequences for the American left. One section in particular was especially relevant. Broadly drawn, and even more broadly interpreted, it prevented the uttering or publication of any "disloyal, profane, or scurrilous" language about the form of government of the United States, and promised long jail sentences or heavy fines to anybody who "by word or act" opposed the war effort, or sided with the nation's enemies.

Predictably enough, press reaction to these new laws was generally favorable, *The New York Times* declared that they would give prosecuting officers "plenty of latitude to frame indictments against traitors," while the *Buffalo News* self-righteously denied that the laws were intended to suppress free speech. Other newspapers admitted that the possibilities for injustice existed but doubted that they would occur. There was general agreement that convictions under the laws must continue if "treason and sabotage are not to flourish and triumph."[12]

On the other hand, most liberals greeted the new laws with apprehension. While the sedition bill was pending, Albert De Silver, the brilliant young head of the National Civil Liberties Bureau, wrote to Walter Nelles, a civil rights lawyer, saying, "You and I will both go to jail if it passes." Roger Baldwin, another official of the NCLB protested to Colonel House, while Norman Thomas, just beginning his career as a Socialist, wrote that the bill was "useless."

In left wing circles the reaction was much the same. After the experience with the Conscription Act, the leftists realized that all future legislation of this type would be largely directed at them. In a telegram to Woodrow Wilson, the New York local of the Socialist party urged him to veto the Espionage Act.

A similar expression of views came from the Socialist aldermen in New York who introduced a resolution requesting amnesty for all political prisoners and those indicted under the Espionage Act. The radical labor unions were also rigorously opposed. *Advance* warned that the new legislation would "put such a tight gag on all newspapers and magazines that any criticism of the government will be prosecuted by federal authorities."[13]

Cases soon arose testing the constitutionality of the new acts. As a group, they provide penetrating insights into the antiradical crusade. For example, the Espionage Act was declared constitutional in the Schenck case when the secretary of the Socialist party was convicted for distributing leaflets opposing the war. The Supreme Court upheld the conviction stating that the leaflets were designed to cause insubordination in the armed forces and to obstruct the draft. Speaking for the Court, Justice Oliver Wendell Holmes said that this constituted a "clear and present danger" to the nation. With the country at war, such statements were not protected by the First Amendment.[14]

Next, the Sedition Act was declared constitutional in the Abrams case. This famous case began in the fall of 1918, when a group of four anarchists and one Socialist, all poverty-stricken immigrants in their twenties, published several pamphlets bitterly denouncing the American intervention in Russia. They threw the pamphlets from the top floor of a building where they were picked up by some workmen at the corner of Houston and Crosby Streets in Manhattan. The workmen notified the authorities and the five were arrested.

Some of the leaflets were in Yiddish; the others were in English. They were highly inflammatory and contained phrases like "the hypocrisy of the United States and her allies." One pamphlet condemned Woodrow Wilson who "with his beautiful phraseology" had so hypnotized the American people "that they did not see his hypocrisy." Another condemned the President's "shameful and cowardly silence" about the intervention in Russia and maintained that the "plutocratic gang" in Washington was behind it all. Still another urged the American people to "Awake, Rise, Put down your enemy and mine."

The trial took place before Judge Henry D. Clayton in the federal courthouse in New York. The defense tried to prove that the American intervention in Russia was not against Germany, therefore, opposition to such a policy could not be construed as interfering with the war. This testimony was thrown out by the judge with the statement: "The flowers that bloom in the spring, tra la, have nothing to do with the case." Judge Clayton took the position that it was illegal for the defendants to try to create public opinion hostile to the government of the United States and to encourage it to recognize "that faction" of the Russian government to which the accused were friendly. Although these statements were not part of the evidence, they tended to prejudice the jury.

Considering the mood of the country and the incendiary nature of the pamphlets, it was unlikely that the defendants would have been acquitted. Abrams and the others realized this and prepared for the worst. When one of the defendants, Samuel Lipman, was being sentenced, he said, "I do not expect anything better." To this Judge Clayton replied, "And may I add, that you do not deserve anything better." The radicals received stiff sentences. Three of them, including Abrams, were given the maximum of twenty years in prison. Another received three years, and Molly Steimer, the only woman in the group, received fifteen years.

As in the Schenck case, the decision in the Abrams case was upheld by the highest court. Here the judges disregarded the doctrine of "clear and present danger." Speaking through Justice John H. Clarke, the Court held that the real purpose of Abrams and his friends was to interfere with American military success in Europe. The language of the pamphlets, he said, clearly "intended to encourage disloyalty and resistance to the United States in wartime."

A strong dissenting opinion was written by Justice Oliver Wendell Holmes. He agreed with Abrams that the only purpose of the pamphlets was to help Russia and not to impede the war effort. The defendants, he wrote, were being punished not for their deeds but for their ideas. He argued that only a small punishment should be inflicted "unless the defendants are made to suffer not for what the indictment alleged, but for the creed that they avow." The defendants went to jail but were released in 1921 after promising to return to Russia.[15]

While these cases were in the courts, the government was busy with many other indictments. All told, there were 1,532 persons arrested for seditious utterances, 65 for threats against the president, and only 10 for actual sabotage. One commentator has written that the "Acts provided more latitude for the federal suppression of dissent" than America had known in its entire history.[16] This opinion was supported by the cases arising in the New York courts.

In the summer of 1917 Scott Nearing submitted a pamphlet entitled "The Great Madness" to the American Socialist Society for publication. This described the way in which financial interests had brought the country into the war as a method of diverting the attention of the workers from more immediate economic problems. Nearing and the American Socialist Society were indicted; however, the case did not come to trial until February

1919. In the intervening period, Nearing was subjected to considerable harassment from local authorities. In April 1918 he was prevented from delivering a lecture at Auerbach Hall in the Bronx. Samuel Orr, a Socialist assemblymen, maintained that the police had threatened to disperse the crowd if Nearing spoke.

Nearing was charged on four counts. Two involved conspiracies to cause insubordination in the ármed forces and to obstruct the recruiting and enlistment services while two others charged actual commission of the offenses. The charges were based on the publication of "The Great Madness." In his trial, Nearing defended his written statements. The jury found the evidence insufficient and he was acquitted.

In another case, an indictment under the Espionage Act was brought against A. I. Shiplacoff and John Reed for using disloyal language about the army and navy and criticizing American intervention in Russia. The court threw out the charges on April 4, 1919. An indictment was also secured against Max Eastman, Art Young, Floyd Dell, and John Reed, who were charged with interfering with enlistments by publishing articles and cartoons in the *Masses*. When notified that an indictment was being drawn up, the publishers offered to delete the offensive material. This request was denied.

The government's case rested upon a considerable number of facts: the sending of a telegram by Eastman on April 6, 1917, in which he stated that he hoped that riotous resistance would follow any attempt to conscript for military service; letters sent by Eastman and Merrill Rogers, the business manager of the Masses Publishing Company, saying that the policy of the magazine would be to oppose militarism and resist conscription; the June and July 1918, issues of the magazine which contained articles by Eastman, Bertrand Russell, and John Haynes Holmes, a liberal minister, urging resistance to conscription; an interview between Rogers and a salesman during which Rogers had said that he would be pleased if the entire naval and military program of the United States would run into difficulties; and a speech by Eastman on August 1, 1917, in which he referred to "We bloody-handed Americans" as only pretending to be fighting in the cause of democracy and defending a war of the working class against the militarists.

Arguments for the defense relied upon denials of any specific intent to obstruct recruiting and enlistment on the part of the defendants, and a denial of any conspiracy on their part. Three of the jurors felt that the government had not proven its case. They voted in favor of the journalists. The government's attorney was dissatisfied with the result. In a confidential memorandum to Attorney General Thomas W. Gregory, Caffey blamed the three jurors and called them "disloyal" and "un-American." The case was set for retrial in the following term of the court; the result was the same and the indictment was dismissed.

Other cases followed the same pattern. In the Pierce case, an Albany Socialist, Clinton H. Pierce, was accused of distributing a famous anticonscription pamphlet, "The Price We Pay," written by the Socialist, Irwin St. John Tucker. It contained a violent attack on the war which was pictured as the work of capitalists. The pamphlet was also used as a campaign document for the Socialist party.

The case arose when Pierce overheard John J. Scully speaking heatedly against the draft in an Albany saloon. Unknown to Pierce, Scully was a member of the American Protective Society; he was planted in the saloon as an agent provocateur. Pierce gave one of his pamphlets to Scully and was promptly arrested and brought to trial. In his charge to the jury, the Judge said: "Does this pamphlet . . . represent the ideas, the beliefs, and the principles of the Socialist Party? If so, it is opposed to the war, the Selective Service Act and the recruiting of the army to carry on the war." Pierce was convicted and the decision of the lower court was sustained by the nation's highest tribunal.

The Pierce case set an important precedent when the Supreme Court adopted a broad interpretation of the phrase "obstructing recruiting" which came to have an all-inclusive meaning. Henceforth, it was not necessary to prove that as a result of certain statements or actions any particular individual refused military service. Liability could be established by writing or speaking against conscription or the war. As in the Abrams case, Justice Holmes, joined by Justice Brandeis, dissented sharply from the principle upheld by the majority.[17]

A similar case arose when Stephen Binder, a New York butcher, was brought to justice for publishing a booklet entitled "Light and Truth." He claimed that the booklet was "written and published as a defiance to our government's misrule and as a bold assertion of the injustice of America's entrance into the world war." Binder was found guilty and received two years in jail.[18]

The same pattern was repeated in other cases. In Jamaica,

New York, Peter Grimm, an admitted Bolshevik and anarchist, was also convicted when he was alleged to have said: "America ought never to have gone to war with Germany. It is only a war of the capitalists." On January 20, 1919, in Brooklyn, a Socialist named Morris Zucker was sent to jail for fifteen years for seditious utterances made in the course of a speech. And in Yonkers, a man believed to be a "Bolshevik agent" was arrested and charged with sedition. The man, an employee of the National Conduit and Cable Company, told a number of naturalized Russian workers that "no Russian should fight in the United States Army." He also said: "If Wilson wants to fight, let him take his own kind." To a group of munitions workers he added, "Russians are crazy to buy Liberty Bonds. They have no value."

Upstate, the story was the same. Stanley Lindenberg, the eighteen-year-old secretary of the Socialist party at Niagara Falls, went to jail for saying that the American flag was a "mere piece of cloth or rag" and the American military uniform was "murderous." At his trial a good deal of evidence was introduced about the activities of the Socialist party. Lindenberg thought this irrelevant and prejudicial to his case, but the court thought otherwise. Meanwhile, in nearby Buffalo, a member of the Socialist Labor party got six years for alleged seditious remarks, and in Syracuse, Miss Julia Armbruster was fined $300 for threats against the president. These are but a few of many similar cases. They show clearly that the government was not solely interested in protecting the country against internal subversion but in suppressing radical dissent as well. The attorney general denied this charge. Gregory said that the suppression of radical opinion was not the *intent* of the Espionage Act; it was merely one of its outcomes. He argued that the indictments were necessary to secure compliance with the law which was being hindered by "local agitators" speaking on behalf of "the I.W.W., the pseudo-Socialists, and similar bodies."

Gregory's own assessment of his part in the administration of the Espionage Act was confirmed by reports coming in from the field. In one of these, the United States attorney for the Northern District of New York wrote to the White House explaining his purpose in seeking the convictions of four Socialists accused of distributing antiwar pamphlets. This official was evidently disheartened by left wing criticism which accused him of carrying on a witch hunt.

My purpose in this prosecution was simply to stop the circulation of such literature during the war. I am convinced that the Socialists will be very careful in this district and probably this pamphlet will not be circulated any more by that party. I tried to make it perfectly clear that the government had no quarrel with the Socialist Party and was not trying to interfere with it as a party, and that it was not seeking the imposition of heavy sentences on first offenders.

I am well aware that the President does not desire that any one shall have the opportunity to pose as a martyr or charge the government with undue activity in muzzling free speech, and I feel that the trial has been conducted so that there is no ground for claims of that kind. The prosecutions and convictions have the hearty approval of the people of this district and it is my desire that the President be correctly informed as to my motive and as to the real facts in this prosecution.

An even stronger defense of the government's policy in securing convictions under the Espionage Act was written by Attorney General Gregory in August 1918. It grew out of a letter sent by Upton Sinclair to Woodrow Wilson in which he tried to convince the president that the jailed radicals were political prisoners and deserved better treatment. Sinclair said that their only fault was that they had "not been able to adjust their minds to the present sudden emergency." He pointed out that they were languishing in filthy prisons and suggested instead that they be sent to farm colonies where they could perform useful work.

Sinclair's letter apparently made an impression on Wilson who sent it along to Gregory for an opinion. Gregory's reply came in the form of a four-page typed memorandum; it was a clearly reasoned defense of the government's policy under the Espionage Act. He argued that Sinclair had an exaggerated notion of the number of prisoners of "the radical-pacifist type" who were in jail for violating the law. He rejected the suggestion that farm colonies be set up, maintaining that these would violate both the letter and the spirit of the Espionage Act which calls clearly for "imprisonment." While the president, under his emergency powers, had the right to establish a special institution for such prisoners, it would have to be guarded and supervised by federal authorities. Anything short of this would not be a "penal institution" as called for by law. For these reasons, the attorney general refused the request for special treatment. He argued that the Espio-

nage Law was a fair reflection of public opinion and that crimes
which obstructed the war must be treated as serious offenses
regardless of the humane motivations which prompted them. "To
do less," said Gregory, "would cast serious doubt upon the law's
wisdom."

What emerges from all of this is a conflict of good intentions.
The left opposed the war as an immoral act carried out by the
capitalist governments at the expense of the workers. This reasoning may have been faulty but it was honestly proposed and sincerely believed. On the other hand, the Justice Department was
equally convinced of the righteousness of its cause. It attempted
to administer the law as best it could. By doing so it not only
discharged its constitutional responsibilities but, at the same time,
appeased public opinion.

The radical organizations also ran afoul of the wartime legislation granting power to the postmaster general to interfere with
deliveries of the mail. By authority contained in Section 12 of
the Espionage Act and amended in the Sedition Act, the government was merely empowered to hold up deliveries of printed
matter in violation of this law. The power to deny second-class
mailing privileges, although not in the Act, was assumed by the
postmaster general. As a result, by the fall of 1918 some seventy-
five papers were interfered with in one way or another. Of these,
about forty-five were socialist papers. Included in the list were
the *Masses,* the *New Republic,* and most of the radical foreign-
language papers.

Among the more celebrated cases in New York was that of the
New York Call which lost its second-class privileges on November 13, 1917. On January 9, 1919, the *Call* made formal application for the restoration of its privileges. The Post Office
Department held the application "under consideration" and then
gave the paper an oral hearing. Six months more elapsed before
a decision was rendered. During the long delay the *New Republic* noted: "It is apparent that Mr. Burleson [the postmaster
general] is stalling for time, afraid to take affirmative action and
thus inviting judicial contest."[19] It was not until June 1921,
during the Harding administration, that second-class privileges
were restored by the new postmaster general, Will H. Hays.

Some radical papers, like the *Jewish Daily Forward,* preferred
to comply with the government's directives. Soon after the passage
of the Sedition Act, its editor, Abraham Cahan, was called to
Washington where he was asked to show cause why his paper

should not be suppressed. This request came as something of a shock to Cahan. He had heard rumors that he was next on Postmaster Burleson's list, but he refused to take them seriously. At the hearing, Cahan denied that he had ever violated either the Espionage or the Sedition Act. But, out of his fear of suppression, he agreed to go along with the government and promised to print the war news devoid of editorial comment.

The representatives of the *New Age,* a socialist publication from Buffalo, were also summoned to Washington. They, too, were asked to "show cause" why their second-class privileges should not be revoked. The editors were indignant. In their view, they had little hope of vindicating themselves. Darcy Milliken, one of the editors, wrote to the Post Office Department requesting a bill of particulars specifying the charges against the paper. He pointed out that socialists also had rights under the Constitution. The Post Office Department answered that under the law it was not required to do more than it had already done; all of the evidence would be presented at the hearing. However, this did not satisfy the editors who protested that this method of procedure would make their defense an "informal one." Furthermore, it would violate the Sixth Amendment to the Constitution which clearly provides that the accused be informed of the charges.

The *New Age* was given its hearing on April 16, 1918. The Post Office Department said that the paper had "consistently followed a policy of attacking the prosecution of the war." It had insisted that the government was "in the power of the capitalist class," that it was insincere in its war aims, and that the workers had nothing to gain from the war even if America was on the winning side. In its reply, the *New Age* denied the accusations. But the government won its case and second-class privileges were revoked.

Difficulties were also experienced by the humorous Jewish weekly, *Der Grosser Kundess* (The Big Stick). Its editor, Jacob Marinoff, was perplexed as to which of its articles had aroused the ire of the postmaster general. He suspected it was because of a satire he had printed on the government's policy of censorship. The article paraphrased the biblical Song of Songs:

> Your cheeks are red as the cheeks of our abashed freedom. Your teeth are sharp as bayonets and as white as milk which we cannot afford to buy for our children. Your eyes gleam as

the fire of black diamonds, coal, which will cost more this
winter than gold. I have met the guardians of the, [*sic*] and
asked them, "Have you not found the reasons for our beloved
war?" And they answered, "Keep your mouth shut!"

A final case concerned the newspaper, *Advance*. Its editor,
Joseph Schlossberg, was an earnest Socialist and pacifist; he, too,
opposed America's entrance into the war. The paper's executive
board felt that Schlossberg had a right to his opinions but with
the threat of suppression imminent he was told to temper his
editorial policy. "There are enough forces in and out of the labor
movement seeking to destroy the Amalgamated Clothing Workers
without the United States government assisting them." Schlossberg did as he was told and censored himself.

In contrast to its ready acceptance of the Espionage Act and
other laws controlling antiwar activities, the New York press was
less willing to accept any interference with the delivery of newspapers through the mail. As newspapermen, they were sensitive
to this type of restriction. The *New York Post* wondered whether
the denial of second-class privileges to the *Call* wasn't the start
of a campaign against other radical and liberal papers. The
New York Sun argued that whatever merit there might be in
trying to suppress the radical papers, more harm than good
would come from the government's efforts. "There is a real danger," it continued, "that inconsequential movements will become
magnified and inconsequential men martyrized by a too broad
application of the censorship and suppression powers now in-
vested in the Post Office Department."

The radical papers were defiant. The *New York Call* proclaimed:

> No absolute monarch at any stage of the world's history
> ever displayed more high handed tyranny in his actions toward
> a subject than the mediocre monarch now mismanaging the
> Post Office displays in mistreating the mail of a citizen. . . .
> To denounce him is to dignify him. In very truth he [Burleson]
> is beneath contempt.

This statement appeared three months before the *Call* lost its
own privileges.[20]

Opposition to the postmaster general came from other sources
as well. During the 1917 election campaign when Morris Hillquit
was running for office, Herbert Croly, a journalist, wrote criti-

cally of Burleson to President Wilson. Croly argued that the suppression of the radical press was actually creating Socialists in New York. He urged a policy of persuasion instead of suppression. Wilson did not change his mind; he continued to support the postmaster general and gave him a free hand.

Debs and the radical trade unions were also violently opposed to censorship. Even the AFL at its convention in Buffalo noted a denial of due process of law. Instead of suppressing the mails, action should have been taken against the editors as individuals. A jury would then decide if violations of law had taken place.

Many leftists complained directly to the president. The millionaire Socialist, William Bross Lloyd wrote:

> Has any nation ever waged a successful war without wholehearted and substantially unanimous support from its citizens? Can such support be gained by law, force, or repression? The first step toward making the world safe for democracy seems to be the attempted extirpation of the Socialist Party and its press.

Lloyd informed Wilson that he would buy no more Liberty Bonds and would spend most of his money supporting the various papers excluded from the mails.

The National Civil Liberties Bureau was also incensed. On July 13, 1917, it held an emergency conference to deal with the problem of mail censorship. As a result, a committee of four lawyers, Clarence Darrow, Frank P. Walsh, Morris Hillquit, and Seymour Stedman, paid a visit to Burleson and pleaded for a more reasonable policy. They asked for departmental guidelines so that the papers might avoid repeating their past mistakes. Burleson would not even consider the suggestion. He maintained that if a paper disagreed with the decision of his department it was free to take its case to court. None of these protests had any effect. The policy of suppression and withdrawal of second-class mailing privileges remained intact until the end of the war.[21]

The hardships created for the left by the Espionage Act convictions and by mail censorship can hardly be minimized. Yet, of all the victims of the wartime Red Scare, it was the IWW which felt the lash of federal suppression most directly. The organization itself, despite its outwardly belligerent appearance, was beset with difficulties. Since 1914 its membership had been falling drastically. In New York state its maintained weak locals in Buffalo, Little Falls, Rochester, and a few other cities. In New York City, it was somewhat stronger; it published a news-paper, the *Rebel Voice,* but its efforts at infiltrating the clothing unions had long since been defeated by the aggressive unions of the AFL.

Despite its decline, the IWW managed to lead a series of war-time strikes in many parts of the country. Soon, the public, the press, and the Justice Department began to feel that the IWW-led strikes were being called in a deliberate effort to obstruct the war effort. To put a stop to this, mass arrests of its leaders took place, accompanied by raids on IWW headquarters.

The raids reached their climax on September 5, 1917, when hundreds of arrests were made. Among those taken were: Hay-wood, Ralph Chaplin, and Vincent St. John. Files, literature, and office equipment were also seized. Convictions were secured against ninety-six Wobblies; the stiffest sentence was drawn by Haywood who went to jail for twenty years.

On October 1, 1917, further developments took place in New York when Elizabeth Gurley Flynn, Arturo Giovanitti, Carlo Tresca, and other IWW leaders were arrested. The order for their arrest was telegraphed from Justice Department head-quarters in Chicago to Captain William M. Offley, chief of the department's Secret Service Division in New York.

The department was justly proud of its catch. Miss Flynn had been active as a strike leader in the West. In 1912 Giovanitti had led the textile strike at Lawrence, Massachusetts; subse-quently, he had been tried and acquitted for a murder which took place during the strike. Tresca, an IWW leader from Italy, had been described by *The New York Times* as "one of the more rabid IWW leaders."[22] He had declared that he was against all govern-ments and once tried to stop ship construction at the Brooklyn Navy Yard.

After their arrest the prisoners were shackled together and sent to the municipal jail, the Tombs, where they awaited the arrival of the indictment coming from Chicago. Within a few days they were free on bail; they set to work immediately to raise a defense fund to pay lawyer's fees. While this was going on, a curious request came from Bill Haywood. From his Cook County jail cell, he advised the New York Wobblies to give themselves up to

the nearest federal marshal and come to Chicago at once to stand
trial. It was not clear why Haywood suggested this. Perhaps he
hoped that the Chicago trial would give the Wobblies greater
publicity if it included the New York leadership. To Miss Flynn,
Haywood's suggestion was "tantamount to a lynching." With the
war hysteria at its height, she thought it better to postpone the
trial as long as possible. "Our plan," she later recalled, "was to
tie the case up in legal knots, in a dozen places, by a fight against
extradition and for severance."

At this point two lawyers arrived from Chicago. One was the
IWW lawyer, George W. Vanderveer, who represented Haywood,
while the other was the United States attorney who tried to secure
extradition through the courts. One of the defendants, Baldazzi,
followed Haywood's advice, discharged his lawyer and went to
Chicago to stand trial. He was convicted along with Haywood and
went to jail. After several years, his sentence was commuted and
he was deported to Italy. The cases of the others never came to
trial.

Undoubtedly, the IWW leadership did not know the real reason why the government was lenient with them. The full story
was contained in a telegram sent by Attorney General Thomas W.
Gregory to the lawyers of the Justice Department in Chicago
requesting a conference to examine the strength of the case against
the New York leadership. "If we have no case whatever as to any
particular defendants," Gregory wrote, "an announcement of such
discovery and abandonment at this juncture would inspire public
confidence in the fairness of the prosecution, and convince some
people that we are strong against those proceeded against." This
suggests that the government was worried about its image and
hoped to maintain public support by strict adherence to law. It
also suggests that the liberal and leftist criticism was having some
effect.

These antiradical activities of the federal government were
paralleled by similar developments within the state of New York.
Newspapers played a part in whipping up hysteria and urging
local officials to suppress antiwar opinion. Of the various municipalities, repression was most severe in New York City. Here, the
liberal policy of 1914 was abandoned when the police banned
all "inflammatory speeches." While the commissioner did not
specify radicals, the implication was clear that they were included
among those who sought to "use the right of free speech to cloak

disorder." It was still possible to speak, but the orator always ran the risk of harassment. In August 1917, for example, the police broke up an orderly street meeting of the Socialist party's Eighth Assembly District. At the meeting, Richard Boyajian, a Socialist, was addressing a crowd of a thousand persons. When the police arrived they told the speaker to move on and stop blocking traffic. A month later a protest meeting was scheduled for the Ebling's Casino in the Bronx. The hall owner cancelled it at the last moment explaining that he had been warned that his license would be revoked if the meeting was held. To the *Call* this was merely an extension of the Red Scare. As proof, it printed the list of speakers which was to include Benjamin Gitlow, a Socialist candidate for the assembly, Edward Seidel, the editor of the radical paper, the *Weekly People,* Louis Fraina, editor of the *New International,* and Charles Sonnenschain, an official of the League for Conscientious Objectors.[23] In mid-December, Emma Goldman, out of jail pending an appeal of her conviction under the Conscription Act, tried to speak at the Bronx casino and found the door barred. A few days later she attempted to hold a reception for Alexander Berkman, and again the doors were shut. When the hall owner was questioned as to why he had locked them out, he answered, "They said when they engaged this place that it was to be a musical entertainment for the United Hebrew Trades, and I found out about it just in time." Again the implication was that pressure had been exerted on him.

Upstate communities adopted a similar course of action. In Albany, a local judge told juries that they must stop "soapbox orators" within the areas of its jurisdiction. He requested that the police commissioner give the name and police records to the grand jury of all those who made "offending speeches." Armed with this information, prosecutions could be carried out more easily. In Buffalo, the City Council voted unanimously to deny the right of Kate Richards O'Hare, out on bail after conviction under the Espionage Act, from speaking in their city. Miss O'Hare was to deliver a standard antiwar speech which she had given many times before. The Socialist local had engaged Elmwood Music Hall early in January; the speech was scheduled for the end of February 1918. Defending their action, the city fathers said that they had voted to deny the use of the hall because of the possibility that Miss O'Hare might make "seditious utterances" and launch an "attack on the federal government." In April,

Franklin P. Brill, a Socialist, was scheduled to speak in Hamburg, New York, on the topic "The Real Meaning of Democracy." This speech had been previously given in Buffalo. Before the Hamburg meeting took place, a leaflet announcing the Buffalo talk fell into the hands of the village president, R. W. Hengerer; he decided to clamp down on the radicals. The Socialist party was informed that the contract for the hall was cancelled and that Brill would not be allowed to speak. Brill and a Buffalo organizer named Heisler then called on Hengerer, and asked him why the speech had been called off. "The people of Hamburg don't want to hear you," he said. Then Brill asked, "How do you ascertain the wishes of the people in this matter?" "I don't have to tell you that," was the curt reply. The Socialists persisted in their arguments but were unable to move him from his firm position. Few protested the decision. One who did was Mrs. Frederick Kendall who graciously offered Brill the use of her home. The Socialists did not accept the offer. They decided, instead, to return to Buffalo where their meeting was heckled by a local mob.

A similar situation occurred at Niagara Falls where a meeting of Russian workmen was broken up by the police soon after a left wing speaker began his address. The police contended that all speeches must be in English.

Thus, it was not surprising that local mobs soon appeared to lend their assistance to municipal governments in the task of suppressing antiwar opinions. As usual, radical speakers were more often than not the targets of mob violence. The *New York Call* quoted a number of servicemen on Fifth Avenue who were heard to exclaim: "If these damned Socialists say anything we will do them in." The press and even city governments did little to stop mob violence. In the opinion of the *Nation,* the press, by virtue of its inflammatory articles, even abetted the mob.[24] The usual tactic of the antiradical mobs was to mill about the crowd at a meeting, heckle the speaker, and then try to disrupt the meeting completely. On certain occasions, victims were forced to kiss the flag. At other times, radicals suffered the fate of the young secretary of a New Jersey Socialist local who was covered with molasses and feathers for refusing to buy a war bond. Some mob leaders like Russell Dunn, active for many years in the New York City area, mixed their antiradicalism with large doses of religious bigotry.

To the leftists the increasing level of mob violence was a cause
of real concern. It was discussed at many meetings of the executive committee of the New York local of the Socialist party.
Impassioned protests were sent to Secretary of War Baker, Secretary of the Navy Daniels, President Wilson, and Mayor John F.
Hylan. In June 1918 mob violence was among the subjects discussed at the state convention of the New York Socialists. The
convention adopted a lengthy resolution which summarized the
many violations of constitutional rights which had taken place
during the war and proclaimed that radicals were being persecuted not for disloyalty to the American people but for their
"loyalty to the struggle against privilege and exploitation."

Despite the rising hysteria, the Socialist party, as we have seen,
approached the election of 1917 with confidence; it presented a
full slate of candidates to the electorate and predicted victory.
For mayor, the Socialists ran Morris Hillquit who was opposed
by three others: the Tammany choice, John F. Hylan, the Fusion
candidate, John P. Mitchell, and the regular Republican nominee,
William F. Bennett.

As usual, Hillquit campaigned vigorously. He argued that a
Socialist victory would be a clear mandate to the government to
open negotiations for a general peace. His appeal was greatest
in the immigrant and working class neighborhoods where he
brought his message to the people via street corner meetings.

During the campaign, the Socialists complained of unfair tactics being used against them. The police, local mobs, and the
patriotic societies harassed them and tried to disrupt their meetings. A common technique used by the mob was to create a
disturbance at a Socialist meeting, then telephone the police
saying that the Socialists were rioting. When the police arrived
they would often find a riot in progress. Louis Waldman, at that
time a Socialist candidate for the assembly, related one incident
which he witnessed personally. A bystander complained to the
officer in charge after he was rudely shoved by a policeman. The
officer wouldn't listen; then the man protested, "But Lieutenant,
I'm an anti-Socialist." "I don't give a damn what kind of a
Socialist you ade," was the reply, "break it up."[25]

Another Socialist candidate, August Claessens, saw many instances of fraud at the polls. He said that some of the Socialist
voters, many of them timid immigrants, were turned away at the
polls by party regulars. Claessens also charged that many Social-

ist ballots, made of paper in those days, were either destroyed or miscounted. He estimated that at least one thousand five hundred Socialist votes were lost in this way.

When the election was over, John F. Hylan was declared the winner. Hillquit came in third, ahead of the Republican, William F. Bennett. Hillquit's total was 142,178 votes which was more than five times the number received by any previous Socialist for mayor. But the very success of the Socialist party seemed to exacerbate public fears of leftist subversion. These anxieties were compounded by Socialist successes in other races when the party sent ten of its members to the assembly, seven to the New York Board of Aldermen, and one, Jacob Panken, to a ten-year term as a municipal court judge. Assessing their victory, the Socialists were jubilant. Eugene V. Debs proclaimed: "The tide has turned. The Socialist Party is rising to power. It is growing more rapidly at this hour than ever before in its history."

Success has its limitations. The Socialists in both the Board of Aldermen and the assembly were soon to discover this. As members of a minority party in the midst of a war-produced hysteria, they sadly discovered that the Red Scare existed even within legislative halls. However, this was not immediately apparent.

Unaware of their eventual difficulties, the new Socialist aldermen approached their new tasks with dedication and enthusiasm. Their leader was Iowa-born, scholarly Algernon Lee. They set up a Socialist Legislative Bureau and hired Evans Clark, a former political science instructor from Princeton, as its director. They made constant use of the municipal reference library and drafted an unusually large number of bills. Few of their measures were "socialistic" but dealt with such needed reforms as a plan for the municipal distribution of ice, regulation of milk prices, free school lunches, day nurseries for the children of working parents, higher wages for municipal employees, and minimum wage legislation. While all of these measures were controversial, their proposals for amnesty for political prisoners and a prohibition against using the police as "strike breakers" created quite a stir.

Within a short time, the new Socialist aldermen succeeded in rousing the ire of the entire Board. Quite apart from differences over ideology, their difficulties can be traced, in part, to their grandiose self-image. The Socialists saw themselves as the guardians of the working masses against the vested interests. As a result, they introduced so many pieces of legislation that the efforts of the regulars looked weak by comparison. When their measures were rejected, they subjected their colleagues to verbal abuse; they accused them of being reactionaries and unconcerned with the welfare of their constituents. Despite the novelty of their left wing views, the press seemed genuinely impressed with their vigorous approach to urban politics.

Open hostility between the Socialists and the regulars broke out as early as January 1918 when the Socialists made speeches critical of Wilson and American participation in the war. One antiwar speech brought Alderman O'Rourke to his feet; he accused the Socialists of being traitors. "I warn the member," said O'Rourke, "not to criticize the President of the United States. I won't stand for it." But the Socialist voices would not be stilled. They continued to abuse the government and their fellow aldermen. For example, at a public meeting Alderman Beckerman said:

> I have spoken to all sorts of criminals, men whose mouths were as vicious as their heads were empty. But now I take my hat off to the gang on the Board of Aldermen. They are vicious and foul mouthed. Not one is interested in, or capable of constructive legislation. And as for their talk of traitors, if there are traitors anywhere they are among the Democrats and Republicans on the Board.

Antiradical feeling at the board came to a head in February when the Socialists refused to participate in a plan to sell war savings stamps. The Socialist position was explained in a speech by Algernon Lee in which he characterized World War I as merely another method of oppressing the poor. This time all of the aldermen were on their feet. There were cries of "traitors," "cowards," and "disloyal to the flag." Alderman Keanneally, a conservative from Staten Island, shook his fist at Lee and invited him to come into the next room where he promised that Lee would "kiss the American flag." Keanneally's further remarks were an open call to violence:

> What is wanted in this city is a patriotic committee that will use the rope on every disloyal person. I don't believe that any man with a spark of Americanism in him, or a drop of red blood in his veins, should sit with any traitors to the flag.

I would not hesitate for one minute in committing deliberate murder of any man who is a traitor. . . . I would consider it an honor to go to the electric chair for such an offense.

Despite an attempt made by board president Alfred E. Smith to smooth over the situation, the aldermen could not be calmed. The board was near riot when the session came to a close. Shortly afterwards, a number of aldermen inquired into the possibility of expelling the Socialists for disloyalty. "I knew it was coming," said Lee, who charged that the aldermen were using the issue of disloyalty as a smoke screen to cover up their own inability to satisfy the people's real needs.

Alfred E. Smith presided over a meeting of the Rules Committee at which the expulsion was discussed. However, nothing came of the plan and it was soon abandoned. As an alternative punishment, the board decided to gerrymander the Socialist districts and run Fusion candidates against them.

Meanwhile, the ten Socialists elected to the State Assembly were also busy. They introduced about seventy-five pieces of legislation in the first session. Here, too, most of the bills were reformist in nature. Among them was a plan to establish a free state university, to provide old age, sickness, and unemployment insurance, and to extend factory legislation. All of these measures were voted down at once, or sent to committee.

The Socialist assemblymen experienced difficulties similar to those faced by the aldermen. They immediately complained that they were being denied their minority rights. As a recognized political party, they were entitled to have one of their members sit ex officio on each committee. When questioned why this had not taken place, Assemblyman Welsh, a non-Socialist member, stated that he did not believe that the principles of the Socialist party would appeal to many people in the state of New York. In addition, the Socialist delegation was not seated together and was assigned seats in the last row where it was "most difficult to hear what was going on."

Unable to effect change directly, the Socialists resorted to a tactic of trying to stop those bills which they found most objectionable. On Lincoln's birthday, for example, they voted against a resolution which declared that World War I was being fought for the same principles for which Abraham Lincoln stood. After the vote was taken, Assemblyman Link, a Republican, delivered a patriotic speech in which he said that he would refuse to sit with men whose "hearts are lined with treason." Link added: "If this thing ever happens again may the Lord have mercy on your souls." He did not specify what he meant, but his message was clear.

In this section an attempt has been made to trace the Red Scare back to the year 1914. In these early years, attitudes towards the left were generally negative but still not intense enough to produce a Red Scare. The period began with a recession accompanied by a high level of unemployment. As the recession deepened, the city made some half-hearted efforts to help the unemployed. When this failed, the IWW stepped in and tried other methods. Under its leadership, the leftists marched on churches and demanded food for the unemployed. But the public did not overreact as it realized that the IWW was defending a just cause.

Neither did the Free Speech Campaign produce a significant increase in antiradical feelings. Most New Yorkers realized that the Colorado miners were being treated unfairly by the corporations. While they disagreed with the IWW's tactics, they sympathized with the cause of its concern.

On the other hand, the unexplained bombings of these years did accelerate antiradical tendencies. When bombs were placed in churches and beneath the seats of local judges, many were swayed by newspaper reports that the left was somehow involved.

Public opinion changed rapidly once preparedness became a national issue. Now, the radical antiwar position came into direct conflict with national security. The public began to equate pacifism with treason. The press and far too many politicians did nothing to discourage the belief that anybody who questioned the war, regardless of his motivation, was disloyal. With the passage of the Conscription Act, and later, the Espionage and Sedition Acts, the federal government joined in the efforts made to mobilize public opinion in favor of the war. While these laws were not aimed at the left directly, many leftists were sent to jail. At the same time, patriotic societies were formed and helped control antiwar and, often, radical dissent.

The experiences of the war years provided a training ground for those interested in carrying on an antiradical crusade during peacetime. The patriotic organizations continued to function and widened their scope. The antiradical mobs, clothed in the mantle of patriotism and realizing that they would not be held account-able for their actions, also remained. So, too, did those rightist elements who realized that the ambitions of the labor movement could be thwarted by emphasizing its radical leadership and its immigrant rank and file. Once these lessons were learned, the stage was set for the more formidable Red Scare of the postwar period.

NOTES

1. Quoted in Philip S. Foner, *History of the Labor Movement in the United States* (New York, 1965), IV, p. 444.
2. In Raymond B. Fosdick, *John D. Rockefeller, Jr.: A Portrait* (New York, 1956), p. 144.
3. *Ibid.*, p. 146.
4. *New York Times*, June 24, 1914, p. 10; *New York Call*, June 23, 1914, p. 6.
5. *New York Times*, July 6, 1914, p. 6.
6. William T. Ghent, *The Reds Bring Reaction* (Princeton, 1923), p. 24.
7. *Advance*, April 13, 1917, p. 4.
8. Quoted in John M. Blum, "Nativism, Anti-Radicalism, and the Foreign Scare, 1917–1920," *Midwest Journal*, III (Winter, 1950–51), p. 46.
9. *New York Call*, June 2, 1919, quoted in Harold M. Hyman, *To Try Men's Souls: Loyalty Tests in American History* (Berkeley, 1960), p. 283.
10. *Kramer et al.* v. *United States*, 245 U.S. 478 (1918).
11. See *Goldman* v. *United States*, 245 U.S. 474 (1918). It should be noted, however, that Miss Goldman, despite her dim view of justice in the United States, was not completely forgotten while she was in jail. The noted labor lawyer, Frank P. Walsh, was one of those who tried to help her. See Walsh to Goldman, July 16, 1917 in Walsh Papers (New York Public Library), Box 16.
12. *New York Times*, April 10, 1918, p. 12; *Buffalo News*, May 8, 1918; *Erie Herald*, May 7, 1918; *Syracuse Journal*, May 7, 1918; *Rochester Herald*, May 7, 1918, clippings in the American Civil Liberties Union Archives (New York Public Library), Vol. 66. Cited hereafter as ACLU Archives.
13. *Advance*, April 20, 1917, p. 1.
14. *Schenck* v. *United States*, 249 U.S. 47 (1919).
15. Horace C. Peterson and Gilbert C. Fite, *Opponents of War, 1917–1918* (Madison, 1957), pp. 227–29.
16. Hyman, *To Try Men's Souls*, p. 268.
17. *Pierce et al.* v. *United States*, 252 U.S. 239 (1920).
18. *United States* v. *Binder*, 253 Fed. 778 (1918).
19. "Burleson and The Call," *New Republic*, January 7, 1920, p. 158.
20. *New York Sun*, October 17, 1917, *New York Post*, October 17, 1917, in the ACLU Archives, Vol. 54; *New York Call*, August 14, 1917, quoted in Peterson and Fite, p. 48.

21. In fact, the *Volkszeitung,* a Socialist foreign-language paper, did not
    have its mail privileges restored until August 15, 1921. See Alexander
    Tractenberg and Benjamin Glassberg (eds.), *American Labor Year-
    book* (New York, 1921–22), p. 11.
22. *New York Times,* October 1, 1917, p. 14.
23. *New York Call,* September 12, 1917, in the ACLU Archives, Vol. 54.
24. *Ibid.,* September 1, 1917; Herbert J. Seligman, "The Press Abets the
    Mob," *The Nation,* October 4, 1919, pp. 460–61.
25. Louis Waldman, *Labor Lawyer* (New York, 1941), p. 41.

Chapter Three

THE RED SCARE
IN NEW YORK: 1919

In New York City, a year after the end of the war, antiradical
activities continued at a heightened tempo. These developments
grew logically out of the wartime experiences and involved three
protagonists: the executive departments of the city, the Board
of Aldermen, and the mob. Their antagonist was the radicals
themselves. At the same time, the Socialist party was undergoing
its most important schism when it split into three parts giving
birth to two new Communist parties. These developments were
all interrelated and acted to widen and deepen the scope of the
Red Scare.

The First World War ended on November 11, 1918. The
soldiers returned and tried to resume the normal course of their
lives. But the economic dislocations of the postwar period made
this difficult.

In New York, conditions were similar to those existing
throughout the country. Returning soldiers were forced to stand
in long lines at employment offices, hoping to be placed in the
few scarce jobs. The housing shortage was extremely severe.
Even the business community was apprehensive as sales volume
decreased and profits fell. There seemed to be no end to the
succession of strikes during 1919, estimated at more than five
hundred in New York City alone. Labor disturbances reached
a peak in October when sixty thousand men were idled. A strike
in the clothing industry just four days after the Armistice was the
first of many industrial disputes in the city. Two strikes on the
waterfront brought all shipping in the port of New York to a
standstill. A pressman's strike tied up the printing industry while
an actor's strike darkened the Broadway theaters. Public opinion
was hostile to the strikers. It was generally believed that radical

77

agitators were behind these strikes and they intensified antiradical tendencies evidenced during the war years.

The growing antiradical hysteria was also heightened by the continued turbulence in the Soviet Union, and by the reaction of the American left to these developments. Since 1917 there had been two revolutions in Russia. The first took place in March 1917, when the Czar was overthrown and a provisional government set up. The American left, while supporting this revolution, was not overly enthusiastic. The March revolution was celebrated at meetings throughout the city. One of the largest took place at Carnegie Hall. Just three days later, one thousand persons assembled to bid farewell to Leon Trotsky who was returning to Russia. Trotsky predicted that he would overthrow the provisional government and stop the war with Germany. His prediction was soon to come true.

Lenin arrived in Russia during April 1917, in the famous sealed railway car that sped nonstop through Europe to its destination at the Finland Station. In America the left followed developments closely, with numerous meetings to decide upon a course of action. There was general agreement that the removal of the Czar had solved only the political problems of Russia. The economic and social problems remained.

The political situation in Russia worsened through the spring of 1917. By July the provisional government was losing ground as it attempted to solve domestic problems while continuing the war against Germany. As Russian enthusiasm for the war waned, Elihu Root and some American labor leaders went to Russia and urged continued resistance. But many Russians were already shouting Lenin's slogan, "All power to the Soviets," and the mission failed. Led by the Bolsheviks, the second Russian revolution took place in November 1917; the Winter Palace was captured and the provisional government was overthrown. Lenin and the Communists were Russia's new rulers.

In contrast to the lukewarm reception given the March Revolution, the American left was highly enthusiastic over the Bolshevik Revolution. Eugene V. Debs' remark was characteristic: "From the crown of my head to the soles of my feet, I am a Bolshevik and proud of it." Even Socialists like Max Hayes and Dan Hogan, who had supported the war, now supported the Bolsheviks.

There were similar expressions of joy in the ranks of the New

York left. Morris Hillquit saw Russia "standing in the vanguard of social progress, in the hands . . . from top to bottom, of the people themselves, of the working class, and the peasants." Louis Waldman greeted the revolution as "an awakening of freedom and self government." Additional support came from the convention of the Socialist party of greater New York where the Russian demand for an end to imperialism was endorsed. Congressman Meyer London was more cautious; he tended to play down the revolutionary character of the Bolsheviks, contending that the demand of the Russian peasantry for land was no more revolutionary than the Homestead Act had been in the United States.

Not only the Socialist party but the Socialist Labor party, the IWW, and the anarchists joined in the chorus of praise for the Russian Revolution. The leadership of the Socialist Labor party, slower than the others to respond, was pressured to do so by its members. To the IWW the revolution represented the triumph of the very class and principles for which they themselves fought. Emma Goldman explained her decision to support the Bolsheviks by remarking: "I sided with them because they had repudiated war and had the wisdom to stress the fact that political freedom without a corresponding economic equality was an empty boast." Many liberals seemed to agree. A typical statement was made by the Reverend John Haynes Holmes who declared in a sermon: "Thank God for the Russian Revolution."

On the other hand, the violence of the revolution and the very novelty of Lenin's doctrines struck a note of fear in the hearts of most Americans. To many, bolshevism represented a fundamental challenge to the American way of life. The important figures of the day, those who were responsible for molding public attitudes, were quick to point out the threat. To Dr. George Clarke Cox, a Harvard professor speaking at a Manhattan YMCA, the philosophy of bolshevism was "insane." The president of Columbia University, Nicholas Murray Butler, saw bolshevism as the world's chief enemy of democracy. The authoritative *New York Times* considered bolshevism a "problem" but found little likelihood of a Communist uprising in the United States. No revolution could succeed, it declared, unless economic conditions were such that the people had little to lose by a radical change in government.[1] One of the strongest opinions was expressed by Senator George E. Chamberlain who suggested in a New York speech that one method of dealing with "local Bolsheviki" might be to "string them up." Few took the trouble to reason beyond this point.

It was not surprising, therefore, that the city government took preliminary steps to lessen radical agitation. In the closing months of the war, Mayor John F. Hylan began by ordering a ban on all displays of the red flag, the international symbol of the radical left. In a letter to Police Commissioner Richard Enright, Hylan also requested that all "unauthorized assemblages" be dispersed. The mayor provided the rationale for his action:

> We are passing through the most important and critical period of our history. Reports from abroad picture the horrors and outrages of unrestricted mobs, and even great neutral nations are facing the dangers of social upheaval. . . . The display of the Red Flag in our thoroughfares seems to be emblematic of unbridled license, an insignia for law breaking and anarchy.

To Hylan the phantom of bolshevism was more than a phantom. As mayor of the city with the largest concentration of radicals, he felt it his duty to prevent disorder which, in his view, could conceivably lead to violence and revolution.

The mayor, however, could only proclaim the law; it was left to others to enforce it. After receiving Hylan's flag order, the police commissioner used his own discretion in carrying it out. Enright interpreted the ban as applying only to "public displays" which meant that the red flag could not be flown at street or park meetings or inside public halls. In his view, the mayor's directive did not refer to flags flying in front of houses or apartments. He ordered the Police Department to enforce this version of the ban; he also told the police to use "extreme vigilance" at all parades, meetings, and other activities conducted by Socialists, anarchists, pacifists, or the IWW. Furthermore, he ordered all precinct police commanders to report at once the time and place of any radical meeting and to prohibit those which might cause disorder or "promote hostility to the government of the United States." Inasmuch as the war was over by this time, these regulations seem unduly harsh.

Protests against these new restrictions were not long in coming. S. J. Block, state chairman of the Socialist party, said that they were as autocratic as anything that the German Hohenzollerns had ever done. Block predicted, incorrectly, that the responsible officials would be defeated at the polls. Usher Solomon, secretary of the New York local of the Socialist party, boasted that if there were parades, the red flag would certainly be displayed. Algernon Lee made his statement by placing before the board an opinion written in 1911 by former Mayor Gaynor that differences of opinion with Socialists was an insufficient reason to deny them their rights. Gaynor had also said that the color of a flag should not alarm people with any intelligence.

These protests seemed to have no effect. If anything, they merely strengthened the resolve of the city fathers to curb radical left agitation. Others were encouraged to take even more drastic steps against radicals when a notice tacked on the bulletin board of the headquarters of the Socialist party was reprinted in the press:

> Verboten, the Red Flag is still flying on the House of Parliament in Vienna. It also flew for a time in front of the Union League Club [an influential private club in New York] while they still thought the Russians were Allies. In spite of the fact that the National Security League [a patriotic organization] tries to forbid the Red Flag in public, that very flag flies in Russia, Germany, Austria, Bulgaria, Roumania, Sweden, Holland, and will soon fly at embassies in Washington, D.C.

Anger mixed with fear increased among many city officials. In the Board of Aldermen, a resolution was introduced by Alderman Keanneally making it illegal to display a red flag anywhere in the city. This provided as punishment a $25 fine, ten days in jail, or both. Both the mayor and the police commissioner supported the resolution passed by the Board. When Enright was asked how he intended to enforce it, he answered that the radicals would soon find out if they violated its provisions.

A confrontation was in the making but it never came to pass. The record reveals that the flag ban was tested only once at a rally in Central Park. The rally was called by the Socialist party to honor Tom Mooney, the convicted San Francisco labor leader. Rainy weather reduced the crowd on the Mall to about seventy-five persons. The police arrested the main speaker for disorderly conduct and the meeting was dispersed. Other than this, the

radical groups honored the ban and did not seek to test it
further.

Similar ordinances banning the red flag were passed by state
legislatures across the country. The New York legislature followed
the trend with a bill introduced by Senator Walter W. Law
making it a misdemeanor to display the red flag at any public
gathering or parade. Governor Alfred E. Smith signed the bill
on May 7, 1919.[2]

While this dispute was in progress, the police added new restrictions with an "unofficial order" to owners of public halls
asking them not to rent to radicals. The Hall Boycott, as it came
to be called, lasted until the spring of 1919. It proved only
partially effective since many radical meetings were held during
this period.

Public discussion of the boycott began as soon as it was imposed and accelerated with time. The boycott was discussed at
many meetings of the executive committee of the New York
local of the Socialist party; the committee decided to publish
a pamphlet informing the people of New York of this latest
violation of their right to free speech. In addition, a motion was
carried to organize a number of protest demonstrations in vari-
out parts of the city.

Since the boycott was "unofficial," there was some question
as to whether it was even in effect. When informed about the
boycott, the district attorney admitted that one had been ordered
but expressed amazement that it was being applied against the
Socialist party. It was his understanding, he said, that it was to
be used only against anarchist groups and locals of the IWW.
The *New York Call* decided to investigate on its own; it called
the Sixty-Seventh Street police station, identified itself as hall
owners and asked for instructions. The police told them not to
rent their hall to Socialists. To the Socialist party this was proof
that the boycott was indeed aimed at them.

The entire situation was discussed at several meetings of the
executive committee of the party which decided to appoint a
committee, consisting of Evans Clark, S. E. Bearsley, Morris
Hillquit, Charles Grossman, and Karl Gottfried, to take further
action. Gottfried, a well-known New York Socialist, was requested to prepare a resolution to be introduced into the state
legislature by the Socialist delegation calling for an investigation
of the activities of the New York City police department. It was

also proposed to request the city's clergy to allow the Socialists to meet in their churches.

The committee reported back on February 3. It had decided to send letters of protest to Mayor Hylan, Police Commissioner Enright and Governor Smith. It had also arranged for a meeting of Socialist attorneys to discuss the legal aspects of the boycott, and had informed the *Nation* and the *New Republic* of their plight. Both of these liberal journals promised to run editorials exposing the ban.

Meanwhile, the policies of the city government were denounced at meetings held throughout the city. Among the speakers were virtually all of the important Socialists in New York including Ella Reeves Bloor, Edward F. Cassidy, Hilda Claessens, wife of Assemblyman August Claessens, Algernon Lee, Scott Nearing, Alexander Tractenberg, Judge Jacob Panken, Assemblyman Charles Solomon, and two Negro Socialists, Chandler Owens and A. Philip Randolph. Some left wing labor leaders like Joseph Schlossberg of the ACW also spoke. At one point, Meyer London suggested a general strike as the only effective means of protest.

This agitation produced few results. Under questioning, Commissioner Enright admitted that he had ordered the boycott; he denied, however, that it was being applied to the Socialist party. Nonetheless, the police at the precinct level continued to pressure hall owners to close their establishments to radicals. On one occasion, the police went even further and tried to prevent a meeting of the National Civil Liberties Bureau. This meeting, which was advertised as a protest against violations of civil rights, was held up for more than an hour until a police stenographer arrived to record every word.

By March many of the city's labor leaders were also up in arms against the Hall Boycott. They reasoned that if the Socialist party, a legal political party in the state, could be denied the use of public halls, the unions, too, might lose their right of assembly. To prevent this, a number of unions sponsored a strong resolution condemning the boycott and placed it before the Board of Aldermen for consideration. This union opposition stimulated a reply from the mayor. In a letter to the bakers' union, Mayor Hylan vigorously denied that the boycott was being used against the Socialist party "or any other organization which desired to assemble lawfully." The Socialists refused to believe him. In their paper, the *New York Call,* they published a list of thirteen halls from which they had been barred. In addition, Evans Clark offered to take the mayor on a walking tour to visit these very same halls.

In Buffalo, a similar situation developed when the local of the Socialist party lost the use of public halls because of Chamber of Commerce pressure. *The New Age,* the organ of the Buffalo Socialists, maintained that the Socialists "should have the same right to their propaganda as other parties. But they haven't. They are at the mercy of the anarchists in the Chamber of Commerce and the City Hall." When questioned about the matter, the city officials denied that anybody was being kept from renting halls to Socialists by intimidation.

Meanwhile, in New York, the Socialist party was experiencing new difficulties when pressure was applied to printing firms not to print radical literature. The *New York Call* found that its printing bill had been raised $1000 a month. To counter this, the *Call* announced plans to buy its own printing plant and sent out an emergency call to its members for additional funds.

Aside from these bans and boycotts, the city fathers had as yet not taken any additional moves to interfere with radical activities. Police activities increased, however, after a series of bombing outrages took place in Philadelphia and a few other cities. Extra police were assigned to guard City Hall and the Federal Court House at Foley Square. More "regulars" were added to the force and a special contingent of reserves was employed to prevent any possible interference with law and order. In a letter to his police chief, Mayor Hylan suggested that an agent of the department be present at all meetings of a radical nature held in the city. This agent would take the names of all radical speakers and note instances of disloyal remarks. Hylan also requested that the commissioner's office read radical papers such as the *Call* and the *Forward* and look for seditious utterances. There is no evidence that the mayor was vehemently anti-radical; he was, in large measure, responding to public criticism that he was being too soft on radicals.

To harden his policy, the mayor permitted the use of the police raid. The earliest raid was a fairly small operation against the Chinese branch of the IWW. This had been set up to organize the underpaid workers in the Chinese restaurants throughout the city. At its head was a talented IWW organizer, Gary

Wu. Curiously, the raid produced no comment in the press, except in the New York Wobbly paper, *The Rebel Worker*. It said the entire raid were merely "another instance of the capitalist class employing their control of the police and the courts to crush the militant labor movement."[3]

In March the police were ready for a much larger raid. Their target was the headquarters of the Union of Russian Workers on Fifth Avenue, a few blocks from the Rand School. The Union was a national federation of Russian clubs which served as a meeting ground for Russian immigrants. Most of the Russians came to the Union to take courses in auto mechanics, music, Russian literature, and to enjoy the companionship of other Russians.

The idea for the raid on the Union was conceived by Sergeant James F. Geegan of the police bomb squad; he worked out the details over a period of two months. Commissioner Enright then discussed Geegan's plans with the district attorney who was to help secure convictions after arrests were made. Immigration officials of the federal government were also consulted about possible deportation proceedings of aliens caught up in the raid.

At the appointed hour, several patrol wagons drove into the area near the Union building. When the police entered the building, they found a number of classes in session. Communication between the police and the Russians was difficult since most of the members did not speak English. There were 162 arrests. These were herded into patrol wagons which sped off to police headquarters.

In their search of the building, the police found many copies of the Union's publication, "The Little Red Book," which they claimed preached violence and the overthrow of existing institutions. The books were torn into little pieces and thrown about the room. On the upper floors, the police entered the editorial offices of a Russian language newspaper which rented space from the Union. Here Detective Geegan found about one thousand dollars in cash collected from the members. The checkbook of the Union was located in the general office. It revealed a recent expenditure of about twenty-five hundred dollars, mostly to publish radical literature. There was no evidence of weapons, bombs, or anything else that might have suggested that the Union was planning disloyalty to the United States.

Four of the members of the Union were held at police head-

quarters; the others were released for lack of evidence. The four
—Mollie Steimer, Peter Bianki, Oradovski, and a man named
Ketzes—admitted their belief in anarchist principles but insisted
that they were committed to nonviolent means. Bianki expressly
repudiated the use of terror which he considered futile; he said
he had nothing against the government of the United States.
In addition, he denied that the URW believed in the overthrow
of existing institutions.

Of all of the New York papers, the *World* was most critical
of the raid which it called an "intolerable abuse of police
power." *The New York Times* could see little difference between
the four who were held and the 158 who were released. "It is
hard to believe," it said, "that they were not all much alike in
mind and aspiration."[4]

In April antiradical activities took the form of a ban on all
foreign language meetings in the city. Once again, Mayor Hylan
responded to pressures, now from patriotic societies that accused
him of being soft on the left. The proposed ordinance was probably intended to disarm his critics. Actually, the mayor designed
the ban to apply only to those meetings in which the government
was criticized and not to meetings held by loyal citizens. But the
ordinance was misunderstood by the public and poorly administered by the police.

The mayor received many letters both supporting and opposing the ban. One letter was written by a man named Thomas
Loughlin who made the common mistake of failing to distinguish
between the radicals and the foreign born. To Loughlin the two
were indistinguishable, and, therefore, he felt that a ban on
foreign language speeches would both promote Americanism
and decrease radicalism. It did not occur to Loughlin, or to many
others at that time, that immigrant radicalism, to the extent that
it existed, was more closely related to poor economic conditions
than to the length of stay in the United States.

Among those groups opposing the ban were the radical
organizations, the foreign language groups, and a number of
trade unions with predominantly non-English-speaking memberships. Some of the trade unions that wrote to the mayor were
the Window Cleaners Protective Association, the Bronx Bakers,
and the ILGWU. The Socialist Consumers League and the
National Civil Liberties Bureau joined the rising chorus of
protest. These organizations were deeply upset and even re-

sentful of the ban. This is clearly seen in the statement issued by
the Amalgamated Clothing Workers:

> We represent 50,000 foreign-speaking workingmen, Jews,
> Italians, Russians, Lithuanians, and others, most of them citi-
> zens of the the United States, others ready to become citizens
> at the earliest opportunity. They contributed millions of
> dollars to the several Liberty Loans. Most of our members
> are raising their families here, and either they or their sons
> were drafted into the army during the war. We feel that we
> have a right to speak for these 50,000 men and women and
> their families and emphatically resent any attempt to besmirch
> the good name of the honest, peaceful, and useful people
> living in this community who have not found an opportunity
> to master the language of the land.

As the annual May Day celebrations of 1919 approached,
feeling was running high against the left. Traditionally, there was
a parade accompanied by many speeches, a custom started in
Europe where the festivities were often marked by labor uprisings
and an occasional assassination. Thus May Day in Europe came
to be associated with fear and, to some extent, this feeling was
carried over to the United States.

All of the radical groups planned for the big day. The IWW
predicted the greatest May Day ever; it promised mass demonstrations and a general strike. The New York Socialists were
more conservative; they merely planned traditional celebrations
and sent fraternal greetings to Socialist and Communist revolutionaries throughout the world.

Public fears were further intensified by a series of bomb
threats reported from many cities across the country. On April 28
a bomb was found in Mayor Ole Hanson's mail in Seattle.
Fortunately, Hanson was not at home at the time. The next day, a
Negro maid opened a package addressed to Senator Thomas R.
Hardwick, chairman of the Senate Committee on Immigration, at
his home in Atlanta; the package contained a bomb which exploded,
blowing off her hand. Hardwick's committee had been proposing
immigration restriction as a means of keeping out bolshevism. Some
thought this was the reason he had been sent the bomb. Among
those who read the news accounts was a postal clerk named
Charles Caplan, riding home after working the late shift. He
learned that the packages in which the bombs were mailed were

about six inches long and three inches wide; they were marked with a false return address to Gimbel's Department Store. Caplan seemed to remember that he had seen similar packages, and indeed he had. Returning to the Post Office, he located sixteen such packages which he had put aside earlier that day for insufficient postage. When the authorities were alerted, it was found that they contained bombs and were part of a nationwide plot to assassinate many prominent Americans. Among those slated to receive the "infernal machines" were Attorney General A. Mitchell Palmer, Mayor John F. Hylan, Police Commissioner Richard Enright, the financiers J. P. Morgan and John D. Rockefeller, Judge Landis of Chicago, Supreme Court Justice Oliver W. Holmes, and Secretary of Labor William B. Wilson. Other bombs had already started their journey through the mails making a total of thirty-six. Soon, post offices throughout the country were alerted. Except for the Hardwick bomb none of the others did any damage. Representative John L. Burnett, chairman of the House Immigration Committee, had a narrow escape when the lid on his package refused to open. This aroused his suspicions and he handed the package over to the police who identified it as a bomb.

From Washington, Postmaster General Burleson publicly praised Caplan for his diligence in discovering the bombs. He suggested that he and other postal employees involved be commended for their watchfulness. Next, federal and local authorities went to work to track down the guilty party. The press followed developments closely as various clues were uncovered. Each new discovery led to a dead end. No evidence was ever presented linking those who carried out the crime with any radical group or individual in New York or elsewhere. In the absence of evidence to the contrary, it is entirely possible that the plot was the work of cranks or lunatics.

Despite the lack of proof of a conspiracy, the police proceeded on the assumption that radicals were involved. Many arrests were made but the victims were usually people of little influence and few friends. One clue led to the Committee of Five, a group of anarchists in the city. All of the accused were soon released when no case could be developed against them.

The press also assumed that radicals were behind the bombings and demanded immediate arrests. A characteristic expression of opinion came from the *Brooklyn Daily Eagle*. It found it hard to believe·that the "resources of the country for the detection of scoundrelism [would] prove inadequate to the task of ferreting out the criminals and bringing them to justice. The horror with which public sentiment regards conspiracies so dastardly," it continued, "should warn the Anarchists, Bolshevists, Syndicalists, or whatever may be the correct designation of the villains now involved that the people of the United States will give short shrift to them and their doctrines alike." The *Brooklyn Standard-Union,* a conservative journal, was close to hysteria and called for severe repressive measures:

> Anybody who preaches overthrowing our form of government here ought to be sent to Russia or else shut up for life in some prison here. . . . There is so much for decent people to do in this land. . . that it is an absurd waste to compel them to devote time continually to watching Bolshevism, cautiously regulating its activities, and patiently deciding in each particular case whether each particular Bolshevist has overstepped the limits of law or not.[5]

This editorial raised a point that is central to our thesis. It was one of the first occasions when any responsible source suggested deportation as the final solution of the radical problem. This could not have been seriously proposed until the government, prodded by public opinion, had grown weary of deciding "in each particular case" whether an individual radical had overstepped the limits of law. That time was soon to come.

As expected, the liberal and radical press provided a different interpretation. The *New Republic* felt that those who mailed the bombs were most likely deranged persons. Normally, it said, such persons would not become violent; they were encouraged to act out their suppressed hostilities in times of social turmoil. *The Rebel Worker,* the official organ of the IWW in New York, suspected that the bombs had been planted by the police to throw the blame on the radicals and embarrass the labor movement.[6]

With the newspapers full of stories about the bombs, it is not surprising that the May Day celebrations were marred by violence.[7] Disturbances began when a group of 150 soldiers and sailors tried to storm Madison Square Garden to disrupt a peaceful meeting called by the Amalgamated Clothing Workers. The troops arrived in a large white bus; they were commanded by a Canadian soldier. They moved forward when a bugler in the group sounded the call "to arms." The police tried to persuade the soldiers to leave by informing them that there were no radicals present at the meeting. After a scuffle, the mob was dispersed.

Later that evening, the soldiers and sailors returned to the Garden where a second meeting was in progress. Leading the mob was a marine carrying an American flag. The police met them head on in the streets and succeeded in repelling wave after wave of "troops" sent against them. At one point rocks were thrown and some arrests were made.

Inside the Garden, the radicals were honoring Tom Mooney, the convicted California labor leader. The speeches were radical but the meeting was peaceful. Dudley Field Malone, a Socialist leader, urged a general strike until such time as Mooney was released. Another speaker, Rabbi Judah L. Magnes, a liberal with prolabor views, denounced people who sent bombs through the mail as "brutal, cowardly, criminals." He said that such people hurt rather than helped the cause of labor. The major address was delivered by Mrs. Rose Mooney who valiantly defended her husband's innocence. The meeting closed after her address without further incident.

Meanwhile, mobs of soldiers and sailors were roaming the streets in other parts of the city. A major incident took place when the new editorial office of the *New York Call* was raided. A housewarming was in progress at the time of the raid. The tone of the speeches and the offerings of flowers and cake reminded one Socialist, Norman Thomas, of the festive celebrations held in any American town when the church debt was being paid off. Suddenly, the mob invaded the premises and drove the people into the street. The attackers formed a semicircle in front of the building and struck people with clubs as they passed between them. Seventeen persons had to be treated for injuries, and one girl went blind from shock. Inside there were fistfights and a man jumped from a window twenty-five feet above the ground to avoid being beaten.

During this attack, a report reached the headquarters of the left wing faction of the Socialist party that they, too, were marked for violence. The advance warning provided time to make the necessary preparations which were carried out under the direction of James Larkin, a veteran of the Irish labor movement. Larkin armed his followers with long iron pipes. Buckets of hot boiling water were kept in readiness. The stairway leading to the first floor was lined with armed men determined to fight to the last man in defense of their headquarters. Thus armed, they eagerly awaited the attack which never materialized.

It is not clear why the left wing headquarters was bypassed by the attacking mobs. One reason may have been that the soldiers who attacked the *Call* then decided to march on the Union of Russian Workers instead. At the Union they lined up the members and forced them to sing "The Star Spangled Banner." Then, they went to another Socialist meeting at Webster Hall and again forced the people to sing the national anthem. This seemed to keep them occupied and the left wingers were overlooked.

Still another mob descended on the Rand School. Anticipating an attack, the school officials had the foresight to lock the entrances but the mob streamed up the fire escapes. Some of the soldiers succeeded in getting into the building only to find a number of classes in session. The soldiers seemed perplexed at the peaceful nature of the school; they were persuaded to leave before they did any damage.

Similar disturbances took place in other boroughs. In the Bronx, a mob attacked a parade whose members carried signs demanding amnesty for political prisoners. There was some fighting and at least one marcher was struck on the jaw by a policeman when he refused to leave the street.

The following day the mayor ordered an investigation of the May Day disturbances. "I knew nothing about it," said Hylan, "until I read it in the papers." Hylan seemed especially distressed that the police had applied force against the soldiers and sailors but he had nothing to say about the brutality directed against the radicals. The *Call* printed many statements from eye witnesses who testified that violence had been carried out against innocent people. It demanded action by the authorities to prevent a recurrence. The *Call* lodged further protests with the Secretaries of the War, Navy, and Treasury Departments and with President Woodrow Wilson, demanding that steps be taken for the future protection of lives and property. The Central Labor Union also denounced the May Day violence calling upon the military and naval authorities to deal severely with any future disturbances of this type.

From Washington, the first response came from Assistant Secretary of the Navy, Franklin D. Roosevelt, who said that he would refer the complaint to the commandant of the naval district of New York. Most other officials maintained that it was a matter for local authorities to handle. The response of the Secretary of the Treasury, Carter Glass, was particularly insensitive. "I am not prepared to say," declared Glass, "that the ultimate responsibility for the disorders to which you call attention rests with the soldiers and sailors rather than with those incendiary publications which they represented." The *Call* answered the charge by expressing amazement at being called an "incendiary publication," and accused Glass of defending hoodlums.

Others as well protested Glass' remark. To Dudley Field Malone, Glass' statement was a "disgraceful contribution to violence and mob spirit in this country." The Methodist Federation for Social Service was also critical; it found it shocking that an important government official should practically condone "direct violence against distasteful opinions." It was time, said the Federation, for thoughtful Americans to speak out against the denial of civil liberties in America. Many liberals expressed similar views.

For the most part, the press tended to excuse the actions of the May Day mobs as a natural reaction to the violence preached by the radicals themselves. For example, the *Brooklyn Eagle* stated:

> The uniformed rioters whether soldiers or sailors, may be himself [*sic*] on the fringes of the law. But with all of his lawlessness he is translating into action a great and overwhelming volume of public sentiment stirred to anger by the frankly violent character of the revolutionary doctrines now everywhere preached in this and other American cities.[8]

Later on, however, the *Eagle* softened its tone, contending that the task of combating violence must not be left to mobs but must be opposed by the intelligent and reasoning forces of the law.

Nevertheless, the events in May did stir some officials in Washington to action. Within a few days, the War Department started an investigation of the attack on the *Call* since military personnel were involved. The managers of the paper were requested to prepare a statement describing the events which would then be submitted to Washington. The *Call* complied with the request but there is no evidence to indicate that anything further was done.

Petitions sent by the *Call* to the city government requesting action were not answered for twelve days. District Attorney Swann replied that he would be glad to receive evidence concerning the attack and promised to take action to indict the guilty parties. Although all of this information had been printed in numerous issues of the *Call*, Evans Clark volunteered to supply the necessary information. Mayor Hylan's letter to the *Call* spoke for itself: "I regret very much that people were injured and you may rest assured that the matter will be given every possible attention." No further action was ever taken by the mayor or his district attorney.

Agitation over the disturbances of May had barely subsided before a new series of bombings erupted in June. Explosions were reported in Paterson, Boston, and Pittsburgh. In Washington, the entrance to the home of Attorney General A. Mitchell Palmer was damaged. Nobody was injured except the man who carried the bomb, who was blown to bits. Parts of his body and clothing were found strewn about the street.

In New York, a bomb intended for Judge Charles Cooper Nott exploded in front of his brownstone on East Sixty-First Street. Judge Nott was not at home at the time but other members of his family were. The blast was so great that it blew out part of the building and demolished the first and second stories. Mrs. Nott was asleep at the time of the blast and was thrown to the floor. She smelled smoke and thought, at first, that the house was on fire. When she came into the hall, she saw the daughter of the caretaker coming down the stairway which collapsed minutes later.

When the police arrived, the remains of two people were found scattered about the street. Parts of their flesh and clothing were found on the window ledge of a nearby building. The man who had set the bomb escaped; he had, however, blown up two people who happened to be passing by.

As in the May Day bombings, there was an immediate investigation. One fact that puzzled the police was why Judge Nott was chosen for the crime. All of the other victims had been involved in antiradical activities in one way or another. This was not true of Judge Nott. The only possible explanation the police advanced was that the assassins had mistaken Judge Charles C. Nott for Judge John C. Knox. Since Judge Knox had handled many cases involving radicals, it was reasonable to assume that the bombs may have been meant for him.

The press reported the details of the June bombings at great length, and editorial opinion was even more frantic than it had been in May. *The New York Times* insisted that the government locate the bombers and punish them. The *Buffalo Evening News* suspected that the culprits would be found among the country's nine million aliens. "The time has come," it continued, "to teach these foreigners a little Americanism." Even more extreme was the *Brooklyn Daily Eagle* which ran a cartoon on its editorial page showing an explosion blowing up a building labeled "American Institutions." In its editorial, the *Eagle* insisted that the plotters be found and "swiftly stamped out." The *New York Sun* was the least subtle; it suggested the same remedy that might be used on a dog with rabies.

Liberal opinion usually tends to be moderate and rational. This proved true in the interpretation of the June bombings. The *New Republic* saw the bombings as a "criminal" rather than a "radical" conspiracy. *The Public* interpreted the bombings in psychological terms suggesting that they were caused by the alienation of the immigrants. It felt that only through equality of opportunity and enlightened Americanism could this alienation be reduced.[9]

By this time, the officials of the left seemed to be wearying of bombs with its accompaniment of charge and countercharge. When a reporter went to the New York headquarters of the IWW to get its reaction, he could not find anybody willing to express an opinion. "What's the use of saying anything," one man complained. "If we said we didn't send the bombs we'd be blamed for it anyway." One Socialist official thought that the bombs may have been the work of an agent provocateur employed by a patriotic society. The left wing faction of the Socialist party retreated behind its ideology; it tended to throw the blame on the "capitalist class" and found it absurd to accuse the Socialists or Communists of carrying out terrorism. Left wing Socialists, they explained, believed in revolution but did not carry out acts of terrorism against individual capitalists. Similar views were expressed by officials of the Union of Russian Workers and the Soviet Bureau in New York. The leaders of the nonradical labor movement were united in condemning the bombings but, perhaps out of fear of retribution, were more inclined to believe that anarchist groups had a hand in them.

Antiradical activities lessened during the summer of 1919 when race riots flared up in several American cities. While these had little to do with radical agitation, the left was often blamed for them. The riots were also important in that they seemed to siphon off some of the anger directed against the left, at least for a brief time. Some believed that "Bolshevik propaganda" had sown the seeds of discontent in black communities. The left answered this charge by pointing out that discontent among Negroes was caused not by radical agitators, but by racial discrimination, Southern lynchings and by the refusal of the black community to submit to these intolerable conditions.[10]

While the race riots of 1919 had little to do with the radical left, there was just enough left wing infiltration into the ranks of those carrying on the black man's struggle to provide some basis for the charge. The very existence of the radical Negro publication, *The Messenger,* a Socialist journal edited in New York, was usually cited as proof that the left was using the discontent in the black communities to further its own ends. Even such a harmless gesture as a $25 contribution made by Morris Hillquit to this magazine was noted as evidence of radical involvement. More proof was found when A. Philip Randolph, the editor of the *Messenger,* campaigned for the Socialist party in Negro neighborhoods.

The IWW also hoped to capitalize on discontent among Negroes. Part of its appeal was its membership policy which opposed discrimination in any form. After September 1919 the Communist party also tried to enroll Negroes as members. None of the leftist groups ever attained much success.

Despite the inability of the left to make much headway among Negroes, its efforts were viewed with increasing concern. Ralph Easley, the head of the National Civic Federation believed that the National Association for the Advancement of Colored People was a radical front. He also became convinced that the *Messenger* was an organ of the IWW. To provide an alternative to radicalism, Easley organized a Negro division in the NCF. He held a number of meetings with Chandler Owen and A. Philip Randolph, both of whom were active in the NAACP.

With the coming of fall, the summer race riots subsided; the Red Scare in New York resumed its former pace. The police continued to interfere with radical meetings and to apologize for their inability to control hostile mobs who continually menaced radical demonstrations and rallies. For example, in September, a man named Manuel Lopez created a disturbance during the

showing of a film depicting the horrors of the Russian Bolsheviks. At one point, Lopez started to applaud when the film
showed the Communists snatching the hats off of the heads of
wealthy Russian women and slapping the face of a Russian
prince. Lopez was asked to be quiet. When he refused, the crowd
slapped and punched the unlucky man.

A month later, the police broke up a peaceful demonstration
protesting the political hysteria then sweeping the country. A
bystander described the scene for the *New York Call:*

> From everywhere policemen came running, striking with
> their heavy clubs, right and left. Then plainclothesmen ap-
> peared and armed themselves with stout poles from some
> fallen banners. They also began beating the people. . . . "Get
> him, knock out his brains, kill him," the crowd shouted. . . .
> One poor fellow was running with his wife. He was so bruised
> that he fell to the ground, and his wife, quite a young girl,
> unable to bear the sight any longer, fell face down in the
> middle of the street and began sobbing hysterically. . . .
> This is what it was over and over again.[11]

In an interesting contrast, the police department reported quite
a different version of the same event. In its view, the extreme
methods were justified on the grounds that the marchers had
neither requested nor received a permit. Their banners were inflammatory and contained material which denounced the government. "This unlawful and menacing assemblage was handled
promptly and effectively by this Department," it concluded.
There were many in the city who agreed with the actions of the
police. One bystander, William F. Leggett, in a letter to the
police commissioner, complimented the department for its efficient handling of the disturbance.

Roughly the same thing happended when the police again
broke up a parade trying to demonstrate against the blockade
of Russia by the Allies. The Socialist members of the Board of
Aldermen protested immediately and introduced a resolution
before the board calling for the resignation of the chief of police.
Their fellow aldermen responded with their usual procedure of
tabling the resolution without reading it. The Socialists insisted
that the resolution should at least be read before being tabled but
their cries of protest went unheeded.

A final bit of protest took place in November when Third
Avenue in New York was decorated with posters calling on the

radicals to secure arms and fight against their oppressors. The posters further predicted a "bloody revolution" as the only effective method of defiance remaining. But the police were not taking any chances. They formed a special "riot squad" to handle any future disturbances which might take place.

Meanwhile, antiradical activities continued within the very halls of the Board of Aldermen. Here, the Socialist party was represented by a small delegation throughout the year. The pattern established during the war was repeated: the Socialists were continually accused of disloyalty and, sometimes, of treason. But, after the failure of the previous try in 1918, no further attempts were made to expel them. As the November elections approached, a number of altercations took place which showed that the latent hostility, previously expressed during the war, was still alive. A clash took place when Alderman McGarry, a Democrat, introduced a resolution providing for the placement of tablets bearing the Ten Commandments and the Declaration of Independence on the walls of the chamber. The resolution was sent to committee where it was tabled. In the course of the debate, a Socialist alderman, B. Charney Vladeck, characterized the signers of the Declaration of Independence as "Bolshevists pure and simple." In the speeches that followed, it was apparent that Vladeck had irritated his colleagues. To Republican Alderman Quinn, the Socialists were "Benedict Arnolds and traitors" who were preaching revolution. The remarks of Alderman Keanneally were more moderate than his wartime attitudes; he said that he would not criticize the Socialists as members of a political party. He merely expressed his opposition to "Bolshevik bomb throwers and destroyers." Alderman Arnon L. Squiers, a Republican, was most vivid when he declared that the doctrines advanced by the Socialists made his "blood boil." His next statement was a prophecy of things to come:

> I cannot stand here and listen to these arguments without replying to them as a red-blooded American. If they don't like it here, let them go back to Russia, as they seem to like that form of government. If they haven't enough money, and I have never seen one of them who did, I am sure that financial aid will be given them to pay their steamship fares.

Squiers' prophecy was soon to come true. Five months later a boatload of radicals was returned to Russia with the cost of their passage assumed by the American government.

These events provide some indication of the growing climate of distrust which existed within the Board of Aldermen. The approach of the November elections did little to clear the air.

In the November elections the balance of power shifted. The Democratic party elected enough of its candidates to ensure a majority on the board. The Socialist delegation was reduced. Two Socialists who were not elected were Edward F. Cassidy and an incumbent, Algernon Lee. Cassidy immediately charged that fraud at the polls was the reason for their defeat. They asked for a recount and hired the law firm of Morris Hillquit to represent them. The Board of Estimate agreed and granted $2,500 to the Committee on Privileges and Elections to pay for expenses. But the committee stalled. When the recount still had not taken place by June 1920, Alderman Vladeck wrote to Mayor Hylan informing him of the negligent behavior on the part of the Committee on Elections. Hylan's reply was cordial but evasive. "I do not believe that I can order the Board of Aldermen to do anything," said the mayor, "however, I have asked the Corporation Counsel to advise me in this respect." Hylan was certainly within his legal rights, but one cannot escape the conclusion that as the mayor of a great city, he should have paid some attention to the spirit of the laws, as well as to the letter.

The situation was to deteriorate further when the Board of Elections even refused to hold a meeting to discuss a recount. At this point, the Socialists were compelled to secure a Supreme Court order to force the committee to meet and to open the ballot boxes. The recount showed that Lee and Cassidy *had* been elected but by this time their terms of office were over and nothing more could be done.

Reviewing the events of the year, one may ask why the left did not offer more resistance to the antiradical hysteria? The succession of demonstrations, meetings, resolutions, and letters of protest seem, in retrospect, far too feeble a response to the intensity of the Red Scare. The explanation for this must take into account the fact that the balance of political power, the instruments of coercion, the press, and public opinion were all on the side of those carrying on the antiradical crusade. The victims—the radicals—were either isolated individuals or, at best, members of weak political parties. Even if they had taken a more vigorous stand, it is unlikely that they could have influenced the course of events.

Still another reason for the relative absence of radical response was an internal conflict within the Socialist party itself. As the only organized radical group in New York that might have stood up before the tide of antiradicalism, the Socialist party was torn by an internal schism. It came in the form of a left wing which crystallized shortly after the Russian Revolution. By February 1919 it was strong enough to hold an all-city convention at Odd Fellows Hall at St. Mark's Place in New York, when the left wing section of the Greater New York Locals of the Socialist party officially came into being. A manifesto and program was adopted and an executive was selected. Thereafter, the left wing operated as a party within a party. It created a speaker's bureau, an International Bureau, and a county organization. It printed membership cards and collected dues, separate from the parent party.

The left wing soon began a struggle to take over the Socialist party. The struggle was repeated in many cities across the country. In New York, it took the form of a battle of the boroughs. The left wing had its greatest strength in Brooklyn, the Bronx, Queens, and in the foreign-language federations; the right wing, under Hillquit and Julius Gerber, controlled the local in Manhattan. As long as the right maintained its base in Manhattan, it more than counterbalanced left wing strength in the outlying boroughs.

The split widened in March 1919 when the first session of the Third International convened in Moscow. From this point on, the left wingers adopted the tactic of disrupting Socialist meetings and hurling charges of "traitor" at anyone who disagreed with what they called their "revolutionary ideas." In the opinion of the left wing anyone who defended the Socialist party was an enemy of the working class.

Throughout March and April tension between the two groups increased. The inner dynamics of this tension were revealed at many meetings. For instance, at the membership meeting of April 4 held in the Bronx, Louis Waldman, a right winger, launched into a bitter attack on the left. He declared, in no uncertain terms, that unless the Socialist party maintained its commitment to democratic ideals, it was finished. Waldman went on to explain that the working class in America had not lost faith in political action. He warned that should the Socialists stray from the path of gradualism and moderation it would never gain their support. Paraphrasing Hillquit, Waldman reiterated the necessity

of securing immediate goals: jobs for returning veterans, the
eight-hour day, and the abolition of child labor. "We cannot ask
the children in the mills to wait until we get socialism," he said.
These arguments were answered by Benjamin Gitlow defending
the left.

By May, Hillquit had decided to strike back at the growing
cancer of communism that was festering within the Socialist party
and threatening to destroy it. He announced his decision in an
article entitled "Clear the Decks" which was published in the
New York Call on May 21, 1919:

> Let us separate honestly, freely, and without rancor. Let
> each side organize and work its own way, and make such con-
> tribution to the Socialist movement in America as it can.
> Better a hundred times to have two numerically small Socialist
> organizations, each homogeneous and harmonious within itself,
> than to have one big party torn by dissension and squabbles,
> an impotent colossus on feet of clay.

Shortly afterwards, at a meeting of the New York state committee of the Socialist party at Albany, Hillquit forced through
proposals which expelled all members of the left wing in the
Socialist party of New York state. The fight soon spread to other
parts of the country. Led by Hillquit, the national executive committee voided an election which the left wing had clearly won,
expelled the entire Michigan state party and several of its
foreign-language federations. This saved the party for the con-
servatives but it reduced its membership drastically. In January
1919 the membership of the party had been 109,589; in July
after the expulsions, it fell to 39,750.

After being expelled, the left wing took immediate steps to
solidify its position: it called for a national convention of all left
wing elements to be held in New York the following June. From
across the nation, Socialists came to plan a course of action.
Many important party leaders were in attendance. New York
sent the largest delegation with ninety-four present.

At the convention, a heated discussion took place over the
following question: Should the left wing take over the Socialist
party or should it form a new Communist party? The question
was not answered at this time but after much debate, the election
of an executive committee, and the adoption of another manifesto,

the convention passed a resolution calling for a general convention of "all revolutionary elements" to meet in Chicago on September 1, 1919, to decide the fate of American socialism.

Two new parties, the Communist party and the Communist Labor party, emerged from the Chicago convention. The Communist party was led by Louis Fraina, Nicholas Hourwich, and Charles Ruthenberg; the leadership of the Communist Labor party was assumed by John Reed, Benjamin Gitlow, and William Bross Lloyd. Debs and Hillquit retained control over the Socialist party which never recovered from the split.

One must conclude that antiradical activities in New York in 1919 were largely a carry over from experiences gained during the war. The same charges and accusations were made. There was the same feeling that the Left was part of a vast conspiracy which was outside of the normal channels of the democratic process. The situation, in 1919, was made worse by poor economic conditions and by a series of crippling strikes. This tended to increase public frustrations and to provide a fertile soil in which antiradical hysteria could flourish. At this point, in the face of continuing agitation by the left, the city fathers took steps to curtail left wing activities by placing a ban on the use of public halls, and by forbidding the display of the red flag. The raids followed logically from these earlier steps.

The Union of Russian Workers was selected as the first major target to be raided. It was a strange choice. The Union was a fairly innocuous institution whose activities were believed to be more sinister than they actually were. Later, during the Palmer raids, the Union was raided again. Perhaps its popularity can be explained by the fact that it was not only a leftist institution but one used primarily by non–English–speaking immigrants. It was this which inspired the police to select it as a victim.

The May Day violence came soon after. We have interpreted this as a direct result of the discovery of bombs in the New York Post Office. Other contributing factors may have been the city's own antiradical efforts and its tolerance towards hostile mobs.

In assessing the role of the mayor, one must conclude that Hylan did not act out of any strong convictions regarding radicalism. Rather, he merely responded to the demands of the public and the press that he adopt a sterner policy towards the "reds." As a politician desirous of winning elections, Hylan understood the currents of the times and tried to adjust his thinking to them. Nevertheless, as the leading political figure in the city, the mayor was personally responsible for his inability, or perhaps his inertia, in dealing with mob violence. It is not enough for a politician to assess the public mood and then to go along with it. Leadership in a democracy requires that elected officials help guide the public towards solutions to problems in which the rights of all are protected. While it must be admitted that the provocation for violence, in the form of the bombings of May and June, was very great, still this does not excuse the mayor for his failure to curb the passions of the mob. The city fathers were extremely negligent in failing to maintain law and order when it was most crucially needed.

The record also reveals that the left was unable to offer any effective response to the challenge presented to it. Let us not make the error of thinking that it didn't want to. These radicals were not social outcasts thirsting for martyrdom. They were, with few exceptions, hard working men and women who sincerely believed that through radical politics they could improve the economic system and their own lives as well. The reason for their lack of response was far simpler. At best, the entire left represented only a small minority of the electorate. The various groups were divided on questions of ideology and torn by schism. In this weakened condition they became defenseless targets for a variety of antagonists.

NOTES

1. *New York Times*, March 12, 1919, p .10.
2. Governor Smith's opposition to the excesses of the Red Scare was far more intense at a later period when he courageously vetoed the Lusk Education Bills. See Chapter V.
3. *The Rebel Worker*, February 1, 1919, p. 1.
4. *New York World*, March 13, 1919, quoted in Kate Claghorn, *The Immigrant's Day in Court* (New York, 1923), p. 416; *New York Times*, March 14, 1919, p. 12.
5. *Brooklyn Daily Eagle*, May 1, 1919, p. 6; Brooklyn *Standard-Union*, May 1, 1919, p. 14.
6. "Bombs," *New Republic*, May 10, 1919, pp. 37–38; *The Rebel Worker*, May 15, 1919, p. 3.
7. A related cause was the call for violence proposed by some super-patriotic magazines and pamphlets. See *New York Tribune*, May 6, 1919.

8. *Brooklyn Daily Eagle,* May 2, 1919, p. 6.
9. *New York Times,* June 4, 1919, p. 4; *Buffalo Evening News* quoted in Don Whitehead, *The FBI Story* (New York, 1965), p. 40; *Brooklyn Daily Eagle,* June 4, 1919, p. 6; *New York Sun,* June 4, 1919, p. 10; "Terrorism," *New Republic,* June 14, 1919, pp. 201–202; *The Public,* June 14, 1919, clipping in the Archives of the ACLU, Vol. 70.
10. Race riots in New York City were avoided during the summer of 1919 due to the ability of the police to keep lines of communication open with the Negro community.
11. *New York Call,* October 9, 1919, quoted in Philip Foner, *The Bolshevik Revolution: Its Impact on American Radicals, Liberals, and Labor* (New York, 1967), Document 44.

Chapter Four

THE RED SCARE
AND THE SCHOOLS

The attempt to ensure the loyalty of teachers in schools and colleges was an important aspect of the Red Scare in New York. This phase of the antiradical crusade began during the war and continued well into the decade of the twenties. The first steps, in the form of regulations and laws, were taken by the State Commissioner of Education and the legislature. This was followed by additional regulations passed by local boards of education. A few colleges also took part in the effort to enforce conformity of opinion.

During the war, school officials were generally concerned with those teachers holding antiwar attitudes. After the Armistice the full weight of the Red Scare fell heavily on teachers, and some students, with radical or union affiliations. The movement against dissenting opinions in the schools gained momentum from the widely held conviction that the drive for "Americanism" was failing, and that more vigorous methods were necessary to prevent the radicals from making even greater inroads among the immigrants.

The First World War precipitated many of these events. At Columbia University, the expression of antiwar sentiment led to the dismissal of two distinguished professors: Henry Dana of the English Department, and James M. Cattell, a psychologist. Both were pacifists, but while neither was a member of a radical organization, the Socialist party was among the left wing groups coming to their defense. The two teachers were also supported by many Columbia students who demonstrated in their behalf. Then Charles Beard, the distinguished historian, resigned his position at Columbia when the university refused to reinstate his two colleagues.[1] Soon afterwards two other professors, Henry

R. Mussey and Ellery C. Stowell, resigned for the same reason.

Meanwhile public school systems throughout the state began taking steps to suppress antiwar statements made by teachers. This development came as a result of a directive issued by Dr. John H. Finley, the State Commissioner of Education, who warned teachers that the state required from them the same degree of loyalty that the army demanded of its soldiers. If any teacher was incapable of living up to these high standards, he did not belong in a public school. Finley's directive was enacted into state law by the Education Act of 1917 which stated that "a person employed . . . as a teacher in the public schools . . . shall be removed from such a position for the utterance of any treasonable or seditious statements. . . ."

In the legislative sessions of 1918 and 1919, a number of related laws were passed; all were part of the same quest for loyalty. One law made American citizenship a requirement for teaching. Another required mandatory attendance in English and civics classes for all non-English-speaking minors. In a third law, the Board of Regents of the University of the State of New York was ordered to prescribe courses in patriotism and citizenship for all schools. A textbook law prohibited the use of books and other materials containing seditious statements. Underlying all these enactments was an implicit fear of foreigners and radicals. As such they were widely condemned by liberal and leftist groups.

As the war progressed, New York City developed its own loyalty program which, in some respects, surpassed the standard of loyalty demanded by the state. At the request of Theodore Roosevelt, the various Councils of Defense, and the American Defense Society, the teaching of German was suspended. In addition all teachers were required to sign loyalty oaths. When eighty-seven teachers refused, the head of the Teachers Union, Dr. Henry R. Linville, went to the associate superintendent of schools, Dr. John L. Tildsley, and requested that the oath be eliminated. Tildsley refused, maintaining that "in a system employing so many teachers of foreign origin, the requirement of a loyalty pledge seemed a necessity." The Teachers Union then wrote to President Woodrow Wilson, a former teacher himself, asking him to frame a loyalty pledge which the teachers could sign without violating their consciences. Wilson never replied to this request.

Actually there was little disloyalty in the New York public schools either during or after the war. This fact was admitted by the Lusk Committee of the New York State Legislature, a body specifically set up to investigate subversive activities. The charge that disloyalty existed was based partly on a report submitted in April 1918 by the influential Schoolmaster's Association whose own investigation revealed the existence of an "oppositional element" in the schools led by Dr. Henry R. Linville and composed of teachers active in the Hillquit-Berger wing of the Socialist party. As proof of the charge, the Schoolmaster's Report referred to many articles in the union's publication, *The American Teacher,* which had supported Morris Hillquit when he ran for mayor. The report also found fault with the pro-union attitudes of many teachers who were labeled "conscientious objectors," "visionaries," and "internationalists."

Even before the Schoolmaster's Report was submitted, the Board of Education began to move against the allegedly disloyal teachers in its employ. The accused fell into three categories: some were pacifists, some held pro-German views, while some were Socialists accused of preaching disloyalty in their classrooms.

Among the so-called disloyal pacifists, the case of Mary McDowell was typical. She was a Quaker and was suspended on March 12, 1918, for expressing an opinion in opposition to the war. At her trial Miss McDowell based her defense on the right of religious freedom guaranteed by the First Amendment. The board asked for her dismissal on the grounds that her pacifism was ill-advised at a time when the lessons of patriotism needed to be taught by deeds as well as words. Miss McDowell was dismissed but her case was reopened after the war and she was reinstated in July 1923.

Miss Gertrude Pignol was among the few pro-German teachers dismissed. She was a naturalized citizen employed in a high school in Brooklyn. Part of the evidence against her was a statement made eleven years before that she was ashamed of being an American citizen. She, too, was dismissed and was never reinstated.

Three teachers from De Witt Clinton High School in the Bronx—Samuel D. Schmalhausen, Thomas Mufson, and A. Henry Schneer—were involved in one of the most celebrated cases of wartime teacher disloyalty. All three were Socialists, were active in the Teachers Union, and had written controversial articles for its journal on the subject of politics and unionism. In addition they were known as militants on the issue of teachers' rights. On numerous occasions they had taken positions contrary to their administrative superiors. On November 13, 1917, they were suspended on the charge of "conduct unbecoming a teacher."

The case against Schmalhausen grew out of an essay which he had assigned to his English classes requiring the students to write "An Open Letter to the President" commenting, within the limits of their ability, on the conduct of the war against Germany. While the themes were being read in class, the supervisor of the English Department, Miss Ellen Garrigues, visited the room and became angry at the lack of patriotism displayed by the pupils. Miss Garrigues collected some of the themes and handed them to the principal, Dr. Francis J. Paul, who, in turn, sent them to Dr. John L. Tildsley, the associate superintendent in charge of high schools. Schmalhausen was put on trial a short time later. At the trial one witness testified that the principal, Dr. Paul, had said: "Now I've got him," which seemed to indicate that he was waiting for just such an occasion to arise.

The most damaging composition was written by a sixteen-year-old boy named Hyman Herman. Young Herman asked: "But how is it that the United States, a country far from democratic (and daily proving itself to be such) and England, the imperial and selfish (and we exclude all minor participants) undertakes [sic] to slam democracy upon a nation whether it likes it or not? What audacity to attempt to force seventy million people to adopt a certain kind of government. . . ." There were other compositions of a similar nature.

Schmalhausen was also charged with having said to Tildsley that he did not think it was his duty, as a teacher, to develop "instinctive respect for the President of the United States as such, or for the governor, or any other federal, state, or municipal officer."

At the trial Hyman Herman, called as a witness for Schmalhausen, testified that he had not gotten his original impressions of the war from his teacher. He also said that he had changed his mind about the war since he had written the composition. Schmalhausen then testified that Wilson's interpretation of the war, as a war for democracy, met with his complete "intellectual approval." He opposed conscription but when the Selective Service Act was passed, he had complied with all of its provisions.

The second of the De Witt Clinton teachers, Thomas Mufson,

came to trial on December 3, 1917. Mufson was charged with thinking it appropriate to remain neutral while his class debated such topics as the purchase of Liberty Bonds, the wisdom of an early peace, the form of government of the United States, and the merits and demerits of anarchism. Mufson defended himself by saying that he did not feel justified in imposing his own views on his students when discussing controversial subjects. He denied, however, that the debate on anarchism took place inasmuch as he considered this subject too difficult for immature minds to comprehend. At one point, Mufson's attorney, Herbert C. Smyth, asked Tildsley: "Assuming that he [Mufson] is in favor of an early peace, should he be discharged for that?" "I should say so," Tildsley replied. The point was also raised that Mufson and the others were among those teachers protesting the loyalty pledges. In addition, Mufson said that Tildsley had asked him whether he was in favor of the "Bolsheviki" and whether, if a king ruled in America, he would not endeavor to inculcate respect for the king even if he had to "knock respect into the pupils' heads?" Mufson said "no."

The third case, against A. Henry Schneer, arose from statements he was alleged to have made regarding patriotism and the propriety of wearing the uniform of the United States Army. The prosecution contended that Schneer objected to persons appearing in uniform when speaking at the school because, in his opinion, it tended to increase militarism. Schneer denied the charges and affirmed his loyalty to the school and the government.

The trial was widely discussed throughout the city and on the pages of the educational journals. The board's position was defended by the Schoolmaster's Association of New York. The teachers were defended by the Teachers Union and by eleven distinguished college professors who requested that a decision be postponed pending further investigation.[2] John Dewey, then of Columbia University, reviewed the entire transcript of the trial and found the charges so vague and irrelevant that they would not have the slightest chance of standing up in any American court.[3] Despite this the board's decision stood, and the teachers were dismissed.

Teachers throughout the state were also subjected to harassment. An important case occurred in Poughkeepsie when a teacher, B. Hiram Mattingly, was dismissed when charged with having made a number of unpatriotic remarks.

The same pattern continued after the war. In New York, Superintendent of Schools William L. Ettinger warned teachers that there was no place in the city's schools for any teacher whose "personal convictions made it impossible for him to be a sympathetic expounder of the cherished ideals and institutions of our national life." As with many other statements made during the Red Scare, there was nothing in this remark that liberals, or even Socialists, would find objectionable. The abuse occurred in its application. This point was made by the *Call* in an article headlined: "Don't Want Teachers With Minds, says Superintendent Ettinger."[4] Ettinger's statement was followed by a directive from Tildsley stating that no person adhering to the Marxist program or the left wing of the Socialist party would be allowed to become a teacher in the public schools of New York. Furthermore, if such a teacher were found already licensed, he would be dismissed. The directive was unclear as to whether it was to include moderate Socialists as well as the extreme radicals. Tildsley's attempts at clarification only added to the confusion.

What accounted for this behavior on the part of the administrators of the New York schools? In part, it reflected the personal convictions of the top leadership. Ettinger, Tildsley and the others were convinced that left wing teachers should not teach in the schools. Their actions can also be explained as a response to pressure exerted by the patriotic organizations. Charges were made continuously that many teachers were using their classrooms to preach socialism and were providing their students with reading matter of a radical nature.[5] Then too, the postwar Red Scare in education was stimulated by a widely held belief that the campaign for "Americanism" was failing.[6] Many citizens were distressed by the fact that immigrants were still joining radical organizations despite the best attempts to educate and assimilate them. While this realization produced a good deal of intolerance, it also led to a reevaluation of the traditional methods of Americanization on the part of a number of sensitive intellectuals. For example, Franklin H. Giddings, a professor of sociology at Columbia University, suggested that citizenship might better be developed by providing immigrants with more jobs and better housing.

The continuing postwar hysteria led to the investigation of individual teachers. Perhaps the most publicized case was that of Benjamin Glassberg, a history teacher at Brooklyn's Commercial High School. Glassberg was also a lecturer at the Rand School and a director of the *New York Call* where many of his articles had been published. At no time did the investigation deny Glassberg's competence as a teacher. It did question the propriety of a number of statements he was supposed to have made in his classroom among which was a remark that the State Department prohibited the publication of the truth about bolshevism and another in which he doubted whether a public school teacher would be permitted to tell the truth about the Russian Revolution. In reply to a student's question as to whether he thought Lenin and Trotsky were German agents, Glassberg said that he didn't think so, but he quoted a number of Communist sources as proof.

Even before the trial began, Glassberg stated that twelve students had been planted in his classroom by the principal to ask controversial questions. He implied by this that the administration was out to trap him. He also accused the Board of Education of trying to force teachers to conform to a prescribed theory of history.

Glassberg's case came to trial on March 28, 1919; it lasted well into the month of May. The teacher was defended by Gilbert Roe, a noted civil rights lawyer and counsel to the Teachers Union. Many of his students attended the trial; some testified against their teacher but most came to his defense. At one point a student said that he had shown Glassberg a newspaper clipping in which Algernon Lee was supposed to have said that the red flag of internationalism might, in a sense, be placed above the American flag. The student asked Glassberg for his opinion. In his reply, Glassberg said that he doubted very much if Lee had ever made such a statement. Other students gave evidence of Glassberg's loyalty saying that he had encouraged the sale of Liberty Bonds and had spoken favorably in class of a fund to help French orphans. When Glassberg's competence as a teacher was explored, all of the students praised him for his abilities.

The trial produced a good deal of controversial comment. One letter, to the editor of *School and Society,* defended the board's action, maintaining that Glassberg should welcome the opportunity of defending himself against his accusers. The letter questioned Glassberg's conclusion that the American government was suppressing the truth about bolshevism. The *New Republic* thought differently; its editors admitted that they did not know whether the teacher made the statements attributed to him, but they questioned whether the "official Board of Education account" of the Russian Revolution "ought to be transmitted by teachers of history as if it were gospel." They called for the dismissal of the nonsensical charges against Glassberg and ended with this flourish: "The Czar is gone, the Kaiser is gone, but the little Czars and Kaisers of our educational system continue in their ways of tyranny."[7] Glassberg was dismissed and never rehired.

The hunt for subversives in the New York City public schools widened after the summer of 1919 to include members of the newly formed Communist party. In a raid on various Communist headquarters, unrelated to the issue of the schools, six female teachers were found to be card carrying members of the Communist party. They were immediately summoned to the offices of the state's attorney general for questioning. All admitted frankly that they were Communists but denied that they were spreading their doctrines in the classrooms. Attorney General Berger passed this information on to Superintendent Ettinger and informed him that, in his opinion, there were many more teachers with Communist affiliations in the school system. Ettinger wrote back asking whether Berger recommended dismissals. Berger replied that he did because the accused teachers would probably teach their revolutionary doctrines "indirectly." This was an important development. In contrast to previous cases which dealt with disloyal teaching, now mere membership in a subversive organization was sufficient to ensure dismissal. What the attorney general was recommending, in effect, was punishment for ideas rather than for acts. Meanwhile, the six teachers were discharged, with others to follow.

Upstate there were fewer such cases but to those involved, whose careers were cut short, they were equally as devastating. In one of these Julia Pratt, of the Buffalo school system, lost her job as a music teacher when she was charged with membership in a Communist organization. In passing on her case, Frank B. Gilbert, a deputy commissioner of the State Department of Education, said that when a teacher is employed in the school system that person becomes the servant of the people. The teacher cannot properly perform the duties of her position if she joins an organization preaching the overthrow of the government by force and violence. Few citizens would have disagreed.

While dismissals of teachers were frequent during the Red Scare, they represented only part of the story. Other aspects of the same trend can be seen in the attempts to pressure both teachers and students into a nonquestioning conformity to the status quo. A characteristic example involved Arthur M. Wolfson, the principal of a large New York high school, who had been in the habit of encouraging discussion among his students on controversial subjects. As the 1920 election approached, the students had finished one discussion by taking a straw vote for president. When Eugene V. Debs, the Socialist candidate, received 354 votes out of 2000 cast, the principal was rebuked by Superintendent Tildsley who told him to suppress the issue of the paper in which the votes were to be published. On another occasion, Wolfson was criticized by his superiors for allowing the students to carry copies of the *New York Call* into the school.

Another incident concerned a teacher named Abraham Lefkowitz who was denied permission to go to Chicago to attend a meeting of the American Labor party. Lefkowitz was going as a delegate of the Central Federated Union of New York. The refusal may have had something to do with the fact that Lefkowitz was active in the teacher union movement. In its protest, the Teachers Union pointed out that thousands of teachers had been granted leaves for less important purposes.

The withholding of permanent certification was another method of insuring political conformity in the public schools. The *New York Call* found considerable evidence that teachers were being denied permanent licenses because they were members of the Teachers Union and for participation in various labor activities throughout the city. There were other reasons as well. Dr. Benjamin Harrow was denied a permanent license when he recommended that his pupils read an article by Thorstein Veblen in *The Dial* entitled "Bolshevism is a Menace—To Whom?" In denying Harrow his license, Superintendent Tildsley noted that *The Dial, The Nation,* and the *New Republic* "seemed to be Dr. Harrow's favorite reading matter," and that he had occupied a front seat at every session of the Glassberg trial.

Even the students were not immune to the effects of the Red Scare in the schools. At Boys' High School in Brooklyn, the administration accused a group of students of leftist leanings when they ran in a student election as the candidates of the Red and Black party. Unwilling to make a full confession, the students were barred from the honor society and were publicly denounced by the principal as "a bunch of ruffians whose ideas will never be realized." Meanwhile, at De Witt Clinton High School in the Bronx, an elaborate student spy system was developed. It was directed by Mr. Dotey, a Latin teacher, whose squad of seventy boys were pledged to seek out subversion. At least two "Bolshevist" students were discovered. One eighteen-year-old student was heard by a Dotey squadman to say that he thought the indicted Socialist, Scott Nearing, was innocent. The same boy was charged ·further with saying, "To hell with the Church and the State." Another boy was caught denying that the women of Russia were nationalized. But justice was swift and sure. Both boys were put on "trial" before Mr. Dotey who lectured them on the values of good citizenship. The Latin teacher then said: "If I were a boy, and I had a sister eighteen years old, I wouldn't let you come within two blocks of my house." The boys were denied their high school diplomas because it was felt that they had repudiated the pledge of loyalty required by the state. Per- haps these were, indeed, small tragedies played out on even smaller stages, but at the time they did not appear so to those who were involved.

As antiradical activities increased in the schools of New York, they encountered fierce opposition from the Teachers Union which accused the board of every sin from violations of academic freedom to union busting. To clear the air, a debate was sched- uled at the Manhattan Hotel on the subject "Freedom in the Schools." Dr. John L. Tildsley represented the board; his oppo- nents were Dr. Linville and Zechariah Chafee, a liberal professor of law from Harvard University. Once again, Tildsley upheld a relativist position on the question of free speech for teachers. There was no place for Socialist teachers in the schools, he main- tained, even if they refrained from expressing their opinions in the classroom. In addition, candidates for teaching licenses in such subjects as English, history, economics, and civics would be questioned concerning their views on socialism, and rejected if their answers were found to be unacceptable. On the question of the discussion of controversial subjects in the schools, another speaker, Dr. George D. Strayer, the president of the National Education Association and a professor at Columbia's Teachers College, said that freedom of discussion might be carried on among adults but not by children of high school age.

Then came the rebuttal. Zechariah Chafee found little to agree with in the remarks of the previous speakers. To the professor from Harvard, free speech was absolute. Any theory of government held by a minority of people, even Marxian Socialism, should be freely debated in the schools. If unpopular doctrines were not studied, Chafee concluded, how would the majority know whether its beliefs were correct? The meeting ended on this note with no indication that anyone's views had been altered.

Still another round in the continuing battle between the Teachers Union and the board took place when the superintendent of schools decided to bar the union from using public schools for its evening meetings. The board took the step because it felt that the union was printing large quantities of "treasonable literature." It denied, however, that its actions were anti-union in nature. The decisions of the board was supported by the *New York Times;* this influential paper said that the union was free to rent halls elsewhere in the city.[8] Soon, however, not only the Teachers Union but the Socialist party as well was being denied the use of schools for meeting purposes. At this point, the board felt obliged to clarify its policy. Guidelines were established for the purpose of safeguarding the schools against dangerous propaganda. To secure the use of a public school for an evening meeting, an organization had to submit in advance a list of all speakers and the subjects to be discussed. The board reserved the right of censorship to ensure "definite support for American institutions and moral teachings." A final guideline prohibited the use of any language but English at meetings held in a public school. As a result of this last guideline, many unions with foreign memberships found themselves barred.

The guidelines were also used to bar unwanted speakers. On one occasion, Will Durant, a liberal with radical tendencies, was denied the use of a public school for a lecture. The left suspected that the board had drawn up an official speaker's blacklist. Their suspicions were confirmed in April 1919 when a list of banned speakers was published. Among the listed were Roger Baldwin, Alexander Berkman, Elizabeth Gurley Flynn, Scott Nearing, and A. M. Simons.

Finally, as the spring of 1919 drew to a close, the Board of Education, as part of its continuing program of "Americanization," designed a questionnaire to test the students' knowledge of socialism. The test was made up of a series of questions, among which were the following: "Who are the Russian Bolsheviks and what are their chief aims?" "Do you believe Bolshevism to be a danger threatening the people of New York? If so, why?" "Tell definitely the sources of your information about Bolshevism." "Explain what led you to believe as you do about the movement." In the instructions to the questionnaire, the teachers were told to call to the principal's attention any papers which show an "especially intimate knowledge of the subject."

The June questionnaire on bolshevism produced few meaningful results. With tongue in cheek, the *Literary Digest* reported that the students "went American by 300 to 1."[9] After an examination of thousands of papers at many schools, it appeared that the principal sources of bolshevism were the *New Republic* and *The Nation,* both liberal journals, the *New York Call* and the *Liberator,* papers in the Socialist camp, the *Communist,* a left wing journal edited by John Reed, and the Rand School. A book by Albert Rhys Williams, *The Soviets at Work,* was also cited many times. A few students attributed their knowledge to left wing rallies at Madison Square Garden, while others mentioned the dismissed teachers at De Witt Clinton and Commercial High Schools.

The quality of the quiz can be appreciated by the fact that the students were given grades from zero to one hundred per cent. As the Teachers Union pointed out, this put a premium on "hypocrisy and ignorance" as those students were graded highest who had no knowledge at all. One young girl was seen studying the "correct" answers in her notebook, while at another school, the "acceptable" answers were placed on the blackboard by a cautious teacher to ensure the desired results. In a perceptive article, a Seattle newspaper concluded that a "reign of terror" existed in the New York City schools.[10]

It is difficult to determine precisely what motivated these various boards of education to call for "100 per cent loyalty" from their teaching staffs. The historical record reveals a multitude of facts but few clues as to the true underlying motives. There is no reason to deny the sincerity of many board members who firmly believed that radical teachers should not be permitted in the school system. Then, too, the boards seemed to be falling in line with the prevailing antiradical hysteria of the day. Boards of education are rarely, if ever, staunch defenders of the nonconventional. Like their staffs, they always seem to be walking a thin line, trying to satisfy the competing demands of various pressure groups in the community. Under such intense pressure, it was unlikely that the boards would have responded differently.

In New York City, there were other factors at work. The Board of Education was, after all, an employer. As a typical employer it was unhappy about the growth of a union in its midst. Since many of the union leaders were also active in the Socialist party, the temptation to link the union with socialism could not be resisted.

Still another cause of discord can be found in the difference in ethnic makeup between the administrators and the teachers. At this period administrative positions were filled by a group of older, more established Americans with Protestant, Anglo-Saxon backgrounds. On the other hand, the teachers were largely recruited from the ranks of the immigrants: there were large numbers of Irish Catholics and Jews. On the whole, the Irish group tended to be more conservative and traditional; by this time they were better assimilated into the American mainstream than their parents were. Thus they tended to support the efforts made to root out the radical teachers. In contrast, the Jewish group tended to be more radical. Many had known poverty in their youth; most were graduates of the free city colleges; others were influenced by the messianic, idealistic teachings of their faith. As immigrants, or the children of immigrants, they were only partially assimilated into the American culture. All of these factors combined to produce a high degree of radicalism among the Jewish teachers which was expressed as loyalty to the labor movement and to the Socialist party.

The left wing orientation of the Jewish teachers, combined as it was with unionism, tended to frighten the administrators. In their apprehension that it might reflect poorly on their own ability to run their schools properly, they were easily persuaded to take strong measures to ensure that all teachers expressed only "acceptable" opinions.

This section, however, raises questions of a more fundamental nature. It goes to the heart of the concept of academic freedom. Which beliefs is a teacher permitted to hold and which ones qualify him for dismissal? Which outside organizations is he permitted to join? Is he allowed to support a teacher's union?

Although the guidelines for their actions were unclear, educational authorities tried to provide answers for many of these questions. They insisted that opposition to the war was a prohibited doctrine, at least while the war was in progress. They also insisted that a teacher was not permitted to speak favorably about socialism, communism, or the Russian Revolution, even if his views were balanced by presenting opposing arguments. Short of dismissal, a teacher was subject to bureaucratic harassment by the denial of permanent certification if he failed to live up to his obligations. Later, membership in the Communist party was added as a further cause for dismissal.

Only the Teachers Union supported by a few other liberal organizations fought the Red Scare in the schools. Under Linville's superb leadership the Union pressed for a clearer definition of teachers' rights. Its tactics of appealing to President Wilson for an acceptable loyalty oath was probably a gesture but, considering the hysteria, was the only option left. When this effort failed, it fought hard to defend those teachers under attack. Its lack of success was due to its inexperience and to its unpopular alliance with the Socialist party.

NOTES

1. See *New York Call,* October 10, 1917, in which Beard was congratulated for the courageous step he had taken. "We stand together against the powers of darkness. The other things we may not agree on are minor and incidental. We, too, would rather be right with you than wrong with them."; for Columbia's viewpoint, see *New York Tribune,* September 24, 1918, in which Dean Stone admitted that it was sometimes difficult to distinguish between academic freedom and the abuse of free speech. He said, however, that the resolution of the conflict lay in mutual responsibility on the part of the University and its professors. Both clippings in the ACLU Archives, Vol. 40.
2. John Dewey, James H. Robinson, Carlton J. H. Hayes, Harry A. Overstreet, W. P. Montague, Thomas Reed Powell, and Morris Raphael Cohen were among the eleven professors protesting the trial. See "New York's Disloyal Teachers," *Literary Digest,* December 8, 1917, pp. 32–33.
3. "Charges Against the New York City Teachers," *School and Society,* December 22, 1917, p. 733. Dewey also said: "I don't know what this is called in 1917 but in the old days it used to be called the Inquisition."
4. *New York Call,* March 23, 1919, in the ACLU Archives, Vol. 40.
5. Letter from Ralph Easley to Vincent Astor, November 26, 1919, in Archives of the National Civic Federation (New York Public Library), Box 56; Joseph Mereto, *The Red Conspiracy* (New York, 1920), p. 354.

6. The traditional methods included the teaching of English and citizenship in both the day and evening schools, as well as lectures on patriotic topics and American history.
7. "Freedom of Speech in the New York City Schools," *School and Society,* February 8, 1919, p. 178; Murray, *Red Scare,* p. 171, quotes the *New Republic.*
8. See *New York Times,* April 9, 1919, quoted in Mereto, *Red Conspiracy,* p. 354.
9. "Bolshevism in New York and Russian Schools," *Literary Digest,* July 5, 1919, p. 40.
10. *Seattle Union-Record,* July 9, 1919, in ACLU Archives, Vol. 40.

Chapter Five

THE STATE LEGISLATURE: LUSK COMMITTEE

The New York State Legislature soon joined municipal authorities in the investigation of radicals by forming a Joint Legislative Committee Against Seditious Activities. The committee was headed by Clayton R. Lusk, a freshman senator from an upstate urban community. Throughout the spring and summer of 1919, the Lusk Committee conducted a wide-ranging series of raids against leftist organizations. The scope of its activities was so vast, its power so great, and its newspaper coverage so extensive, that it quickly overshadowed all previous local efforts. The committee attracted nationwide attention and, in large measure, set in motion the forces leading to the expulsion of the five Socialist members of the assembly the following year.

The idea for the Lusk Committee was conceived as early as January 9, 1919, at a meeting of the Union League Club in New York. This club, one of the most influential in the city, appointed a committee of five members to study radicalism in the state. At its head was a New York lawyer, Archibald Stevenson, whose background seemed to qualify him for the task. During the war Stevenson had served as chairman of the Committee on Aliens, a branch of the New York Mayor's Committee on National Defense. In 1918 he was made a special agent of the FBI studying enemy propaganda. A year later, he appeared as a witness before the Overman Committee of the United States Senate, which was then engaged in an investigation of the left. Stevenson was introduced as a former member of army intelligence. Among other disclosures, he informed the Overman Committee that bolshevism was rampant among New York workingmen and urged that strong remedial measures be taken. He then read a list of sixty-two eminent citizens who, in his opinion, held "dangerous, destructive, and anarchistic sentiments." Among the listed were many well-known liberals including Jane Addams and Lillian D. Wald, two famous social workers, Charles A. Beard, Harry Overstreet, the writer, Frederick C. Howe, a government official, and Oswald G. Villard, the editor of *The Nation*.

These allegations created such a furor that Secretary of War Newton D. Baker was forced to deny publicly that Stevenson had any connection whatsoever with the War Department. Baker also disavowed the list saying that he found on it "names of people of great distinction, exalted purity of purpose, and lifelong devotion to the highest interests of America and mankind."

With Stevenson at its head, the Union League Committee conducted a two-month investigation and presented its conclusions on March 13, 1919, at its monthly meeting. After hearing the report, the full membership voted unanimously to petition the state legislature to appoint a special committee to deal with the leftist challenge. On March 20 the Lusk Committee was officially formed when the president pro tem of the Senate, J. Henry Walters, introduced a concurrent resolution providing for a legislative investigation to trace "secret information received from official sources" that bolshevism with heavy financial backing "was making rapid headway in New York and was soon to become a menace to organized government in the state and nation."

The resolution was adopted unanimously, practically without debate, and without resort to the usual practice of sending it to the finance committee, despite its $50,000 appropriation. The acting minority leader, State Senator John J. Boylan, was especially enthusiastic, contending that the state should devote all of its resources, if necessary, to destroy the threat of violent revolution. Further proof of the need for the committee was offered by Senator Walters who maintained that "a concerted, well-organized movement with vast ramifications and heavy financial support designed to overthrow the State and national governments" actually existed.

In the light of later developments, it is important to emphasize the exact wording of the resolution granting power to the Lusk Committee. This said in part:

Be it resolved that a Joint Committee of the Senate and the Assembly be created . . . to investigate the scope, tendencies, and ramifications of such seditious activities and report the results of its investigations to the Legislature, and be it further

resolved, that the said special committee shall have power . . .
to compel the attendance of witnesses and the production of
books and papers . . . and shall otherwise have all of the power
of a legislative committee as provided by legislative law, including the adoption of rules for the conduct of its proceedings.

The wording is significant because nowhere did it state that the
Lusk Committee had the power to conduct raids or to make
arrests. These activities are administrative in nature. Their continual use by the Lusk Committee was a clear violation of the
doctrine of separation of powers and was the first of its many
violations of due process of law.

The resolution then went to the lower chamber where greater
opposition developed. Here the Democratic minority leader was
compelled to apply pressure to keep his party in line. The greatest
opposition came from the two Socialist members of the assembly,
August Claessens and Charles Solomon. Solomon said that if the
assembly really wanted to stop the spread of "what you call
Bolshevism," it should study the causes of social discontent which
stemmed from the high cost of living, unemployment, inadequate
housing, and "the intensity of the struggle for existence." He
challenged the assembly to state what it had done to remedy these
conditions.

The resolution passed the assembly but not before its appropriation was reduced to $30,000. Two Socialists and eight Demo-
crats voted against the measure.[1] *The New York Times* appeared
pleased with the outcome. If New York City was indeed the
center of bolshevik activities, it maintained, the "public should
certainly know the facts."[2] Radical opinion, on the other hand,
was forcefully expressed by August Claessens in an open letter
to his constituents:

> After having administered a stinging rebuke to the slowly
> awakening labor forces in this State by burying every moderate
> and conservative request the workers begged of them, this
> colossal aggregation of asses, the Republican majority, stupidly
> capped the climax by ramming through the Legislature a reso-
> lution appropriating $30,000 for the investigation of the spread
> of Bolshevism in this state.

The committee itself consisted of four senators appointed by
the president pro tem, and five members of the assembly appointed by its speaker, Thaddeas Sweet. Sweet also appointed

Clayton R. Lusk, a freshman senator from Cortland as chairman. The reasoning behind the choice of Lusk was never clarified. His background was in business and he had been in the legislature only since January 1919. He had no previous experience in the investigation of radical activities. His views, however, were sufficiently conservative for the position, and he expressed his nativist attitudes towards radicals by continually referring to them as "alien enemies."

Late in March Senator Lusk held a series of conferences with the state's attorney general, Charles D. Newton. At one meeting a decision was made not to employ special counsel for the committee but to ultilize the services of the attorney general instead. Although the reasons for the choice of the attorney general were never revealed, there are two possible explanations: the assembly's cut of the original appropriation by $20,000, and the fact that the attorney general was actively engaged in the organizational stages of the investigation and was, therefore, a logical choice. Then a staff was chosen which included, in addition to Newton, his deputy Mr. Berger, Clarence L. Converse, formerly a private detective for an express company, and Archibald E. Stevenson, fresh from his appearance before the Overman Committee. At the suggestion of the attorney general, Chairman Lusk hired additional staff members to examine foreign newspapers, periodicals, and documents. The committee also received the assistance of district attorneys and police departments throughout the state. The Department of Justice and the Immigration Bureau in Washington provided further help.

As to the cost of this operation, the committee admitted in January 1920 that its expenditures had been $80,000, a sum far in excess of the original appropriation. Additional funds were obtained as a private loan from an Albany bank. The state controller distributed the proceeds of the loan in $10,000 installments. No accounting was ever made of the entire cost of the committee whose expenses included the printing of its final report in four heavy volumes totaling more than 4,000 pages.

In addition to its investigations, the Lusk Committee carried out a series of spectacular raids. The reason for the raids was explained in its final report: "It became apparent that the criminal anarchy statute of this state was being constantly and flagrantly violated." So, in order to secure evidence which would "assist prosecuting officers" in the preparation and presentation of cases involving violations of law, the committee sought search warrants to be used against the various organizations alleged to be centers of revolutionary propaganda. This constant use of the search warrant deserves comment. The normal channel of the investigating committee is the public or private hearing implemented by the subpoena or the subpoena *duces tecum*. While the subpoena was used by the Lusk Committee on certain occasions, and served the same function, the search warrant was considered preferable, probably for its dramatic effect. Armed with these weapons, the committee was able to go far beyond its powers and assumed many executive functions. Unable or unwilling to distinguish between legislative and executive prerogatives, the Lusk Committee continually acted as if it had police powers which, of course, it did not.

The New York bombings of May and June encouraged the committee to speed up its work. Early in June, Chairman Lusk told reporters that the first meeting of the committee, originally scheduled for July, would be held within a week's time. The senator claimed that the committee already possessed evidence proving that certain radicals within the state were actively engaged in spreading subversive propaganda. They were so successful, he added, that their "followers and sympathizers in New York City . . . were numbered by the hundreds of thousands."

The committee obtained its first search warrant on June 12 from City Magistrate Alexander Brough. The warrant was drawn against the offices of the Russian Soviet Bureau on Fortieth Street, in the old World Tower Building. In charge of the office was Ludwig C. A. K. Martens, appointed on January 2 as the representative of the Bolshevik government to the United States. Earlier in March, Martens had contacted the State Department in order to present his credentials, but the department, unsure of which side was going to win the civil war then in progress in Russia, declined to recognize Martens, preferring instead to negotiate with the provisional government. Martens' mission received the hearty support of the Socialist party of America, and, later, of the Communist party. Although Martens spoke at many Socialist and left wing rallies, he was probably correct when he said that his main function was to secure diplomatic recognition for the Bolshevik regime. Time and again he protested that he was not engaged in carrying out a Communist revolution in the United States. In general, Martens' statements were more moderate than those of his staff. At a rally, one of his associates, Gregory Weinstein, was supposed to have said: "We have come here to tell Comrade Martens that we have come prepared to take over this great country, as the working class is taking over Russia." Later, Martens denied under oath ever hearing Weinstein make this statement.

The raid on the Russian Bureau took place at three o'clock on the afternoon of June 12, when police and private detectives employed by the Lusk Committee arrested everybody in sight. Among those arrested were Gregory Weinstein, formerly editor of the Russian periodical, *Novy Mir,* Santeri Nuorteva, an aid to Martens, A. A. Heller, the commercial attaché, and Mr. Horowitz, their attorney. The accused protested vigorously and demanded to see the search warrant authorizing the raid. This was produced and Mr. Horowitz was permitted to examine it. The Russian agents were then taken to City Hall. Meanwhile, the police began a thorough search of the offices of the Russian Bureau and literally cleaned out the premises. Every desk, index file, and box was opened and all the papers removed. Among the items seized were books, pamphlets, bankbooks, and a large bundle labeled "diplomatic correspondence." The police also took a large red flag, neatly stored in Martens' office.

When the arrested Russian agents arrived at City Hall, they found a meeting of the Lusk Committee under way. By this time Evans Clark was able to secure the aid of counsel. The law firm of O'Gorman, Battle, and Vandiver was employed to defend the staff, and Charles Recht was to represent Martens. Edwin Stanton, a son-in-law of State Senator O'Gorman and a member of his law firm, asked that he and Recht be permitted to be present at the hearing while their clients were being examined. They were barred by Attorney General Newton. This, too, was an obvious denial of due process and still another glaring example of the Lusk Committee's abuse of its power. The committee remained in session for three hours. Martens and Heller were questioned about Soviet propaganda in the United States. Another witness, Hugh Frayne, an AFL organizer, quoted from anarchist and IWW publications to prove that the bureau was engaged in an attempt to overthrow the government of the United States by force and violence. Frayne testified further that anarchist, syndicalist, and Socialist "elements" in New York and elsewhere were allying for the purpose of establishing a proletarian dictatorship in this country. He also discussed the operations of the IWW in New York City. "Do you mean to tell us," asked Lusk, "that this organization that advocates the overthrow of the government has a headquarters in this city, and that its literature is openly circulated?" "They operate as openly as any business establishment," replied Frayne.

There was some indication that Senator Lusk was apprehensive about the methods used during the first raid and aware of encroaching on the executive function. When asked by reporters who had ordered the raid, he admitted issuing the subpoenas, but denied any knowledge of the search warrant. For this information, he referred the reporters to the attorney general. The attorney general said that he didn't know but he suspected that the search warrant was secured by Archibald F. Stevenson. As Stevenson sat next to Lusk all through the hearing, the implication was clear that this was no mere administrative oversight.

A day later the directors of the bureau were permitted to return to the building and found state troopers still guarding the premises. When news of the raid reached George Tchitcherin, the Soviet Foreign Minister, a formal protest was lodged with the State Department. Senator King of Utah was also concerned and sent letters to the attorney general of the United States and to the secretary of labor asking for the deportation of Martens and other representatives of the Bureau. "It is time that these disturbers of our peace and enemies of our country . . . be driven from this land whose hospitality they have so grievously abused," said the senator. In New York, the *World* was worried over the amount of property taken but felt that it was probably necessary. "There is an evident understanding between revolutionary elements in the United States that does not include the American people," it said.[3] A few days later, the bureau brought suit to vacate the search warrant which was denied.

The Lusk Committee held its second public hearing after it had carefully examined the material taken in the raid on the Russian Bureau. This hearing was similar to the first and to others held during the succeeding months. Many vague charges were made. A miscellaneous assortment of evidence was presented and many names were introduced of people supposedly active in seditious activities. Topics raised were soon abandoned as the committee veered off in other directions. It was alleged, for example, that Martens and other members of the Soviet

Bureau were in close touch with organizations in this country
working along militant lines for the attainment of revolutionary
aims. A number of letters were presented from Socialist headquarters in the city pledging the locals to work "directly" towards
the establishment of a Soviet type of government. Archibald
Stevenson testified that the bureau was interested in the fate of
the IWW members then on trial at Chester, Pennsylvania, for
May Day disturbances.

At hearings held the next day a letter from a Soviet "secret
agent" was translated. It dealt with efforts made by the Bureau
to stimulate trade between the United States and the USSR. As
Martens was negotiating with dozens of American corporations
concerning the possibility of Soviet-American trade, one can only
speculate as to the purpose of this disclosure. Stevenson then
produced the Bureau's New York mailing list, also taken during
the raid. He said that a similar list existed for each state. Among
those names on the list were Carleton J. H. Hayes, a professor
at Columbia University, Lillian D. Wald, Paul V. Kellogg, the
editor of a liberal publication, the *Survey,* and Norman Thomas.
None of these was ever called to testify in his own behalf but, by
the doctrine of guilt by association, it was assumed that being on
a list meant support for the organization doing the mailing. Further proof of the Bureau's subversive character was deduced from
requests for speakers made by many radical groups. The committee believed this to be clear evidence of the fact that the left,
after years of division, was banding together to form a unified
conspiracy.

On the night of June 20, 1919, Martens spoke at a large demonstration at Madison Square Garden protesting what he called
an interference with Russian internal affairs in the United States.
A second protest came when two translators on the staff of the
Lusk Committee resigned their positions. Both men denounced
the committee's methods as "czaristic" and "disgraceful," and
said that the Lusk Committee would strengthen rather than
weaken American Bolshevism. The committee replied that the
translators had been fired because of a loss of confidence in them.

Hearings of the Lusk Committee resumed on June 26. At this
session, the committee challenged the sincerity of the Bureau's
stated purpose of trying to improve Soviet-American trade. As
proof, Archibald Stevenson presented memoranda which showed
that the Bureau had contacted several liberals and Socialists in-

cluding Frank A. Vanderlip, Dudley Field Malone, Amos Pinchot, Rabbi Judah Magnes, Gilbert Roe, and Lincoln Colcord, for the purpose of having them arrange meetings with senators and business leaders. It was pointed out that Malone was a speaker at a Madison Square Garden rally attacking the Lusk Committee, that Pinchot and Magnes were pacifists, and that Colcord, a liberal journalist, wrote frequently for the *Nation*. While this evidence may have convinced some, its effect was weakened somewhat by the disclosure that the Russians had also been introduced to a number of conservative bankers through their left wing contacts. This fact seemed to diminish the importance of the original charge and rendered the committee's activities less newsworthy.

While the investigation of the Russian Bureau was in progress, the Lusk Committee conducted its second raid against the Rand School. The school was housed in an old building, the People's House on East Fifteenth Street. In its classes, the Rand School taught that socialism would evolve peacefully and not by revolution. Among the many teachers who had served on its faculty were Morris Hillquit, Algernon Lee, Charles Beard, George R. Kirkpatrick, a prominent educator, Lester F. Ward, a sociologist, and the psychologist, John B. Watson. Its building contained a library and a bookstore. *The American Labor Yearbook,* one of the many publications of its Research Department, claimed that its graduates were spread across the United States with "several holding positions of responsibility in the Socialist Party and in trade union organizations." While the major stress of the curriculum was on economics and history, its appeal to immigrants can be seen in a number of "practical" courses such as English, Correction of Accent, and Public Speaking.

While the activities of the Rand School satisfied its supporters, some public defenders of law and order reacted differently. In the bookstore, one antiradical writer discovered a pile of birth control pamphlets "several feet high." In addition, he found that the IWW publication, *One Big Union,* was being sold and enough "foul and revolutionary matter to satisfy the filthiest and most bloodthirsty wretch in the United States." "For years," he continued, "this school . . . has been sowing the seeds of class hatred and class discrimination now springing up around us."[4]

To carry out the raid on the Rand School, Clarence Converse obtained search warrants from Judge William McAdoo.[5] The warrants were broadly drawn to include the Rand School, its parent organization, the American Socialist Society, and *Worker's World,* a publication edited in one of its offices. Also mentioned in the warrants were the Socialists, Scott Nearing, Louis P. Lochner, Algernon Lee, Norman Thomas, Irwin St. John Tucker, and James O'Neal. None of these people was present at the time of the raid. At the appointed hour, fifty policemen and committee agents entered the premises. The school, its offices, and the bookstore were searched and vast quantities of books and records removed. Except for the fact that the agents were unable to pry open the school's safe, the committee considered the raid a success.

Armed with another search warrant, agents of the Lusk Committee, led by Archibald Stevenson and Deputy Attorney General Samuel A. Berger, returned two days later to open the safe. Isadore Sacklin, the lawyer for the school, read the new warrant and, after protesting its illegality, demanded that two passing city policemen protect the school's property. The policemen refused and a safe expert was brought in. After the safe was opened, Algernon Lee began to compile a list of its contents. Lee protested that none of this material related to the advocacy of violence. "Oh, that ain't what we're after," one of the troopers replied. "We want to get at the source of financial support for the Rand School." This, too, was obtained from a list kept in the safe, containing the names of many prominent people. All of the documents were taken to the offices of the Lusk Committe where they were arranged and indexed.

Almost at once the liberal and radical press rallied to the defense of the Rand School. The American Civil Liberties Union issued a manifesto in its behalf signed by a number of prominent people. Civil rights leader Albert De Silver bitterly protested the raid and the ease with which the warrants were obtained:

> To anyone who is familiar with the activities of the organization having their offices at 7 East Fifteenth Street such suggestions of disloyalty are nothing more or less than nonsense. . . . It should not be possible for Mr. Stevenson to secure search warrants by such simple methods as having one of his subordinates make oath to such a bizarre conclusion.

A distinguished non-Socialist lawyer, Samuel Untermyer, then stepped forward to defend the school. It was well known that

Untermyer was donating his services, but Chairman Lusk could not resist charging that the selection of such an expensive lawyer proved that the Rand School had "powerful financial backing from sources yet unknown to the public." This charge, like so many others, was never followed up by the committee.

Untermyer immediately began court proceedings to recover the property taken from the school. The defense charged that the search warrants were illegal, that they had been obtained on false grounds, and that it was unlawful for the city magistrate to turn over property seized in this manner to a legislative committee or to anybody else.

The attorney general also started court proceedings to annul the charter of the American Socialist Society which conducted the Rand School, and to enjoin the society from continuing its operations. In his suit, he charged that the school advocated the overthrow of the government, used anarchists as lecturers, sought to arouse rebellion among Negroes, obstructed recruitment during the war, and employed convicted law violators as teachers.

Despite the insistence of both Untermyer and State Supreme Court Justice McAvoy that the case be argued at once, Attorney General Newton asked for a delay of several months along with a temporary injunction against the school. By this move, Newton hoped to close the school and prevent the American Socialist Society from publishing while the case was being argued. When Justice McAvoy declined to grant the temporary injunction, Newton agreed that the case should be argued in two weeks. A date was set and a special term of the Supreme Court ordered. Justice McAvoy then enjoined both parties from discussing the case before it came to court, but in less than a week Mr. Newton informed the press that he had found new evidence that the Rand School was fostering revolutionary teachings.

Despite his new discoveries, the attorney general showed no inclination to try his case in court. After several unsuccessful attempts to obtain a postponement, the case finally came to trial on July 28, 1919. Deputy Attorney General Berger then moved to postpone the case on the grounds that Mr. Newton wanted to amend his complaint by incorporating new evidence to be obtained by examining the officers of the American Socialist Society and by a commission set up to examine witnesses outside the state. Both Mr. Untermyer and Justice McAvoy indicated their willingness to accept oral arguments, and even a week's postponement, but the attorney general requested a further delay. Eventually, the court realized that the attorney general was stalling due to the weakness of his case. "What I'd like to know is why isn't the case ready now?" asked Justice McAvoy. "Tell me specifically what are the amendments that are necessary to your complaint?" Berger's answer was vague: "We are not prepared at this moment. We prefer ———————." "Of course, I know you prefer," came the retort from the bench. Mr. Untermyer intervened: "The defendant asks that this action be dismissed and that the order granting leave to begin these proceedings be vacated." At this point Judge McAvoy dismissed the case against the American Socialist Society. The *New York World* commented: "It proves to have been a raid chiefly on the ordinary right of free speech, and is thus calculated to produce quite as much Bolshevism as it suppressed."[6]

During the raid on the Rand School, Lusk Committee agents and police were also raiding the left wing section of the Socialist party. By coincidence, this took place on the same day that the national left wing convention was meeting in another part of the city. News of the raid forced the left wing to hold the remainder of its meetings in semisecrecy.

The raid on the left wing was similar to the one on the Rand School. It was directed by Sergeant Charles McVey of the state police, and by members of the New York City bomb squad under Sergeant Geegan. Documents, pamphlets, and a trunkful of letters were taken, many from the office of its secretary, Maximilian Cohen.

At the same time, a second raid was carried out against the headquarters of the IWW. This was led by a Lusk employee, Henry Grunewald, of the Adams-Grunewald Investigating Agency, accompanied by six state troopers and several of his own agents. Upon entering the offices, two IWW officials jumped through the window, and a third escaped through a rear entrance. No effort was made to stop them as the aim of the raid was to secure evidence, not prisoners. Soon, the raiders discovered a batch of stamped envelopes with instructions to "return to J. P. Morgan and Co. if not delivered in five days." These envelopes were used to send out IWW mail. The Lusk investigators thought they had uncovered an important clue, when they noted the similarity between the instructions on the envelope and the false return address stamped on the back of the bomb packages sent in May and June. Their suspicions proved to be wrong. Then the material was sorted and analyzed. Neither the left wing of the Socialist party nor the IWW tried to contest the raids through the courts.

At a subsequent hearing of the Lusk Committee, Archibald Stevenson presented a document which Senator Lusk called its most important piece of evidence. This was written by a Negro, W. A. Domingo, a lecturer at the Rand School and a contributing editor of the *Crisis,* a radical publication, and appeared to be a detailed plan designed to spread left wing propaganda among blacks in the South. The Lusk Committee hoped that this evidence would strengthen its contention that the Rand School by its incitement of Negroes was part of the radical conspiracy. However, this conclusion was not supported by the document itself which was, simply, a series of nine proposals by which Negroes were to be made more socially conscious and receptive to the message of socialism. There was no suggestion of violence; rather, the stress was on a peaceful evolution to socialism.

The hearings continued through July when additional evidence was presented from documents seized in the raids on the left wing and the IWW. For example, in a letter from Maximilian Cohen to John Reed, a plan for a huge May Day meeting at Madison Square Garden was revealed. The plan was never realized. Even more sensational was a bulletin which called for armed revolution, the opening of prisons, and the incarceration of John D. Rockefeller and that "hypocritical Woodrow Wilson." At a later hearing, documents were presented which showed that the IWW was trying to organize an international "revolutionary" maritime union, and was making a special appeal to Negroes. Articles from various foreign language magazines were also read. Fairly typical was one from a Finnish magazine which said: "To hell with the teaching of peaceful revolution. . . . A rioting mob is the one and only possible means for organizing . . . open and decisive blood battles between the capitalists and the working class." Lusk regarded this as a clear violation of the state's criminal anarchy statute.

In executive session, the Lusk Committee decided that some of the more inflammatory material would be handed over to the district attorney's office which would decide whether to press for indictments. A report from committee agents operating in Buffalo that radicals were preparing to organize Soldiers and Sailors Soviets similar to those in Russia was included in this category. This was the first indication that the committee was planning to investigate radical activities upstate. Measures against the anarchists in the IWW were also contemplated. A special investigator from the Deportation Bureau of the Immigration Department, A. B. Schell, attended all meetings of the Lusk Committee and gathered information about the Wobblies to secure deportation of its alien members. Lusk was certain that he had information which the government could use but he hesitated to release it before a scheduled August meeting of the grand jury. It was this grand jury that brought charges of criminal anarchy against two anarchist editors, Gus Alonen and Carl Pavio, based partly on information supplied by the Lusk Committee. The two men were sent to Sing Sing prison with sentences ranging from four to eight years.

At later hearings of the committee, emphasis was placed on radical propaganda in New York City. Deputy Attorney General Berger testified that there were forty to fifty radical publications in the city with about three million readers. Only two, he said, were self-supporting while the others were subsidized by "dilettante Reds." Berger maintained that these radical papers were mailed everywhere, even to Gary, Indiana, then in the grip of a nationwide steel strike. By this disclosure, he implied that the New York left was supporting labor disturbances in other states. A few arrests were also made at this time. Among the more prominent leftists seized were Peter Bianki, Naum Stepanuk and Peter Krawchuk, all editors of an anarchist sheet, *Khliev y Volya.* The three were indicted by a grand jury in New York on charges of criminal anarchy and were later deported to Russia.

In light of these events, at least one publication, *The Nation,* questioned whether the American people were losing their desire for freedom and becoming "spiritual autocrats." Perhaps the time had come to restore a measure of sanity throughout the land.[7] Events proved otherwise as the Lusk Committee prepared for its most spectacular raid on seventy-three branches of the newly formed Communist parties.[8] The timing of the raids was important. It was set for Saturday night, November 8, when the Communists would be attending meetings, parties, and dances celebrating the anniversary of the Bolshevik uprising. The raids caught them off guard. They knew that they were under investigation but did not know how far the authorities would go in making arrests and securing convictions. This explains the success of the 700 uniformed policemen, plainclothesmen, agents of the narcotics and bomb squads, members of the Justice Department and Immigration Service who participated. The offices of more than fifty radical publications, called by Berger "the backbone of the Red movement in this country," were also raided. The police confiscated so much printed material that according to one newspaper account they literally staggered under its weight. Senator Lusk was jubilant: "The time has come for the people of this country to take a definite stand on this question in order that we may know who our enemies are and deal with them as they deserve."

In his memoirs, Benjamin Gitlow recalled the moment when he arrived at police headquarters which was "alive with excitement."[9] Gitlow and his friend, James Larkin, were herded into an auditorium where they were joined by Communists arrested in other parts of the city. Seated on a platform in front of the room was Archibald Stevenson and other members of the Lusk Committee. In all, about a thousand arrests were made but only thirty-five people were detained without bail on the charge of criminal anarchy. Of these, twelve were later convicted, a few more deported, and the rest were released for lack of evidence.

Of those arrested, most were not disheartened. Unaware of the long prison sentences facing their leaders, they called out to their fellows in adjoining cells, bombarded their jailors with insults, and spent the night singing revolutionary songs. For a few, however, the raid was a harrowing experience. This is indicated by the testimony of Theodore Conceivich, a minister of the Church of All Nations, who told of the effect of the raid on one of his parishioners, a twenty-five-year-old man named Joseph Polulech. Conceivich said that Polulech was:

> . . . attending a night school run by the Communist Party. He was studying English and algebra. He was not a Communist but was made an officer of the school because of his faithfulness and intelligence. On the night of the raid everybody present was arrested, Joseph Polulech among them. I and others protested to the Lusk Committee. We received no reply to our protest.

Joseph Polulech was later deported from the United States as a radical alien.

The Lusk Committee appeared satisfied with the results of its latest work. Nothing in the record indicates that they were disturbed by the small number of radicals actually held in jail compared to the number arrested. Neither did they seem concerned that all of the Communist literature seized was readily available in bookstores throughout the city. On the contrary, Archibald Stevenson complimented the police for their "generous cooperation" and called the raids a success.

A few newspapers were critical. The *New York World* noted that while the search warrants were legal, a warrant which "incidentally" scoops up one thousand people because they "happened to be on the premises" played into the hands of revolutionaries everywhere. The *New York Post* also had second thoughts. "It is very much a question whether the public is being served in a spirit of panic." It said further that mass raids of this type could only create "a state of public alarm unjustified by the tactics and surely not conducive to a sane and efficient defense of democratic government against a lunatic fringe of society." In a letter to the *New York Call,* Theodore Debs, the brother of the leader of the Socialist party, voiced additional misgivings over the "administrative persecutions" of the Lusk Committee.[10]

By the end of the year, the Lusk Committee shifted its focus to an examination of radicalism in upstate communities. Throughout the month of December, they carried out raids on radical centers in Buffalo, Utica, and Rochester. The procedure was much the same as in New York. Each raid was followed by a public hearing with many revelations of subversion and radical infiltration into various institutions. Left wing trade unions came under especially heavy attack. The Amalgamated Clothing Workers was singled out as a good example of a union whose leaders preached radical propaganda while organizing the mills.

The Lusk Committee returned to New York in January 1920. Further raids against the offices of four Communist newspapers were planned. Search warrants were obtained stating that the papers advocated the overthrow of the government by force and violence. The raids cleaned out the offices of *The Communist World, The Elore, Der Kampf,* and the *Robitnik.* It was obvious that the committee hoped to put these papers out of business when their entire current issue was seized. This was another example of the committee's conception of itself as an executive law enforcement agency rather than a legislative committee.

In April, the Lusk Committee published its findings. Barely ten percent of the report consisted of material relating to its work. The remaining ninety percent reprinted a wide selection of material gathered during the raids and secured from witnesses.[11]

Volumes I and II were filled with documents pertaining to "Revolutionary and Subversive Movements." Most of the documents related to European, not American developments. The others dealt with left wing movements and labor unions in the United States. Among the documents were Lenin's "Letter to the American Workingman," the constitutions of the Socialist and Communist parties, and the manifesto of the left wing of the Socialist party. Perhaps the strangest part of the report concerned the activities of peace organizations and agencies like the American Civil Liberties Union specializing in the protection of civil rights. These were lumped together with the radical parties with no attempt to distinguish between their objectives or methods.

The last two volumes were concerned with what the committee called "Constructive Movements and Measures in America." Included were achievements in labor-management relations, the cooperative movement, the open and closed shop, compulsory arbitration, and guild socialism. The report detailed almost a thousand different programs in citizenship training conducted by educational, religious, and social organizations throughout New York state. The final volume concluded with information on compulsory citizenship education, displays of the flag, courses in the English language, and other patriotic measures in all forty-eight states.

Despite the stated desire of the report to "eliminate personalities," many persons were named with the clear implication that they were disloyal. Liberals were lumped together with Socialists, Communists, and anarchists. Among these were Roger Baldwin, Dr. Judah L. Magnes, the Reverend John Howard Mellish, a Protestant clergyman, and Jane Addams, whose name appears more times than Lenin's.

Under a section entitled "Socialist Propaganda in Educated Circles," the ACLU was presented as a subversive organization. Two documents, "The Challenge" and "Civil Liberties," were reprinted to support this charge. In actuality, these two pamphlets were merely attempts by the ACLU to define its position in relation to the issues of the day.

According to the Lusk Committee, craft unions were loyal and

American, while industrial unions were subversive. The Industrial Workers of the World, the Amalgamated Clothing Workers, and the International Ladies' Garment Workers Union were in the subversive category and were lumped together as proponents of One Big Union or syndicalism. This error was partly perceived by the Committee when it added that the Big Union contemplated by the ILGWU was to be limited to the "needle trades."

Shortly after, as a result of these disclosures, the state legislature passed a number of bills implementing the committee's suggestions. The first two dealt with educational reforms. One required that teachers in public schools secure a special certificate before January 1, 1921, certifying that they were persons of good character and loyal to the institutions of the state and nation. In another bill, all schools not under the supervision of the Department of Education or maintained by a religious denomination were obliged to secure licenses from the Board of Regents of the state. The measure was obviously aimed at the left wing schools. The committee emphatically denied that its proposals were intended to suppress free education, bar educational progress, or revert to "medieval methods."

Two final bills dealt with other related matters. One empowered the Appellate Division of the State Supreme Court (in Albany) to remove from the ballot any political party whose platform was unconstitutional or unlawful. Another created a state secret service, uncontrolled by the attorney general's office, to seek out and prosecute criminal anarchy and sedition. Both bills passed by wide majorities.

Vigorous and sustained opposition to the Lusk bills developed at once. Quite naturally, the Teacher's Union was opposed to any licensing of teachers while the New York Bar Association frowned on the measure to license schools. The bar was quick to point out, however, that opposition to the bill did not imply acceptance of the radical doctrines taught in these controversial schools. Additional protests came from many labor, educational and civic groups throughout the state, such as the New York State Federation of Labor (AFL), the New York Central Trades and Labor Council, the Workmen's Circle, the Public Education Association, the Ethical Culture Society, the Citizens Union, the Federal Council of Churches, and the City Club. An ad hoc group, the Emergency Educational Conference made up of more than sixty unions, was also formed to lobby against the school bills.

Many were equally disturbed over other aspects of the legislative session. A host of bills including proposals for an eight-hour-day and a minimum wage had all gone down to defeat. In the light of the legislature's failure to discharge its obligations, the Women's Trade Union League announced that its membership of 35,000 would no longer "dilly dally around trying to have bills passed by a reactionary Legislature controlled by Speaker Sweet and the manufacturing interests of the state." *The Nation* agreed, predicting that the defeat of the measures for social justice would result in gains for the Socialist party and might even lead to the formation of a new labor party. Furthermore, it felt that the defeat of the bills would breed "cynicism" and might result in an "American form of political nihilism."[12]

The legislature's poor record was also noted by the League of Women Voters which sponsored a movement to unseat Speaker Sweet at the next election. The League charged that Sweet was supported by Mark A. Daly, a lobbyist for the Associated Manufacturers and Merchants of New York and by Clayton R. Lusk. Lusk himself was unsympathetic to the League's stand on social legislation. His position was consistent with his general attitude which placed every issue in the context of the radical or foreign conspiracy. "Why are these women backing welfare measures?" he asked. "Not to benefit any class of people. It is all part of the German propaganda to break down the government of the United States." Sweet was reelected in spite of the opposition.

When the Lusk Bills reached the desk of Governor Alfred E. Smith, he was deluged with an avalanche of mail urging passage or defeat. Smith held public hearings and, after careful consideration, vetoed all of the bills stating that those supporting the measures were "prejudiced," "hysterical," and "mainly interested in the control of liberal thought."

The governor's veto messages explained his reasoning in greater detail. To Smith, the school licensing bill, obviously aimed at the Rand School, was a "vicious" measure which encroached heavily on freedom of expression. "The safety of this government," he continued, "rests upon the reasoned and devoted loyalty of its people. It does not need for its defense a system of intellectual tyranny, which, in the endeavor to choke error by force must of necessity crush truth as well."

In his veto of the bill requiring loyalty oaths for teachers, Smith found this to be a type of class discrimination which deprived educators of their right of free speech. To require such an oath would encourage meekness and conformity, and would strike at the very foundations of democratic education. In a similar vein, he opposed the bill permitting the courts to remove a political party from the ballot on the grounds that it would give to the judiciary an excessive amount of power. Finally, while the governor found the addition of a special police force justified in time of war, he found it abhorrent in peacetime when it might lead to a police state.

In the 1921 session of the legislature, the Lusk bills were again presented for consideration. Despite opposition by the same groups that lobbied against the 1920 measures, the new bills passed on the last day of the session. By this time, Governor Smith was out of office, having been replaced by a Republican, Nathan L. Miller, who signed them on May 12.

Armed with this new legislation, the attorney general decided to test it on the Rand School. Meanwhile, on the advice of Morris Hillquit, the school's legal counsel, the administrators decided to ignore the law and open the school at its usual time. On October 24, the state began an action in the Appellate Division of the Supreme Court in the form of an application for a permanent injunction to restrain the Rand School from operating without a license.

The school suffered a defeat in the first phase of the case, when the injunction was granted and then affirmed by the Appellate Division. The question of whether the Rand School was entitled to a license was not raised. All that was decided was that the school was required to apply for one since the statute was, as yet, constitutional.[13] A further appeal was planned.

However, in November, 1922, Alfred E. Smith was reelected Governor on a Democratic platform pledged to the repeal of the Lusk laws. The courts took no further action but, instead, awaited the fate of the controversial measures. Shortly after the opening of the legislative session of 1923, bills were introduced repealing the Lusk laws. The Republicans opposed vigorously and voted solidly against the measure. Although the vote was close, there were enough Democrats in favor to secure repeal. Governor Smith again called for public hearings. He was unimpressed with the opposition and signed the repeal measures. Smith said that he was "vindicating the principle that within the limits of the Penal Law, every citizen may speak and teach what he believes."

Thus, the Rand School case was finally decided not in the courts but at the polls.

Smith's final veto of the Lusk bills brought the era of the committee to a close. Its work had gone on for about two years. During this time, the committee tried to save the people of New York state from the "radical threat." The major difficulty seemed to be that the threat, in actuality, was far less severe than the committee supposed. This explains why its results were meager by any standards.

What had the Lusk Committee accomplished? Few persons were either convicted or deported. The radical organizations were shaken up but survived the raids. The Lusk bills were short-lived and were soon repealed. Even the Rand School continued to function for a number of years in spite of its difficulties in the courts.

Even more significant was the fact that the Lusk Committee, in its desire to achieve results, violated a number of basic constitutional principles. The committee, for example, exceeded the powers originally granted by the legislature and assumed many police functions. It behaved as if it were a part of the executive branch of the government which, of course, it was not. Then too, by its indiscriminate use of the search warrant and its series of raids, it trampled over the constitutional rights of many individuals.

The pattern was set during Lusk's first raid against the Russian Bureau. In this raid, truckloads of "evidence" were removed from the premises and the offices were turned upside down. One wonders, if left wing radicalism was such a threat, why the office of the Russian Provisional Government was not included in the raid? Perhaps this can be explained by the fact that Washington was engaged in delicate negotiations with the provisional government at this time and Lusk was cautioned against intervening. Nevertheless, the raid on the Bureau produced little of value. It failed to provide any greater insights into the radical conspiracy.

The Rand School raid was equally devoid of results. The school had always been moderate in its approach and was not a center for subversion. Indeed, it might be argued that it served a fine purpose as an outlet for urban discontent. Why, then, did so many consider it threatening? Basically, the school was considered dangerous because it challenged conventional thinking. It preached socialism at a time when laissez faire capitalism was highly regarded. Then, too, it was not afraid of coming to grips with the most controversial social questions of the day. Such topics as race conflict and birth control were considered to be appropriate issues for discussion. This liberal approach threatened so many people's beliefs and so many vested interests that the school gathered a host of enemies over the years.

The raid on the Communist party was, perhaps, more rationally explained. Like the Palmer raids, it helped dismantle the party's structure and drove many Communists underground. But even here, the raid was undertaken in violation of strict constitutional safeguards. It was defensible only in terms of the means justifying the ends.

Lusk's motives are not easy to determine. There is no reason to doubt his sincerity, his patriotism, or his honest conviction that the left presented a real threat. On the other hand, he may have used the committee to advance his own political ambitions. Other men have risen to high posts on lesser issues. Even if he had no ulterior motives, Lusk was certainly an unwise choice for such a sensitive post. As a freshman senator with no experience in radical or urban problems, he was ill-equipped to handle such a difficult job.

Still another troublesome aspect of the Lusk Committee investigations was the loose manner in which the public hearings were conducted. One is struck by the fact that the proceedings were marked by what can only be described as a carnival atmosphere. Many of the charges made were wild and vague; few were ever followed up to any logical conclusion. Then, too, character assassination was all too frequent. Those named were not invited to appear at the hearings or to reply to the charges in any other way. Furthermore, little or no attempt was made to develop a professional approach to the problem. If left wing subversion was the issue, then experts in this area should have been called. Instead, the witnesses were often biased and continually made inflammatory statements based on partial evidence. As to the material taken in the raids, this, too, was of little value. Much of it was printed by the committee in its final report, and while it provided a good, historical summary of the trends in American and European radicalism, it did not suggest any radical conspiracy. The press only compounded the errors through its sensational reporting. It made no efforts to develop perspective or to isolate significant elements, but reported, at face value, all of the evidence presented at the hearings. This attitude was not conducive to a careful investigation carried out by a responsible legislative committee.

A final shortcoming of the Lusk Committee was its inability to define the scope of its investigation. Subversion was never defined, so when the question was approached in terms of a vague, amorphous "threat," it was difficult, in the absence of overt acts or other activities of a conspiratorial nature, either to prove or disprove the charges.

The times were, however, not marked completely by despair. The people of New York were fortunate in having a man of the calibre of Alfred E. Smith as their governor. Smith wisely and courageously vetoed the Lusk bills and, at the same time, indicated how unwise it was to try to legislate acceptable political beliefs. He popularized the idea that poor economic conditions, not left wing agitation, was the real cause of radicalism. As a liberal thinker attuned to the problems of the urban slums, Smith realized that the radical threat would have subsided if the legislature was willing to confront the issues of low wages, unhealthy factory conditions, and inadequate housing. Had it done this, the efforts of the Lusk Committee would have been unnecessary.

Another disturbing note was the relative absence of protest on the part of the public. With the exception of a few liberal publications, few questioned the activities of the committee. One must conclude that the public was either in sympathy with the Luskers or else frightened into silence. As to those in sympathy, in retrospect, we cannot be too critical of them. One must remember that these were times of crisis. The bombings of May and June raised real fears of social upheaval. When the bomb throwers were still at large some months after the incidents, could the public be blamed for trusting the one public figure who said he would try a new approach? On the other hand, should we condemn those who remained silent? In part, no, for if those in positions of political leadership were unwilling or unable to stand up against the hysteria of the times, the average citizen could hardly have been expected to do more. Nevertheless, the silent ones must share some of the blame. They represent the saddest aspect of the Lusk Committee era. Most probably, many remained silent out of fear that their protest might be misconstrued as sympathy for the radical cause. Certainly, more citizens should have spoken up, for, in the last analysis, every man's freedom is jeopardized when those not directly involved fall silent.

NOTES

1. The Socialists were: Claessens and Solomon. The Democrats were: Johnson, Leiniger, Lyons, McCue, McLoughlin, Muller, O'Hare, and Schwab.
2. *New York Times,* March 27, 1919, p. 8.
3. *New York World,* June 14, 1919, p. 12.
4. Mereto, *Red Conspiracy,* p. 358.
5. McAdoo was the Chief Magistrate and a former Commissioner of Police. He was first appointed by Mayor John F. Hylan.
6. Quoted in "By Stevenson Out Of Lusk," *The New Republic,* June 15, 1962, p. 66.
7. Alice Edgerton, "Individual Liberty in America," *The Nation,* October 11, 1919, p. 494; "The Resuscitation of Liberty," *ibid.,* October 25, 1919, p. 539.
8. Information for the raid was secured partly from an informant named Morris S. Nessim, a left winger arrested earlier on November 1. Among other items, Nessim provided the Lusk Committee with a list of Communist fronts and organizations.
9. Benjamin Gitlow, *I Confess: The Truth About American Communism* (New York, 1940), p. 60.
10. *New York World,* November 11, 1919, p. 10; *New York Post,* November 11, 1919, in ACLU Archives, Vol. 54; letter from Theodore Debs, November 20, 1919 in David A. Karsner Papers (N. Y. Public Library), Box 2.
11. Senate of the State of New York, *Revolutionary Radicalism,* Report of the Joint Legislative Committee Investigating Radical Activities (Albany, 1920), 4 vols.
12. "Education from Albany," *The Nation,* May 8, 1920, p. 613.
13. *People* v. *American Socialist Society,* 202 N. Y. App. Div. 640 (1922).

Chapter Six

THE UNSEATING OF THE FIVE SOCIALISTS

In 1920 five Socialists were expelled from the Assembly of the New York State Legislature. This event attracted nationwide attention and was an important development in the history of the Red Scare. However, in contrast to the favorable response received by the Lusk Committee, the expulsion elicited a feeling of shock from the press and the public. This negative reaction represented a turning point in national attitudes and, more than any other single event, hastened the end of the antiradical crusade.

The expulsion took place during the legislative session of 1920, four days after the Lusk raid on the radical newspapers. The episode could scarcely have occurred without the sensational publicity generated by the Lusk Committee.

Socialist legislators were not new to New York. In varying numbers, they were present at every session since 1916. In 1919 there were ten Socialist assemblymen, all from New York City. This was reduced to five in the November election. Those elected were: August Claessens, Louis Waldman, Charles Solomon, Samuel De Witt, and Samuel Orr. With the exception of De Witt, all had served in previous sessions of the assembly.

August "Gus" Claessens was easily the most colorful personality of the five. Born in Switzerland, he came to the United States as a child. As a young man he tried various occupations including acting, painting, and peddling. He studied at the Rand School where he was later employed as a teacher. After joining the Socialist party he became known as a popular speaker and Socialist agitator. Although not Jewish, he would amaze his audience by delivering many of his speeches in Yiddish. Claessens was an active legislator: in previous sessions he had introduced many measures for social reform including a proposal to eliminate capital punishment.

Charles Solomon came from the Brownsville section of Brooklyn. Born on the Lower East Side, his earliest ambition was to be an actor. To pursue his career, he attended the American Academy of Dramatic Arts. Solomon discovered his aptitude for public speaking after joining the Socialist party. Subsequently, he became a secretary to the Socialist congressman, Meyer London and, later, to the Socialist delegation of the New York Board of Aldermen.

Louis Waldman was born in a little Ukrainian village not far from Kiev. He came to the United States in 1909 "with the sounds of the pogroms" still in his ears. In New York he worked in a variety of sweatshops for eleven hours a day at two dollars a week. After work he attended night school, became active in the garment worker's union, and participated in its earliest strikes. Through the influence of Meyer London and Morris Hillquit, he joined the Socialist party, hoping to improve the economic and social conditions of his family, his fellow workers, and his community.

Samuel Orr had a background in the study of law which he pursued at New York University. He was active in many liberal and left wing organizations: the Educational Alliance, the Workmen's Circle, and the Socialist party.

Samuel De Witt was a newcomer to the legislature. His background was in business where he sold machine parts. But his sympathies were with the working class and he came to the legislature determined to pass laws in its behalf.

These were the men chosen to represent their Socialist constituencies in the Bronx, Manhattan, and Brooklyn. They were jubilant when the election returns were announced and interpreted their victory as a mandate for a total change in the moral, political, and intellectual climate of the state. They were not only opposed to capitalism but to political corruption in every form. They called for a "vast social revolution to effect change." August Claessens spoke for them all when he said:

> We are going into the Assembly and we will tell it to them. . . . We won't waste much time, Comrades, talking to the bunch that [sic] sit there with stolen property, but we will use our position in the Assembly to reach the "Henry Dubs" and

speak to them. And I can assure you, Comrades, we won't sleep one night while we are in Albany, but every night we will be speaking in Troy, Schenectady, and Amsterdam, rousing the members wherever we possibly can.

Such rousing statements were hardly calculated to put the non-Socialist assemblymen at their ease and helped to widen the breach already existing between the two groups.

The new session of the legislature began on January 7, 1920. Along with other members, the Socialists took the prescribed oath of office, swearing to uphold the Constitution of the United States and the laws of the State of New York. The oath includes the following words: "No other oath, declaration or test shall be required as a qualification for any office or public trust." Afterwards, the Socialists took their seats and participated in the organization of the House. They listened to an address by the Governor and helped select the various officers including the speaker, Thaddeas C. Sweet. This business took about two hours.

Then, without warning, Speaker Sweet directed the sergeant-at-arms to present the Socialists before the bar of the house. The sergeant obeyed. Reading from a prepared resolution, the speaker said: "You whom I have summoned before the bar of the House are seeking seats in this body. You have been elected on a platform which is absolutely inimical to the best interests of the State of New York and the United States." This was followed by an enumeration of the charges to the effect that the Socialist party was not a regular political party, that it admitted aliens and minors into its ranks, that its elected officials were bound by instructions of the party's executive committee, that it was disloyal during the war, and that it was in sympathy with the Communist International and its program of violence and civil war.

The Socialists protested but were told by the speaker that they would be allowed to reply to the charges at the proper time. Meanwhile, the house would vote on a resolution which, if adopted, would declare their seats vacant pending a hearing before a Committee of the Judiciary. At this hearing, the Socialists would be given an opportunity to prove their right to a seat. Louis Waldman explained that according to the rules of the assembly, an elected member could only be unseated after charges were filed against him, a hearing held before the Judiciary Committee, and the entire house voted for expulsion. There was no procedure for suspension pending a hearing. In addition, Waldman observed that no charges had been made against the Socialists, only against the party with which they were affiliated. Waldman was overruled by Speaker Sweet. But he had made his point.

Next, the speaker recognized Simon Adler, the majority floor leader, who presented the resolution drawn up in advance by Attorney General Newton. This repeated the charges and called for the creation of a Committee of the Judiciary to investigate. The Socialist seats were declared vacant. Surprisingly, there was no debate on what later proved to be a question of national significance. The resolution was put to a roll call vote: 145 Democrats and Republicans voted in favor of the measure while four of the five Socialists and two Democrats from the Bronx, William S. Evans and J. Fairfax McLaughlin voted against it. Louis Waldman did not vote. After the vote, the speaker requested that the five Socialists retire to the rear of the chamber. When they refused to move, the speaker commanded the sergeant-at-arms to escort them out. They were led out one by one. As Louis Waldman passed up the aisle, a few of his friends from the Democratic side said to him, "Sorry, Waldman, we just couldn't help it." This passing remark seemed to indicate that despite the almost unanimous vote in favor of expulsion, a few members were already having second thoughts about the propriety of their decision. Nevertheless, by its vote, the legislature had effectively disfranchised some 60,000 voters in the City of New York.

The expulsion of the Socialists was carefully planned. Speaker Sweet must have discussed it with other members of the assembly.[1] The attorney general was consulted and drew up the resolution. There is some evidence that the idea may have originated with Archibald Stevenson. It may also have been suggested by a similar case in the House of Representatives where a seat was denied to the Socialist congressman, Victor Berger. With the newspapers full of stories about the Berger case, the New York legislators were encouraged to act in a similar fashion.

To many, the speaker's action came as a complete surprise. August Claessens offered one explanation: he felt that the Socialists were unlike the usual breed of politicians sent to the assembly at that time. They were scrupulously honest and insisted that their colleagues maintain equivalent standards of honesty and integrity. Then, too, they espoused their Socialist philosophy with messianic fervor which must have irritated the non-Socialist members.

Waldman was also surprised. His thoughts were hostile as he stood in the well of the assembly. To Waldman, Sweet looked like a "sleek, white-haired mortician." He remembered Simon Adler, the Republican floor leader who had introduced the resolution, as having "a meticulous hair-do and a smug smile of self-satisfaction." Waldman could not help being amused by the thought that the Socialists were being accused of advocating revolution and class violence, the very issues which had split the party and which they had violently rejected at Chicago in 1919. "I looked at Tad Sweet," he continued, "and saw a marked resemblance to the ignorant New York policeman who had clubbed an antisocialist because he didn't care 'what kind of a Socialist' he was. All he needed was a blue uniform and a club." Waldman attributed the expulsion to Sweet's desire for statewide political recognition. He believed that Sweet was riding the crest of an antiradical wave stirred up by the Lusk Committee which would carry him on to higher office.

As the Socialists left the chamber, they were followed by the press; the reporters realized at once the importance of the story. They accompanied the Socialists to their hotel rooms and subjected them to a succession of questions. Waldman and Solomon broke away long enough to draft a formal statement to the press on behalf of the delegation. The statement did not satisfy the reporters who returned with them to New York City. At Grand Central Station, they were met by a small demonstration of party members and additional reporters who, in the interim, had been alerted to the historic decision taken at Albany. Next, the Socialists went to party headquarters at the People's House on Fifteenth Street where all available officials assembled to plan a course of action. One member said: "Things are going to hum as they never did before." Julius Gerber maintained: "This action of the New York State Assembly, if permitted to stand, will go further to make anarchists and create anarchy, then Emma Goldman, Berkman, and thousands of anarchists could have accomplished in a lifetime." To Algernon Lee, the assembly's vote was "as black an act against the fundamental principles of American government as was ever committed."

The left wingers drew up a joint protest in which they called the expulsion an act of "organized violence" against the very essence of democracy and the "sacred right" of the ballot. They repeated the fact that the Socialist party was totally committed to achieving its ends by peaceful and legal means, that the law of the land had been distorted, and that the suspension had perverted the assembly's rules.

The Socialists soon found support in many quarters. Charles Evans Hughes was one of the first to denounce the assembly's action. In an Open Letter to Speaker Sweet, Hughes went to the heart of the matter:

If there is anything against these men as individuals, if they were deemed to be guilty of criminal offenses, they should have been charged accordingly. But I understand that the action is not directed against these five elected members as individuals but that the proceeding is virtually an attempt to indict a political party and to deny it representation in the Legislature. This is not, in my judgment, American government. . . .

I understand that it is said that the Socialists constitute a combination to overthrow the government. The answer is plain. If public officers or private citizens have any evidence that any individuals are plotting revolution and seeking by violent means to change our government let the evidence be laid before the proper authorities and swift action be taken for the protection of the community. . . . But I count it a most serious mistake, not against the individuals charged with violation of law, but against masses of our citizens combined for political action, by denying them the only resource of peaceful government, that is, action by the ballot box and through duly elected representatives in legislative bodies.

The letter was sent to the *New York Tribune;* it was reprinted in other papers. The *Tribune* was deeply impressed, saying that Hughes' letter achieved the level of a state paper and should be a guide for the future. The following day Governor Alfred E. Smith held a conference with leaders of the state Democratic party after deciding to issue a statement condemning the ouster. Some of the leaders protested but the governor's views prevailed. In his letter Smith argued that if the Republicans possessed information which led them to believe that the Socialist assemblymen were subversive, they should have submitted the charges to the legislature and conducted a trial by orderly processes. Meanwhile, the Socialists should have been permitted to retain their seats as they were innocent until proven guilty. The opposition to the expulsion was gaining new adherents. The press was next to speak up.

Press reaction to these events was extensive. In New York City, the majority of the papers reversed their previous stand in defense of the Red Scare and came out against the action taken by Sweet and the assembly. Running through their editorials was the theme that while socialism was an abomination, the arbitrary action of suspending the Socialists by extralegal means was even worse. The *New York World,* for example, headlined its story, "A Blow At Free Government," and called Sweet's performance "Bolshevism Masquerading in the Livery of Americanism." The *Tribune* characterized the suspension as an act of "official lawlessness." It reported a protest movement developing among the city's clergy. The New York *Evening Journal* called it the "most serious assault upon the liberties of the American people since a British King and Parliament forced our fathers to protect their freedom with arms in their hands." The *Evening Post* denounced it as a "sinister threat against the fundamentals of democracy and representative government," while the *Brooklyn Standard-Union,* conservative on most issues, decried it as "utterly wrong in principle and lamentable as a matter of policy." One can only speculate how shocked Thaddeas Sweet must have been after reading these editorial opinions.[2]

A small minority of New York City papers supported the assembly. *The New York Times* said that the guilt or innocence of the Socialists would be determined in the trial and warned the Socialist party that the "majority of the American people are not disposed to yield before any revolutionary threats." The *New York Commercial,* a leading business journal, said that the case of Victor Berger, the Socialist congressman expelled from the house for violation of the Espionage Act, was analogous to the present case and urged their expulsion.[3]

Upstate, the situation looked far more encouraging to Sweet, where twenty-two out of thirty-four representative editors gave immediate if varying degrees of approval to the speaker's action. The rest protested.[4] The *Albany Knickerbocker,* for example, insisted that the "Socialist Party is a political party under the laws of the State of New York, having the same standing in the eyes of the law as the Republican and Democratic Party."

After an exhaustive survey of the nation's press, *The Literary Digest* reported that most papers opposed the suspension. The *Newark Evening News,* for example, ascribed the actions at Albany to "present day anti-Red hysterics," and directed its readers to the fact that the British Labor party, a Socialist party, was in power in England. "It would be just as wise for Parliament to expel the British Labor Party, bag and baggage, as it would be for the New York State Legislature to suspend its Socialist members." Further west, the *Pittsburgh Leader,* a Republican paper, compared the action of the assembly to Southern lynch law.[5]

Individuals and organizations on all sides of the political spectrum soon joined the press in a series of vigorous protests. The New York Bar Association, the state Federation of Labor and the Central Federated Union lined up with the Socialist party and the radical labor unions in this rising chorus of dissent. Nicholas Murray Butler, a strong foe of radicalism, declared that the expulsion was unwise although undertaken for the "highest motives" and for "patriotic reasons." Frank P. Walsh wrote that the "action of the New York Republican Legislature [was] not surprising. The habitual and unbridled violation of the commonest constitutional rights of the working people since the signing of the Armistice naturally leads to such assaults upon institutions and representative government." Even the capitals of Europe were interested in the fate of the Socialists. In a cable to the *New York World,* George Bernard Shaw concluded that "Americans [were] savages still" and like all primitive societies, prosecuted opinions as a matter of course. It was "high time," he thought, "for the Mayflower to fit out to sea again."[6]

After this barrage of criticism, some members of the assembly began to wonder whether they had acted wisely. Led by the Democratic floor leader, Charles Donahue, they moved to rescind the suspension of their Socialist colleagues. Thirty-three assemblymen voted in favor while seventy-one voted against it. Unwilling to face the consequences of such a controversial issue again, forty-one legislators absented themselves from the assembly while the vote was taken.

A few days later, additional support for the Socialists came from the Socialist members of the Board of Aldermen. Although reduced in number after the election of November 1919, they

succeeded in introducing a resolution calling for the impeachment of Speaker Sweet and the Republican floor leader, Simon
Adler. The resolution did not pass, but the Socialists received
some support from a few Democrats who thought it would prove
embarrassing to their Republican opponents. This stormy session
of the aldermen was presided over by its newly-elected president, Fiorello LaGuardia, who later expressed views favoring
suspension. "If the five suspended Socialists are guilty of the
charges made against them, they should be indicted, convicted,
and shot," he said.[7] This extreme statement seems unusual in the
light of LaGuardia's later liberal record.

The periodicals were slower to reflect upon the events in
Albany. *The New Republic* felt that the final decision of the
Judiciary Committee would be to unseat the Socialists. It predicted dire consequences if Speaker Sweet, Senator Lusk, and
Archibald Stevenson continued to control the state's policy towards radical legislators. Furthermore, it was heartened that so
many distinguished citizens like Charles Evans Hughes, Ogden
Mills, Alfred E. Smith, and Henry L. Stimson, all well-known
lawyers, had taken strong stands against legislative expulsion.
The conservative *Review of Reviews* was more cautious. While
agreeing that the legislature had the right to expel its bolshevist
members, it questioned whether the Socialists fitted this descrip-
tion. The *Review* looked forward to the trial to clear up the
question.[8]

In the meantime, Charles Evans Hughes, following up his
original letter to Speaker Sweet, called a meeting of the Bar Association of the City of New York to plan a further course of
action. Hughes proposed a resolution which called the suspension
"un-American" and condemned it in the strongest terms. This was
opposed by a group of lawyers led by William D. Guthrie and a
lively debate developed on its merits. Guthrie said that the
accused would have a fair, open, and impartial hearing. He
found the resolution out of order in view of the fact that the
assembly had voted overwhelmingly for expulsion. He also maintained that the Socialists could not truthfully take the oath of
office while adhering to their stated ideology. If the Socialists
were seated, the oath would be converted into a "travesty" which
might be taken by any revolutionary Socialist or Communist.
Guthrie warned that if Hughes' resolution passed, the prestige of
the bar association would be diminished.

Guthrie's remarks were persuasive, and some members supporting Hughes began to waver. To stop the trend, Hughes permitted an amendment to the second paragraph of the resolution. In its amended form the resolution pledged the bar's support only to those elected officials whose parties employed legal and constitutional methods to bring about social change. This made it more palatable to many of the waverers and since it clearly included the five Socialists under attack, it passed by a vote of 174 to 117. Next a special committee was appointed to draw up an amicus curiae brief to be presented to the Judiciary Committee at the beginning of the trial. The special committee was headed by Hughes and included Ogden Mills, Morgan J. O'Brien, Joseph M. Proskauer, and Louis Marshall, all distinguished members of the bar.

The Socialists were also busy preparing for their defense; they started a fund-raising campaign to pay legal and other expenses. The *New York World* came to their assistance setting up a special fund and calling for contributions. A strong endorsement came from a former governor of New York, Martin H. Glynn, who sent in a check for $25 and added a note emphasizing the need for "fair play." The Socialists then contacted Morris Hillquit, resting at Saranac Lake after a bout with tuberculosis, who was asked whether he felt well enough to take charge of the defense. Hillquit replied that he would.

The hearing before the Judiciary Committee began on January 20, 1920. The atmosphere was one of tense excitement. The large hall was filled with members of both houses of the legislature, public officials, and a throng of private citizens lucky enough to secure admission. A horde of newspapermen from all parts of the country was also in attendance. People milled about the room and spilled out into the adjoining corridors.

At a large table in the hearing room was Assemblyman Louis M. Martin, formerly of the Lusk Committee, who was chairman of the Subcommittee of the Judiciary in charge of the trial. To Hillquit, Martin "looked exceedingly unhappy and uncomfortable in his role." Hillquit speculated that Martin may have had some private qualms about what he was expected to do. But if he had such qualms he did not reveal them but remained calm throughout the trial. Martin was surrounded by the other members of the subcommittee named by Speaker Sweet. There were ten Republicans and three Democrats, all members of the bar.

The Judiciary Committee also retained the services of a distinguished group of lawyers to act as counsel. They were: John B. Stanchfield, a criminal lawyer, Arthur E. Sutherland, a former Justice of the Supreme Court, former Attorney General Carmody, Martin Conboy, an important figure in legal and political circles, State Senator Elon R. Brown, Attorney General Newton, and Martin W. Littleton, a successful lawyer and one of the outstanding orators in the country.

The Socialists were ably defended by a team headed by Morris Hillquit. In some respects, this trial was the highlight of Hillquit's career. He was not only defending five of his friends but his Socialist philosophy and his life's work. Assisting Hillquit was the Chicago Socialist, Seymour Stedman, formerly the party's choice for the vice presidency of the United States and the defense attorney in the Espionage Act trial of Eugene V. Debs. Others on the Socialist side were Gilbert E. Roe, a progressive Republican and the former law partner of the elder Senator LaFollette, Walter Nelles, prominent in civil rights cases, and the Socialist attorneys, S. John Block and William Karlin.

The Socialists prepared their case carefully. They sensed what the final outcome would be, but decided to use this opportunity to explain their Socialist principles in as forceful a manner as possible. As in everything else they did, they brought a sense of mission to their task and prepared to inform the country about their party and its doctrines.

Charles Evans Hughes was the first to speak. He asked permission to submit the brief drawn up by the special committee of the bar association. The brief was lengthy; in summary, it contained the following arguments. The Socialists had been duly elected. Prior to their suspension, no charges had been lodged against them. They possessed all of the qualifications prescribed by the Constitution. They had not been guilty of any violation of law, nor had they been guilty of any misconduct while members of the assembly. While the legislature was the sole judge of the qualifications of its own members, this power was not absolute, but must be used in accordance with the principles of due process. All questions regarding disqualification were best submitted before a member was admitted to membership. After the oath was administered and a member was admitted to the privileges of the house, he could not be deprived of those privileges except by expulsion. A member could only be expelled upon the presentation of proper charges and after an opportunity to be heard. A member, after taking the oath, could not be denied the privileges of the house because of an alleged opinion, state of mind, or intent claimed to be inconsistent with the oath. A member could not be expelled for his political opinions as the Constitution clearly stated that "no oath, declaration, or test shall be required as a qualification for any office or public trust."

The brief cited many historical and legal precedents and recommended that the Judiciary Committee restore the five Socialists to their seats immediately. If any wrong had been committed, they should be brought up on charges in the proper way.

As persuasive as the brief was, Chairman Martin would not permit it to be read. He also refused to allow the bar association to participate in the trial in the capacity of amicus curiae, maintaining that there were many other organizations that had requested the same privilege. Without further recourse, Hughes distributed copies of the brief to the committee and the press and walked out of the chamber, with great dignity, followed by his colleagues from the bar association.

Hillquit made the next move; he attacked the entire proceeding charging that the members of the committee had been appointed by the assembly. As both judge and jury, they could not possibly render an impartial verdict. Hillquit noted that certain members of the assembly had publicly stated that the Socialists were guilty even before the trial had begun. One man, Assemblyman Louis Cuvillier, had said that if the five Socialists were found guilty, they ought not to be expelled but should be "taken out and shot."

Hillquit's first challenge was overruled. He followed it with a motion to dismiss the proceedings on the grounds that it was "without warrant in the Constitution, or in the statutes of the State of New York, and was, therefore, totally illegal and void." This motion was argued extensively and was, as Hillquit later admitted, "the heaviest legal battery" which the defense could produce. During the debate, Hillquit cited many precedents from the proceedings of the national Congress and from the New York Assembly itself, to illustrate the dangers inherent in this course of action. For example, he denied that the case of Victor Berger was analogous to the present case in any way. He pointed out that Berger had presented himself to the house "with a sentence of twenty years for imprisonment for violation of the Espionage

Act" pending, while the five Socialist assemblymen had never been convicted of any crime. He charged further that the trial was merely an attempt to emasculate the Socialist movement. Hillquit also developed the point that the Socialist movement was not trying to destroy the government by revolution but was interested in effecting orderly and peaceful social change.[9]

Hillquit's arguments were answered by Mr. Stanchfield and Mr. Littleton. Stanchfield denied that the Socialists were entitled to representation. He said that the assembly had "the unqualified power" to expel any member, with or without cause. Littleton called the statements of Charles Evans Hughes and the bar association "bewildered" and refused, once again, to listen to them. He rejected Hillquit's legal precedents as "hair splitting" and repeated the charges that the accused had taken the oath of office openly but were really the agents of a subversive organization called the Socialist party. Secretly, they sought to destroy law and order in the country.

In the second day of the trial, Seymour Stedman argued the case for the Socialists. He said that even if all of the charges were proven true, there would still be insufficient legal grounds for removing the Socialist assemblymen. Stedman cited many legal precedents supporting his cause but the committee was not impressed. Mr. Block then asked for a bill of particulars specifying in greater detail the actual offenses committed by the defendants. This motion, along with many others, was turned down by the chairman.

Then Martin Littleton took the floor. He repeated the charge that the Socialists gave their allegiance "wholly and solely to an alien and invisible empire known as the International," and were pledged to destroy the government by "force if necessary, perhaps by peaceful means." Littleton stressed the point that the Socialist party was on record as sympathetic to the Bolshevik Revolution. He maintained that the Socialists agreed with the present Russian program; therefore, if the Judiciary Committee could offer evidence as to what Lenin and Trotsky stood for this would be proper grounds for expulsion. Whether the Socialist party carried out its activities peacefully, masquerading as a political party, would make little difference. The end result would be the same.

Louis Waldman later recalled that when Littleton reached that part of his speech in which the Socialists were presumed to give their allegiance to a foreign power, some members of the press looked skeptical while others "tittered audibly." The public seemed to enjoy the hearing and applauded loudly at several points.

Littleton then pointed out that the Socialist party stood indicted by its declaration of April 1917, when it characterized World War I as a "criminal war" conducted for the benefit of capitalists. When the party urged resistance to the war, it was, in effect, giving aid and comfort to the enemy. Next, he referred to section 13, subdivision A, of the Socialist party constitution which provided:

> A member may be expelled from the party or may be suspended for a period not exceeding one year for the following offenses: for failing or refusing when elected to public office to abide or carry out such instructions as he may have received from the dues paying organization, or as prescribed by the state or national constitution.

To Littleton, it was close to treason for the Socialists to do the bidding of a party infested with aliens.

Stedman was to reply to Littleton, but Hillquit could not contain himself. Rising to his feet, he tried to define treason. In his attempt, he compared the Socialists to men like Patrick Henry and Thomas Jefferson who wanted freedom from England. Their doctrines were considered disloyal at the time. So, too, were the ideas of William Lloyd Garrison who sought to deprive slave holders of their property. If Garrison and the other abolitionists had not protested, chattel slavery would still disgrace the nation. Hillquit maintained that the Socialists had a right to express their views freely. They stood for economic independence, emancipation of the working class, and freedom for the whole community. "It sounds treacherous and traitorous to you, but it is our right to hold these doctrines, and you are not our judges anymore than we are yours."

Soon after this exchange, Littleton left the trial to fulfill a prior commitment. Theodore Roosevelt, Jr., a member of the Judiciary Committee, left soon afterwards. Roosevelt had become increasingly disillusioned with the trial. He felt that the committee was not acting fairly. The *New York World* speculated that Roosevelt's departure might precipitate a movement for reseating the

Socialists. Hillquit also left in order to resume his convalescence at Saranac Lake. The defense was left in the capable hands of Seymour Stedman and the other lawyers.

Subsequently, the trial dealt mostly with the presentation of evidence, composed of a miscellaneous collection of documents, many of which had already been presented before the Lusk Committee. Among them were transcripts of speeches made by the defendants, the votes of the Socialists in previous sessions of the legislature, speeches by Eugene V. Debs, Lenin, and Trotsky and other speeches.

At one point, Julius Gerber was subpoenaed to produce the national constitution of the Socialist party. He was questioned about section 1, paragraph 5, which stated:

> All persons joining the Socialist Party shall sign the following pledge: "I the undersigned, recognizing the class struggle between the capitalist class and the working class, and the necessity of the working class organizing itself into a political party for the purpose of obtaining collective ownership and democratic administration and operation of the collectively used and socially necessary means of production and distribution, hereby apply for membership in the Socialist Party."

This was cited as further proof that the party was no regular political party but a full-fledged subversive conspiracy.

The conspiratorial and subversive nature of the party was further emphasized by Article 10, subdivision B, which forbade members, at the risk of expulsion from the party, from voting for any but Socialist candidates. Actually, the party had no method of enforcing this provision even if it wanted to. In 1912 and again in 1916 Socialists abandoned the party en masse to support President Wilson and the provision was not used against them. The secret ballot made it totally void. Still another damaging bit of evidence was found in Article 7, section 3, which provided that Socialist members of legislative bodies must vote "as a unit" under the direction of their elected chairman. This, too, was introduced to prove that the Socialists were not free agents but subject to party discipline. Presentation of evidence of this type continued for some time. The prosecution was building its case proving that the Socialist party stood beyond the pale of legitimate politics. At one point, Mr. Stanchfield tried to secure the party's membership lists. This request led to the following exchange:

> Stanchfield: Mr. Gerber, you have been served with a *subpoena duces tecum* commanding you to produce records showing the names of dues paying members of the Socialist Party in the counties of New York, Kings, and the Bronx?
> Gerber: I have.
> Stanchfield: Have you produced the papers therein called for?
> Gerber: Not yet, it weighs about two tons.

Actually, Mr. Gerber was only sparring. Although the party had complied fully with every other request made by the committee, it was not inclined to expose its membership lists to public scrutiny. By doing so it felt that some members might be harrassed by their employers. This was clearly indicated in Seymour Stedman's testimony.

Speeches made up an important part of the evidence for the prosecution. The Judiciary Committee seemed to be operating under the theory that the Socialists were responsible for everything that was ever said or written by any member of the left. Exhibit 27, for example, dealt with a meeting held at the Hunt's Point Palace in the Bronx celebrating the second anniversary of the Russian Revolution. Among the speakers was Wilfred Humphries, for "fourteen months with the Red Cross in Russia," A. Rhys Williams, an "eye observer of the Russian Revolution," and two Socialists, Gertrude Robinson and Norman Thomas. Another was the transcript of a rally held at the Park View Palace. The speaker's list included Santeri Nuorteva, a secretary of the unrecognized Bolshevik Embassy at Washington, the indicted Socialist, Scott Nearing, and the defendant, August Claessens. The chairman was Alexander Tractenberg, later a member of the Communist party. Claessens' speech, already presented to the Lusk Committee, was quoted in full as proof of the Socialist involvement in revolution.

Evidence of incriminating speeches made by Louis Waldman and Charles Solomon was also presented. In one of these, delivered at a meeting celebrating the success of the Russian Revolution, Waldman said:

> If you commemorate the birthday of the Russian Revolution, if you revere your Russian comrades, if you applaud Lenin

and Trotsky [applause by the crowd], if you believe in the worthiness of their cause . . . then it is your duty to enter the Socialist movement in America to make it more like Russia is today [great applause].

Along with documentary evidence and speeches, a number of expert witnesses were called before the Judiciary Committee. Their testimony strengthened the case against the defendants. The Socialists protested in vain that many of these witnesses were recalling from memory events that happened years before, that no records were kept, that the remarks were quoted out of context, and that they were irrelevant to the issues presented in the resolution for expulsion. The transcript of the trial proved this. For example, in February 1917 Claessens engaged in a public debate with a lawyer named Frank Wasserman on the topic "Socialism versus Capitalism," during which he was alleged to have said that "the Constitution" was a "mere scrap of paper," and that the people would soon take over the government by force. Wasserman's evidence against Solomon was also hearsay in nature. During the latter part of 1919 he met Solomon on a street corner in the East New York section of Brooklyn where he was delivering a speech. He heard Solomon say: "Bolshevism is under way, the revolution is under way." In other statements, he indicated that the revolution would come much sooner than expected, and compared it to the American Revolution of 1776. In the face of such vague evidence, it was difficult for Stedman to cross-examine the witness. He tried as best he could:

Stedman: Do any of the Socialists advocate violence?
Wasserman: Why, yes.
Stedman: Name a party declaration.
Wasserman: Not a party declaration, no sir. There isn't any party declaration. . . .
Stedman: Did you ever hear of Socialists rifling the ballot boxes?
Wasserman: They haven't had the opportunity yet, I guess.
Stedman: Have you ever heard of the Socialists engaged in mob violence?
Wasserman: Yes, mob violence, yes.

But when pressed by Stedman, the witness was unable to think of a single instance.

Another sensational witness was a young lady who swore that

in 1917, shortly after America's entrance into the war, she heard Charles Solomon make an inflammatory speech on a street corner. A detachment of American soldiers walked by and the officer in charge asked for the use of the platform for recruiting purposes. Solomon refused, adding the comment that "the gutter is good enough for you." The soldiers left hurriedly and Solomon supposedly celebrated the victory by spitting on the American flag. S. John Block raised an objection to this testimony and it was stricken from the record; there was no indication, however, that it was stricken from the thoughts of the members of the Judiciary Committee.

The most important witness called by the prosecution was Peter W. Collins, a former official of the Electrical Workers Union and the AFL. During the war he was employed by the Wilson administration as an industrial expert. Later, he resigned from the AFL to become a professional antiradical agitator. He once offered Eugene V. Debs $300 to debate with him; on another occasion he said that there was no real difference between socialism and communism, that bolshevism was only socialism in action.

Collins was called back to the witness stand a number of times. His testimony was quite rambling but he tried to develop the idea that socialism like communism was committed to violence, mass action, and the general strike. By showing that Marx advocated violence, he tried to prove that the Socialists were wedded to the same concept. Collins charged that the Socialists had infiltrated the labor movement in order to destroy its effectiveness. Once this happened, it was to be replaced by a more radical organization.

The press reported the trial in detail. *The Literary Digest* sampled press opinion across the country; in an interesting article, it tried to summarize the editors' views. Most papers felt that the trial had stirred the average American's sense of justice and fair play. Their editors believed that minority rights had been violated during the proceedings. Only a few papers defended the Judiciary Committee, stating that the trial would prove, once and for all, whether the Socialist party was a menace to American liberties.[10] As the trial dragged on, more papers spoke out against the committee. The Socialists fought hard but were pessimistic about their chances of winning.

After the prosecution had presented its case, the defense was given its chance to present evidence and interrogate witnesses.

By this time, Hillquit had returned to the trial and was called by Stedman to testify. Hillquit sketched the history of the International Socialist movement and described the relationship of the Socialist party of the United States to the parties of other countries. Then, he explained its attitude towards Soviet Russia, its stand on the war, and its economic and political program. Hillquit was cross-examined by Martin Conboy who asked whether Hillquit had ever taken money for his services while employed as counsel to Martens and the Russian Bureau. Hillquit said he had not. By this line of questioning, Conboy hoped to reinforce the point that the Socialist party was beholden to a foreign power.

Other witnesses followed Hillquit. Algernon Lee discussed the economic theories of socialism, while Otto F. Branstetter, the national secretary of the Socialist party, explained the structure, composition, and methods of the party. Branstetter surprised the committee by informing them that a party census showed that 73 per cent of its members were American citizens, thus refuting the charge heard so often during the Red Scare that the Socialists were all aliens or foreigners.

Still another witness was Norman Thomas who showed that there was no antagonism between socialism and religion. Contrary to the popular view, he stated that the party took a neutral stand on religion. To the party it was a matter of individual choice. He argued that the best way to carry out the Christian ethic was to organize a cooperative commonwealth which was also the goal of socialism. Then Thomas explained how he, himself, had been converted to socialism. As the father of five children he found it to be compatible with morality and family structure. The audience was deeply impressed with his sincerity and his depth of knowledge.

The last witnesses for the defense were three of the five Socialists on trial. Louis Waldman gave an account of the inner workings of the Socialist caucus in the assembly. This was important in light of the charge that the Socialists were required to vote as a bloc. Waldman said that the caucus provided a method by which the Socialists could study bills and arrive at a consensus on how they would vote. Once the decision was made, all voted the same way. As final witnesses, Solomon and Claessens gave testimony on their social, economic, and political beliefs.

A highlight of the trial was Morris Hillquit's summary for the defense. Hillquit was on the stand throughout the entire day and evening of March 3. His address was broad in scope and covered all of the issues of the trial. Hillquit began by stating that the trial had already amassed over 2,000 pages of evidence, "some of it relevant, some irrelevant." He thanked the Judiciary Committee for permitting him the opportunity to add to it. He then got down to business: "We have gotten far from the facts in this case." He reviewed the contents of the original resolution under which the Socialists were expelled. He reminded the committee that the only authority for expulsion was that which flowed from the original resolution. The five must be tried on the charges but these had been subject to change halfway through the trial. In the original resolution, the Socialists were merely members of a conspiracy called the Socialist party. By the time the trial was over, they were an active part of that conspiracy. In other words, the accusation had been reinterpreted to fit the facts. Hillquit denied the legality of this procedure. What right, he asked, did the committee have to review the votes of members cast in previous sessions of the legislature, or to make their actions the basis of criticism. "If ever there was a sacred right recognized in the political fabric of our country, it is the untrammeled right of an elected representative to any legislature . . . to speak his mind freely according to the dictates of his conscience. . . ."

Next, Hillquit challenged the committee's evidence. By extracting items out of context and by delving far into the past, it had developed a false case of conspiracy against the Socialist party. At no time did the committee attempt to balance this negative presentation with instances of Socialist support for American democracy.

At a later session, Hillquit discussed each of the charges contained in the indictment. He emphasized that socialism was created by the breakdown of capitalism. He defined "revolution" as an act carried out for the welfare of humanity and, again, stressed the use of the ballot in bringing it about. There would be no recourse to violence but socialism would be brought about by the conversion of the majority to its doctrines. Confronting the charge that the party tried to regiment its elected officials, Hillquit explained that this was merely a method of pressuring these officials to live up to their promises and to the party's platform.

On the question of Socialist opposition to the war, Hillquit affirmed the right of the people and a political party to criticize the government. By analogy, he showed that opposition to war was well within the American tradition. Charles Sumner had opposed the Mexican War. Why couldn't the Socialists oppose World War I? Even Woodrow Wilson, he reminded the committee, was elected on a platform that promised to keep the nation out of war. Then, he discussed the charge that the Socialist party was part of the world Communist conspiracy. He pointed out that the party was not a member of the Third International but if the day ever came when it would join, he pledged its independence. Socialists were no more internationalists, he said, then were bankers, businessmen, scientists, artists, or members of the AFL.

On March 30, 1920, some three months after the suspension of the Socialists, the Judiciary Committee delivered its report. By a vote of seven to six, it had decided to expel them. The next day the entire assembly met to take action on the report. The debate lasted all night and the vote was not taken until the following morning. During the night the emotional atmosphere became charged. At one point, Theodore Roosevelt, Jr., arose to denounce the committee's recommendations and to insist that the expulsion would completely negate the principles of representative government. At other times, the assemblymen spoke to empty chairs. Hillquit recalled that the legislators were "drunk with patriotic fervor." The *New York Globe* noted that they were drunk with "spirits."[11] Near morning the empty chairs became filled. There were shouts of "Little Lenins, Little Trotskys," as the assemblymen vied with each other in pouring out hatred at the five Socialists. The final vote showed that the Assembly had decided to unseat all of them. The vote against Waldman was 115 to 28, against Claessens and Solomon 116 to 28, against Orr and De Witt 104 to 40. An analysis of the vote revealed that the Republicans voted against Waldman 98 to 11; the Democrats divided, 17 for and 17 against. The Republicans voted against Orr and De Witt 90 to 20, while the Democrats voted *for* them 20 to 14. Of the 28 votes cast for reseating Waldman, Claessens, and Solomon, 23 were New York City Republicans and Democrats. Of the 40 cast for reseating Orr and De Witt, 28 were New York City Republicans and Democrats.[12] These figures suggest another possible explanation of the expulsion beyond that of a confrontation between right and left. The Socialists received their greatest support from assemblymen in New York City. These legislators, both Republicans and Democrats, may have voted for reseating out of a fear of antagonizing their predominantly liberal constituencies. Still another possibility can be seen in the conflict between the upstate, Republican counties and the Democratic cities. Today, the Socialists were being censured but tomorrow it might be their turn. Others shared this apprehension. Thoughtful Republicans like Ogden L. Mills and Charles E. Hughes were distressed with the results of the trial. The *New York World* called it "Nothing Short of Calamity."[13] To Alfred E. Smith, the trial had been merely a "formality" as the result was expected.

The situation remained unchanged until September 1920, when Governor Smith called a special session of the Legislature to consider the statewide housing crisis. This necessitated the calling of a special election in the five districts left vacant by the expulsion of the Socialists. Although opposed by fusion candidates, all five Socialists were reelected. After being sworn in by the secretary of state, they again presented themselves to the assembly. Thaddeas Sweet noted a "changed attitude" in the five and asked that they be seated. This did not suit some members of the assembly who introduced a resolution again calling for their expulsion. The resolution was carried after a bitter debate in which the Socialists themselves took part. By a vote of 90 to 45, Solomon, Claessens and Waldman were expelled again, but the assembly voted 87 to 48 to seat Orr and De Witt. Those seated later resigned, refusing to sit in a body from which their legally elected colleagues were barred.

Two months later, in the regular November elections, the Socialists, still smarting from the second defeat, made a special effort to get their candidates elected. In spite of heavy campaigning by the opposition, four of them prevailed against fusion candidates. They were: Samuel Orr, Edmund Seidel, Charles Solomon, and Henry Jager. On the opening day of the session of 1921, several resolutions were introduced to unseat Orr and Solomon because of their previous expulsions, and to unseat Assemblyman Jager on the grounds that he was not a resident of the state. As a newcomer to the legislature, Seidel faced no action aimed at unseating him. The resolutions were reported to the Judiciary Committee where testimony was taken on Jager and, after numerous hearings, the subcommittee in charge reported in favor of seating him. The Socialist party felt that no inquiry would have been made regarding Jager's residence had he not been a Socialist. Then, the subcommittee considered the resolution on Orr and Solomon. Despite a move to discharge the resolution from the Judiciary Committee, they refused to vote on it and the resolution was permanently shelved. With this step the episode was closed.

In retrospect, it is hard to have much sympathy for the actions of the lower house of the legislature in voting to unseat its Socialist members. The picture becomes doubly sad when it is recalled that five districts in New York City remained unrepresented throughout most of the year. Although clothed in the legality of an official trial, in the final analysis, the expulsion was a direct result of the antiradical hysteria rampant throughout the country. One can only admire the Socialists for defending themselves as best they could while realizing the ultimate futility of their efforts.

While the expulsion was part and parcel of the statewide and national Red Scare, it benefited from experience gained previously by the Lusk Committee. The trial fed upon a popular desire for excitement, and for vicarious participation in the suppression of a conspiracy. For the press, it provided exciting headlines when the war news was no longer available. While providing excitement, and possibly a scapegoat for public frustrations, the trial tended to deflect concern from the real issues of the day. These were the inequities of the economic system, poverty amidst plenty, and the failure of the legislature to address itself to these pressing issues. Instead, the house busied itself with a cleansing of its ranks and was thus relieved of its real responsibilities. This explains, at least partially, the motives of the legislators in the expulsion and trial. But there were other motives as well. It is possible that Thaddeas Sweet, like Senator Lusk before him, used the publicity generated by the trial as a means of personal aggrandizement. As the savior of the legislature, Sweet may have hoped to secure the governorship. If this was his intention, it was never realized.

Still another important current can be seen in the geographic distribution of the vote. Most of the support for the Socialists came from districts within New York City. Sweet drew his support mainly from the heavily Republican counties upstate whose

newspapers continued to back him even after the New York
City papers, and many others across the country, had changed
sides. This division suggests that a conflict between the hinter-
lands and the cities may well have been a hidden element in the
dispute. It was compounded by the fact that the five Socialists
and their constituents came from immigrant stock. The temptation to lash out at these radical, urban immigrants was too great
to be resisted.

Considering all this, one wonders why the expulsion did not
come earlier, during the war, perhaps. Surely, with the Socialists
agitating against the war, a sufficient excuse existed. The Board
of Aldermen, it will be recalled, had considered such a step for
its own leftist members. But the board was divided, and, in its
lack of unity, it abandoned the plan. The assembly's case was
strengthened by an increase in its Socialist membership during
the war. The expulsion of Victor Berger provided further en-
couragement. With antiradical hysteria increasing around the
country, it felt it could proceed.

The five Socialists were, in some measure, responsible for their
own predicament. Unlike the mild-mannered Meyer London, the
Albany Socialists behaved like bulls in a china shop. They refused to act in a diplomatic manner. When they spoke of their
colleagues it was in unflattering terms. They deluged the assembly with bills and by their efforts pointed out the legislature's
failure to pass meaningful legislation. In a more tolerant age, the
five Socialists might have been welcomed, even encouraged. The
very function of a minor party in a democracy is to pull the
major parties away from a center position by forcing them to
consider controversial measures. Unfortunately, the hysteria of
the age did not permit this.

In a sense, the trial reflected a certain naïveté on the part of
many Americans. Such a trial would have been inconceivable in
Europe, where Socialists were not only seated in many legislative
bodies but controlled a few governments. On strictly legal grounds,
the Socialists seemed to have presented a far stronger case. They
insisted that they represented a legal, political party which was
widely supported by thousands of voters. The Judiciary Committee relied on the conspiracy theory: that the Socialist party,
despite its protestations to the contrary, was an unlawful conspiracy controlled by a small group of insiders who owed their
allegiance to a foreign power. The prosecution must have real-

ized that its case needed strengthening, for it changed the indictment during the trial in a subtle way. At the conclusion of the trial, the Socialists were not only members of the conspiracy called the Socialist party but were an active part in it.

There was little doubt that both sides were addressing far wider audiences than those actually in attendance. The assembly was making a bid for recognition, while the Socialists were using the trial to spread their ideas. Hillquit's summary for the defense provided an illustration of this. In many ways, it was the highlight of the trial. As we have seen, he based his arguments on the right of dissent. The opinions of the majority, he maintained, must be challenged from time to time. If they were not, how would the majority know whether its ideas were correct? The function of the party was to test popularly held ideas by disputing them.

The Socialists expected that the trial would turn out as it did. But their efforts were not wasted. The trial had national significance in that it helped precipitate a change in attitudes towards the Red Scare. Many realized, perhaps for the first time, that the antiradical crusade had gone too far. If Socialists could be expelled today, whose turn would it be tomorrow? Once this fact became clear, it was only a matter of time for the pendulum to swing in the opposite direction.

NOTES

1. Assemblyman Simon Adler presented the resolution. He must have known beforehand what he was going to read.
2. *New York World,* January 8, 1920, p. 12; other opinions quoted in Hillquit, *Loose Leaves,* pp. 250–51; see also *Brooklyn Daily Eagle,* January 8, 1920, p. 6.
3. *New York Times,* January 10, 1920, p. 16; for other press opinion see "Albany's Ousted Socialists," *Literary Digest,* January 24, 1920, p. 19, and *New York Herald,* January 8, 1920, p. 10.
4. Thomas E. Vadney, "The Politics of Repression: A Case Study of the Red Scare in New York," *New York History,* IL (January, 1968), pp. 61–62.
5. Press opinions in Louis Waldman, *Labor Lawyer* (New York, 1944), p. 96; see also n. 3.
6. *New York Sun,* January 20, 1920, p. 6, quotes Butler; Walsh to *New York World,* January 9, 1920, in Frank P. Walsh Papers (New York Public Library), Box 33; "Albany's Ousted Socialists," *Literary Digest,* January 24, 1920, p. 19, quotes Shaw.

7. In *New York World,* February 12, 1920, clipping in Socialist Aldermen's Scrapbook (Tamiment Library, New York), Box D 35.
8. "The Mob in High Places," *New Republic,* February 4, 1920, pp. 279–81; "The Progress of the World," *Review of Reviews,* February, 1920, p. 128.
9. Hillquit's final statement was: "You can no more kill the Socialist movement in the United States, than you can kill social progress, the development of industry, and the growth of civilization generally."
10. "Socialism on Trial in Albany," *Literary Digest,* February 7, 1920, pp. 14–15.
11. *New York Globe,* April 1, 1920, quoted in Waldman, *Labor Lawyer,* p. 108.
12. The party distribution of votes for Claessens and Solomon were similar to Waldman's.
13. Quoted in Waldman, *Labor Lawyer,* p. 109.

Chapter Seven

THE
FEDERAL GOVERNMENT:
PALMER RAIDS

The intervention of the federal government in the activities of the Red Scare was a logical outgrowth of previous efforts made by the states. This phase of the antiradical crusade was, of course, national in scope. Here, only those aspects relating specifically to the state of New York will be discussed.

The role of the federal government is conventionally associated with President Wilson's attorney general, A. Mitchell Palmer, who, in December 1919 through January 1920, organized a series of spectacular raids upon radical headquarters throughout the country. A few of those arrested were deported on a converted army ship, the *Buford*, which was brought into service for this purpose. Those not deported were largely frightened into silence or else driven underground. The Palmer raids were unique in that they were the first to be directed against the newly formed Communist parties. These left wing groups were based largely in New York and, as such, form an important part of this history.

Like the expulsion of the Socialists from the assembly, the Palmer raids were, in many respects, counterproductive. Many Americans began to feel that perhaps the means did not justify the ends, especially when they entailed excessively harsh punishments and wide violations of civil liberties. As a result, the Palmer raids helped hasten the end of the Red Scare hysteria.

While the Palmer raids were unique, they relied heavily on experience with radicals gained during the war when many convictions were secured for violations of the Espionage and Sedition Acts. With the passage of the Immigration Act of 1917, Congress provided an additional weapon. This Act, with its 1918 amend-

169

ment, provided for the deportation of any alien who advocated anarchism, syndicalism, or violent revolution, or belonged to any organization which did. Under the Act's authority, aliens were arrested and detained in the Western regions of the country. They were transferred to Ellis Island in New York at the end of the war whence many were deported. These steps were taken quickly and legally and attracted little attention.

In February 1919 a second group of about fifty alien radicals was rounded up. Many were members of the Industrial Workers of the World. They were put aboard a special train, the "Red Special," which sped swiftly across the country and arrived at Hoboken, New Jersey, on February 12; the anarchists were transferred to a ferry boat and taken to Ellis Island.

In contrast to earlier deportations, this attracted more attention; now that the war was over, the excuse of national security could no longer be used. The National Civil Liberties Bureau, the forerunner of the American Civil Liberties Union, was the first to take an interest in the plight of the aliens and sent a lawyer, Walter Nelles, to investigate. Nellies reported that few lawyers could be found willing to defend such unpopular clients. This situation was not limited to the West. Even in New York, the *Journal of Law* warned lawyers to avoid cases involving Wobblies who, in their view, were "dangerous adversaries of our government and of our fundamental rights and liberties."[1]

Nelles encountered immediate difficulties at Ellis Island where he was not allowed to see the prisoners. He then went to court to secure writs of habeas corpus and protested further to Secretary of Labor William B. Wilson that the rights of his clients were being infringed. The writs were contested by Byron Uhls, the officer in charge of the Island, who argued that the aliens had already received their hearing and that their cases were closed.

Soon Nelles was joined by Caroline Lowe, a western lawyer for the IWW, who had come East to assist those interned on Ellis Island. Miss Lowe went to court to secure the necessary writs but she was as unsuccessful as Nelles had been. Even with letters from the defendants in her possession, she was unable to persuade Judge John C. Knox of her legal right to represent the aliens. Knox denied the writs "without prejudice" which meant that if the lawyers could prove that the government was deporting any of the aliens illegally, they could apply again.

In New York, left wing groups opposed the deportations but, apart from a series of written statements appearing in their press, could do little or nothing for the accused. The Central Federated Union of New York, representing the AFL unions, presented its grievances at a Conference of Governors and Mayors at the White House; it complained that the IWW was being persecuted for its prolabor activities. Secretary of Labor Wilson maintained that the IWW was not being punished for strikes but for its efforts to overthrow the government.

Later in February, the federal government kept the pot boiling by arresting fourteen more Wobblies in New York City. The arrests were made just four days after an attempted assassination of Premier Clemenceau in France by a "Bolshevik agent." Many approved the arrests fearing that the New York Wobblies might be part of an international conspiracy to kill Allied and American officials. Again, protests were lodged by a number of journals. *The Nation* called for legislation protecting against such arbitrary action while the *New York Globe* warned that the government might be carrying its "anti-radical business too far."[2]

In the meantime, the commissioner of immigration for the New York region, Frederick C. Howe, returned from a European trip. Howe was a liberal; he had held his post since 1914 and was genuinely concerned with the fate of the people entrusted to him. He began an immediate review of all cases of anarchists being held for deportation. Next, he went to Washington and urged Secretary of Labor Wilson to reopen the cases. The secretary agreed. Howe also pursued a liberal policy towards the aliens interned on Ellis Island. He permitted them to roam about in the company of their lawyers.

As a result of Howe's intervention, fourteen of the men were released. Later a district court judge released another and, shortly after, almost all of the warrants for deportation were cancelled by the Labor Department or the courts. Howe's liberal policies led to calls for his resignation. Conservative circles in the government demanded that he explain why he had let so many radicals go free. Other aspects of Howe's background aroused even greater suspicion. Senator King of Utah wanted to know why he was present at a number of radical demonstrations held in New York City.[3] The New York City district attorney questioned one of his speeches and wanted to know why he associated with radicals like Emma Goldman and Elizabeth Gurley Flynn.

As a result of this criticism, the Labor Department requested Howe's resignation. On leaving the department, Howe asked that his successor be a person genuinely friendly to immigrants. Secretary Wilson ignored his advice and appointed Byron Uhls, setting the stage for a far more hostile policy towards alien radicals.

The roundup of IWW members continued throughout the year. As we have seen, very few were actually deported due to the liberal policy of the Labor Department and its Immigration Bureau. An increasingly large segment of the American public found this policy too lenient and demands were made of the attorney general for more vigorous action. There were suggestions that prosecutions continue under the Espionage Act but Attorney General Gregory refused on the ground that the Espionage Act was a wartime measure and inapplicable in the postwar period. He added that if the Congress wanted "Bolshevik agitation" suppressed, it should legislate the needed authority. Gregory did issue orders to agents of the Justice Department to continue their surveillance of radical activities. Agents also began to infiltrate the left wing organizations. Some were so successful that they managed to rise to positions of leadership within the various movements.

Congress, too, was getting impatient with the cautious attitude adopted by the attorney general. Soon after the Armistice, a number of congressmen demanded that he play a more active role. In part, this protest stemmed from the traditional resentment against the expansion of the executive wartime powers. With peace, Congress reasserted itself, and used the campaign against bolshevism as one method of reestablishing its position.

A more immediate response came from the Senate Judiciary Committee headed by Lee Overman, a senator from North Carolina. The Overman Committee began its work in January 1919, when it conducted an inquiry into the wartime propaganda efforts of German-Americans. After the adoption of a resolution sponsored by Senator Walsh of Montana, its attention shifted to include "pacifists, Socialists, and radicals" and even "free love college professors." The committee held many hearings and called witnesses who told of the horrible conditions existing in the Soviet Union. This was linked up with radical activity in the United States. As the Seattle general strike was then in progress, the disclosures of the committee seemed to make sense.

Among the many witnesses called by the Overman Committee

was the solicitor general of the United States, W. H. Lamar, who told of a plot to overthrow the government; he also expressed apprehension about the many newspapers published by the IWW. Archibald E. Stevenson, soon to play an important role with the Lusk Committee, was another important witness. Stevenson presented a list of radicals and organizations which, he claimed, desired to overthrow the government. Still another witness, Dr. W. C. Huntington, from 1916 to 1918 the commercial attaché of the American Embassy at Leningrad, produced an order addressed to all Russian Soviets which decreed that all persons failing to support the Bolshevik regime be slaughtered. Huntington said that the executions were carried out at night in darkened cellars with the firing squad using Maxim silencers. This type of testimony helped heighten public fears of similar disturbances in the United States.

Other witnesses before the Overman Committee developed the point that New York City was the center for radical activity. This charge was made by the Reverend Dr. George S. Simons, who, as an official of the Methodist Episcopal Church in Russia, was one of the last Americans to leave the country after the revolution started. Simons stated that the Jewish immigrant population of the Lower East Side provided a fertile field for radical agitators, many of whom had gone back to Russia at the beginning of the revolution and were prominent in Bolshevik ranks. One committee member, Senator Walcott, was greatly interested. He asked Simons whether agitators from the Lower East Side could be held responsible for the triumph of bolshevism in Russia. Simons replied that the Bolsheviks could not have come to power except for "certain support received from the City of New York and from Germany."

Simons' testimony was confirmed the next day by two American vice consuls who had spent time in the Soviet Union. One told of a New York cobbler who had lived on the Lower East Side of Manhattan for thirteen years. He was last seen as a "commissar" of a Russian city and was noted for his record of cruelty. They identified many of the Bolshevik leaders as "apostate Jews" again implying that Russian communism was a Jewish movement with links to the immigrant population of the Lower East Side. At least one of these apostates had boasted that he expected to return, and give America the same type of government that the Russians had.

The testimony taken before the Overman Committee was

widely reported in the press. Many were offended by the charge
that bolshevism was a movement of Jewish origin. It was challenged by Louis Marshall, a distinguished constitutional lawyer
and head of the American Jewish Committee, who presented evidence of the loyalty of Russian and American Jews. Marshall said
that Jewish participation in radical causes was no more relevant
than Christian involvement in the same causes; no conclusions
could be drawn from either act. He characterized the charge as
group libel, maintaining that he could prepare a list of prisoners
at Sing Sing and show that every religious and ethnic group was
represented; the list would tell nothing about the group. Finally,
Marshall showed that although Jews made up only 3 percent of
the population, more than 5 percent had served in the armed
forces where they distinguished themselves for bravery and
heroism.

Within a day, letters of support for Marshall began coming in
from distinguished people throughout the State. Among those supporting him were Governor Alfred E. Smith, Charles E. Hughes,
William G. McAdoo, and the Reverend James M. Byrnes, the
pastor of St. Mary's Roman Catholic Church in New York.

Meanwhile, the work of the Overman Committee continued.
One result was the Overman bill, the first peacetime sedition bill
since 1789, which was introduced in the Senate. Under its terms,
no one could advocate the violent overthrow of the United States
government or the destruction of industrial property; no one could
display a red flag or mail any printed statement which supported
revolution. The National Civil Liberties Bureau and other liberal
and radical groups urged rejection of the bill. Although it was
widely supported, its sponsors were unable to muster a sufficient
number of votes and it died in the Senate in March 1919.

That same month another development occurred which proved
to have grave consequences for the future. Attorney General
Gregory resigned to go to Paris to assist with the Versailles peace
conference. He was replaced by A. Mitchell Palmer, the former
custodian of alien property. Gregory had not requested Palmer
for the job as he felt that his assistant attorney general was more
deserving. Wilson chose Palmer on the advice of party leaders in
order to strengthen the northern wing of the Democratic party.[4]

Palmer was not unqualified for the high office. Thus far, he had
proven to be a distinguished public servant. He was ambitious;
from his earliest years he hoped to make his mark as a statesman

or a lawyer. At Swarthmore College he had graduated at the head of his class. His views were progressive but he shared the distrust of foreigners held by many contemporaries. For example, in a Swarthmore commencement address, Palmer thought it proper to excuse an angry New Orleans mob that had lynched eleven immigrants after they had been acquitted of a murder charge. These attitudes persisted; even later, he continued to believe that foreigners were criminally inclined. Yet his xenophobia was mixed with a good measure of concern even for the "lowest born" person coming to these shores. Even they, said Palmer, were entitled to justice and fair play in the American tradition.

Once in office, Palmer continued the liberal policies of the former attorney general. In some respects, he was even fairer and more liberal than Gregory had been. He personally reviewed the cases of all those indicted under the Espionage Act and recommended clemency where he felt that the verdict was unjust or too severe. The effects of his actions were immediately apparent; in the first few months hundreds of suits were abandoned. In addition, Palmer ordered the release of ten thousand enemy aliens arrested during the war. But nativism continued to pervade his thinking and he repeated, in writing, the charges made before the Overman Committee, that the Russian Revolution was carried out by a small clique of "outcasts" from the Lower East Side of New York.[5]

Palmer began to adopt a more aggressive attitude after June 1919. This policy was quite different from the liberal stance he had taken on first coming into office. The reason for the change is not easy to explain. The rising hysteria throughout the country, the disclosures of the Lusk Committee, and the succession of strikes all played a part. Then, too, the Congress and the president were subjected to increased pressure after the May Day bombings heightened fears of a radical conspiracy designed to eliminate the national leadership. With his Quaker background, Palmer was repelled by the atheism and violence with which bolshevism was often associated. Possibly, he hoped to rise to the presidency through the publicity he would receive. Regardless of the precise motivation, the attorney general soon became a willing instrument of those advocating repressive measures against the left. His changed attitude was reflected in the following statement: "Those who cannot or will not live the life of Americans under our institutions . . . should go back to the countries from which they came." Considering the public mood, one really cannot blame him for changing his mind. But he still hesitated to throw the entire weight of his great office against the left. It is also significant that even in December and January, at the height of the Red Scare, he was criticized more for his inactivity than for his violations of civil liberties.

To the public and press, the June bombings were a cause for real alarm. They did not share Palmer's caution but demanded action. Palmer was unable to resist such pressures any longer. To prepare the Department of Justice for an assault on the left, he appointed William J. Flynn, the former head of the Secret Service, as chief of the department's Bureau of Investigation. He also appointed Francis P. Garvin of New York as assistant attorney general. These two men were required to coordinate all investigations relating to subversive activities.

The nerve center of operations was the General Intelligence Division, the forerunner of the Federal Bureau of Investigation. At its head was a twenty-four-year-old special assistant to the attorney general, J. Edgar Hoover. Hoover was instructed to study subversive activities in the United States and determine a course of action. Control over the Bureau of Investigation remained with Flynn whose agents passed along to the GID all information concerning Communists, anarchists, and IWW groups within the United States.

There was, of course, little chance of a Communist uprising in the United States at this time. Despite the many statements in favor of revolution made repeatedly by the more extreme elements of the left, their propaganda was mostly rhetoric, more suitable to the European than to the American environment. It was never accompanied by overt acts. Moreover, not one case of bombing violence was ever traced to a radical source. Nevertheless, Palmer decided that more action was called for. On June 17, 1919, he held an all-day conference with Hoover, Garvin, and Flynn; they discussed the bombings at length and agreed upon a broad policy for the elimination of dangerous radicals. Previously Palmer had asked for, and received, an additional appropriation of $500,000 to be used for the investigation and prosecution of radicals.

Hoover was also busy. After taking charge of the GID, he began systematically organizing all available information concerning radicals. All names were placed on cards and an impressive index of more than 200,000 entries was devised. In addition, the division distributed press releases describing leftist activities, as well as copies of the Manifestoes of the Third International, the Communist party, and the Communist Labor party. Under Hoover's direction, information pertaining to race riots and strikes was also made available. These were linked with left wing activity and contributed to the intensity of the Red Scare hysteria.

Congress became more active after the bombings of May and June when four sedition bills were presented for its consideration. The first was the Aswell Bill which prohibited bomb throwing and other attempts to destroy life and property. The Myers bill denied the use of the mails to any publication printed in German. The Walsh bill was the most far reaching; it outlawed the IWW and other revolutionary organizations. Finally, the King bill duplicated the measure submitted earlier by the Overman Committee. However, the Senate was preoccupied with other matters and none of the bills passed. The *New York World* was pleased with the outcome:

The time has not come when the American people will willingly assent to the retrenchment of the rights of free speech and lawful discussion.

What was needed, said the *World,* was an

. . . effective way to deal with crimes directed against the government. For national safety it is not necessary to magnify into crimes all reckless words, spoken or written, of irresponsible agitators hunting notoriety.[6]

Palmer wisely refused to support any of these sedition bills. He felt that they were too drastic and proposed a bill of his own which was introduced promptly into the house. Palmer's bill attempted to call seditious any "act of force against any person or any property." This section was so severe that it even drew the opposition of Samuel Gompers and the AFL who thought that it might be used as an antistrike weapon. The Federation closed ranks with the National Civil Liberties Bureau and others to ensure enough opposition for the bill's defeat.

The approach of the Fourth of July heightened national fears of a possible Bolshevik uprising. To meet this threat, Flynn met

178 CRUSADE AGAINST RADICALISM

with police chiefs of major cities and arranged for the collaboration of law enforcement officers. New York followed the national pattern, mobilizing 11,000 men for continual duty throughout the day. A navy guard protected all public buildings and the state militia was readied should the disturbances within the city prove too difficult to handle. But the fateful day came and nothing happened.

Throughout the summer, the public and certain congressmen continued to denounce the attorney general for his inactivity. A New York patriotic society protested the "loose manner in which the Department of Justice is conducting the campaign against Bolsheviks, anarchists, and traitors seeking to destroy the government."

The Justice Department was anxious to give the public what it wanted. The only question was: on what legal authority? At first, Palmer tried to use Section 6 of the Federal Criminal Code. This old law dating from the 1860s was designed to prevent a genuine civil war. It was tested against three members of the El Ariete Society, an anarchist group in Buffalo, whose manifesto said in part: "Proclaim yourselves openly an anarchist. Let the revolution come. Hail to the immaculate and redeeming anarchy." The government lost its case. Federal Judge Hazel contended that such language did not constitute a conspiracy to overthrow the government.

This defeat left two alternatives to the government. It could use the Espionage Act, but Palmer was unwilling to use this wartime measure. It could also try to deport aliens under the immigration statutes. The decision to use the deportation provisions of the Immigration Act was made early in June 1919. This was not the preferred method, but in the absence of new sedition legislation, it was all the government had at its disposal.

Legislation against alien subversion was a fairly recent development. It had not been seriously considered by the Congress until an anarchist, Leon Czolgosz, had murdered President McKinley in 1901. Despite the fact that the assassin was native-born, Congress listed "anarchism" as one of the offenses for which an alien could be *excluded* from the United States. Although the term was not defined, there was general agreement that this referred to revolutionary aliens. The revised Immigration Law of February 1917 included philosophical anarchists and provided for their deportation from the country.[7] A further amendment, in the Act of October 1918, extended the law to include all aliens teaching or advocating the overthrow of the government by force or violence. Consequently, after 1918 an anarchist could be deported for believing in anarchism or supporting an organization which did. Procedurally, the deportation trial was administrative in nature. The Justice Department gathered the facts and passed them on to the Immigration Service of the Labor Department which held a hearing. If the government won its case, the alien would be shipped out.

The defeat in the case of El Ariete was one of the significant factors that convinced the Justice Department to use the deportation provisions of the Immigration Acts. The resignation of Frederick C. Howe was another, since the Justice Department could now expect more cooperation from the Immigration Service. A meeting was held that included high level officials from the Immigration Service and the Justice Department and plans for the raids, arrests, and deportations were finalized. Confidential instructions were sent out by Flynn to all Justice Department employees informing them of the decision taken. In October, Palmer was informed by the GID that the Union of Russian Workers advocated revolution and it was decided that many of them would be deported. Secretary of Labor Wilson agreed to hold the necessary hearings.

Just how subversive was this organization against which the raids were planned? The Union of Russian Workers was a nationwide federation of Russian clubs with headquarters on East Fifteenth Street in New York. It was founded in 1907 and operated under a set of "Fundamental Principles" which stressed the class struggle and the necessity of revolution. While its principles were revolutionary, the organization itself was quite peaceful in nature. Members were not required to agree with its objectives or to take any pledge of obedience to its leadership. They were not even required to read the principles of the organization. In fact, many of the members, poorly educated as they were, had not read them. While some of the Russians came to the Union to listen to radical speeches, others came to attend classes, or to read books available in the reading room. This was not the first time that the Union was raided but it was the first raid to culminate in deportations.[8]

After serving the proper warrants, the Department of Justice carried out a massive raid on the various headquarters of the

Union around the country. This took place on November 7, 1919, and was timed to coincide with the anniversary celebrations of the Russian Revolution. The main blow fell in New York where the raid was directed by William Flynn, assisted by Sergeant Geegan of the New York City bomb squad. At the appointed hour, police cars arrived, and agents moved towards the building. Those inside did not have the slightest idea of what was coming as the police saturated the building from top to bottom. The students were told to line up in the hall, while desks were ripped open, doors taken off, and even a few carpets taken up in the search for documents, explosives, and other weapons. Then the people were questioned: "Are you a citizen?", "How long have you been in this country?", and "What were you doing in this building tonight?"

At first, the Russians submitted meekly to the questioning. Then, a few of them spoke up and demanded to know the purpose of the raid. They were told to "shut up if you know what is good for you." There is also evidence that a considerable amount of violence accompanied the raid. On the top floor a class in algebra was in progress. The students were lined up against the wall and searched. They were then ordered downstairs and, on the way down, had to run between a line of policemen who beat them with improvised clubs torn from the bannisters of the building. Gravely mistreated was a fifty-year-old teacher who was not only beaten but thrown down the stairs, suffering injuries in the process. No reply was made by the attorney general when questioned about the violence but he did comment on the damage done to the building. Palmer blamed it on "boys" who came into the building at a later time.

About two hundred Russians were arrested. They were bundled into patrol wagons and taken to the New York office of the Department of Justice. Kate Claghorn, a liberal writer of the period, has written that many were subjected to the "third degree."[9] Those who could prove their citizenship were released; only thirty-nine were held for deportation hearings.

For nearly an hour after the raid, policemen were still carrying books, pamphlets, and other literature from the "People's House" of the Union. The press reported that "several tons" of material were taken, "filling several huge trucks." All of it was said to be anarchist literature.

The police were unwilling to discuss the raids. They claimed they were under orders from Washington to maintain silence. William J. Flynn also would give little information except to say that the raids were "satisfactory." *The New York Times* gloated; it claimed that the raids delivered the "most serious blow yet aimed at criminal anarchists."[10]

While the raid on the Union was in progress, agents of the Justice Department aided by police were striking at many other locations throughout the city. Scores of homes were broken into and searched. While some warrants were legally secured, many homes were searched without warrants, an obvious violation of the Fourth Amendment to the Constitution. In all, police arrested about 650 people in New York City. Many were arrested in a haphazard manner because they roomed with suspects or lived in an apartment formerly occupied by a party member.

The following day, agents struck at the Russians Seamen's Union on lower Fifth Avenue which was broken into and searched. The story was much the same. Mirrors, furniture and fixtures were smashed, and the entire office was a shambles when the police finally left. Raids were also carried out in New Jersey and in surrounding communities.

Palmer's agents staged a second raid on the headquarters of the Union of Russian Workers on November 25. The newspapers reported that the police found a large quantity of explosives, acids, and chemicals used in the manufacture of bombs hidden in a "secret room." The police speculated that at last a clue would be found to the Spring bombings. There is no indication that anything ever developed out of this. The left ridiculed the disclosures of explosives. Said James Larkin: "We don't use such weapons. We use mental bombs to blow new ideas, a new ideal into life."

Upstate, the Palmer raids followed a similar pattern. The local papers applauded the arrests and assured their readers that the aliens would soon be sent to the "land of snow and radicalism."[11]

The violence used during the raids was only one of many violations of constitutional liberties. Another pertained to the matter of bail. To prevent aliens from obtaining bail, various surety companies had been warned by the government of "official criticism" if they wrote bonds for alien "reds" involved in deportation proceedings.

Other violations occurred when warrants were issued. The procedure was slipshod in nature, with little regard for the rights of those involved. In most cities, the number of arrests exceeded the number of warrants. Some were not issued until after the actual arrests had been made.

Still other violations of rights occurred on Ellis Island where the aliens were interned awaiting deportation. Even before the raid on the Union of Russian Workers, the *New York Call* sent Eugene Lyons, a popular writer, to the island to investigate. Lyons reported that the inmates were being held in filthy conditions. The food was unbelievably bad and there were worms, "real, wiggly worms," in the soup. "Is your linen changed often enough?" Lyons asked. "Linen," the aliens replied, "there is no linen! There is a heavy blanket which is changed at rare intervals. . . . The beds are old and ugly and filled with horrible vermin." Lyons also found evidence of riots "about which the public knows nothing."[12] Fights among inmates, undoubtedly caused by the impossible conditions, were frequent. The police restored order by the use of clubs. There were also a number of attempts to escape. In one of these, five men tried to swim to the mainland. One was struck by a passing boat and drowned, while the others were captured. In a later attempt six men actually succeeded in swimming across the harbor to freedom.

After the Palmer raids of November, conditions on Ellis Island became even more crowded. The authorities were alarmed and pleaded with the Justice Department to postpone further raids until more room could be provided. At one point, seventy-three inmates staged a hunger strike and refused to cooperate with the government until a wire barrier, placed between them and their visitors, was removed. Police said that the barrier was erected after one of the prisoners received a steamship ticket from a visitor, permitting his escape. Next, the prisoners held a meeting and proceeded to organize "The First Socialist Community in America." They issued an ultimatum stating the government would be held responsible if they were harmed in any way. Through their lawyer, Isaac Shorr, they dispatched a letter to Washington which described their plight and warned that they would refuse to cooperate until such time as the barrier was removed. Later on, however, six radicals defected. As they left the dormitory to go to the commissioner's office, they were booed and hissed by some while others sang the Internationale.

The strike was called off after a few days. Eventually, all of the aliens received hearings. To prove its case, the government had to show that the alien either believed in anarchism or was a member of a group which did. It soon became apparent that many of the deportees were unfamiliar with the principles of the organization in which they held membership. Most disclaimed any belief in violence. The record supported this conclusion. Take, for example, the case of Ivan Duboff, arrested in the raid on the Union of Russian Workers while attending a class in automobile repair. Duboff admitted his belief in anarchism but he asserted that the coming revolution would be similar to the "American Revolution of 1776 when the American people liberated themselves from England." Beyond this, he expressed little interest in anything that might take place in the country. "How can I sympathize with America when they [sic] oppress me so much." He was found guilty and deported to Russia.

In another case, Joseph Polulech, a twenty-seven-year-old native of Russia employed for seven years as a packer for the American Distributing Company, was arrested in a raid on the Russian People's House. He was charged with membership in the Union of Russian Workers when his name was found in its membership book. Unable to raise bail, Polulech was held in jail from the time of his arrest until December 21, 1919, when he, too, was deported.

The case of Tom Turka was similar. Turka was a Russian alien who joined the Newark branch of the Union of Russian Workers. He wanted to study auto mechanics and enrolled in a class in New York since it was not offered in Newark. It was apparent that Turka had no interest in violence. He believed that a change of government would come when a majority of the people supported the idea. His conception of "revolution" was a radical transformation in the "minds of the people." He believed in the concept of class struggle but not in anarchism which, he maintained, his lack of education prevented him from understanding. When asked whether he was in sympathy with the principles of anarchism as far as he understood them, he said: "I sympathize with whatever is good for the working class," and "I believe that when the people will get [sic] more education, they may not need any government." In a final statement, Turka said that he would support a revolution based on a heightened public awareness but would never participate in one accompanied by force and violence.

These cases were typical of the 249 passengers deported by the federal government. Their stories revealed that they were all persons of little consequence, aliens without friends or influence, who possessed only a hazy knowledge of the doctrines of which they were accused. On the whole, they appeared confused and bewildered by the hearings and left the country without a clear understanding of just why they were considered a threat to the security of the United States.[13]

There were, however, two exceptions. Among the more famous and knowledgeable of the *Buford* deportees were Emma Goldman and Alexander Berkman. The government believed them to be at the very center of the radical conspiracy.

Miss Goldman came to this country from Russia in 1885. She went to work in a factory in Rochester, New York, where she labored sixty-three hours a week for a wage of $2.50. This experience left her with lasting and bitter impressions. Soon after, she began to take an interest in labor problems and joined the anarchists after the Haymarket Riots of 1886. Her first arrest followed a speech delivered to a group of striking garment workers. She was convicted of "inciting to riot and unlawful assembly" and sentenced to a year in prison on Blackwell's Island. After her release, she devoted all of her time to the cause of anarchism. Her belief in its doctrines was deeply felt. This can be seen in her statement, "I consider anarchism [to be] the most beautiful and practical philosophy that has yet been thought of in its application to individual expression and in the relation that it establishes between the individual and society. Moreover, I am certain that anarchism is too vital and too close to nature ever to die."

In 1892 Miss Goldman was preparing for a trip to Russia when the Homestead Strike began. With Alexander Berkman she conceived a plan to kill Henry C. Frick, the head of the Carnegie Steel Company. Berkman did shoot at Frick but the millionaire survived.

In her many years of service to the cause of anarchism, Miss Goldman rarely questioned any of its tenets. A brief period of doubt ensued after President McKinley was assassinated by a professed anarchist. At his trial Leon Czolgosz said that he was directly influenced by the preachings of "Red Emma." Her loss of faith proved to be only temporary and for the next two decades, until her deportation, Miss Goldman continued to espouse her anarchist dogmas.

Berkman's career was similar. He plunged into anarchist activities in 1888, soon after his arrival in the United States. After his attempted assassination of Frick, he was sentenced to prison for twenty years and released in 1905, after serving only thirteen. The paths of the two anarchists crossed again during the war when both were jailed for violation of the Conscription Act. By the time of their release the war had ended. Soon after, they became involved in the deportation proceedings.

To be eligible for deportation, proof of alien status was required. Miss Goldman was married to an American citizen but his citizenship had been revoked many years before. It was not certain whether hers had been revoked at the same time. The question was put to Louis F. Post, the assistant secretary of labor, who decided against Miss Goldman. In Berkman's case there was no problem as he had never taken out citizenship papers and the government ruled that his original passport was irregular. Next, it was necessary to prove a belief in anarchism. When questioned by Eugene Kessler, an immigration inspector, Berkman admitted his belief in anarchism as a goal but denied that he advocated violence as a means of bringing it about. He then offered a formal definition of anarchism as he accepted it: anarchism was the "philosophy of a new social order based on liberty unrestricted by man-made law; the theory that all forms of government rest on violence and are therefore wrong and harmful as well as mercenary."

Miss Goldman's hearing took a different turn; when questioned before immigration officials on Ellis Island, she refused to answer any questions, stating that her social and political opinions were private matters that did not concern the government. She did not feel compelled to justify her opinions but accepted responsibility only for her thoughts when expressed in action. Next, she denied that she had ever participated in violence or encouraged anybody else to do so. At the end of the hearing, she handed the following written statement to the officials:

> If the present proceedings are for the purpose of proving some alleged offense committed by me, some evil or anti-social act, then I protest against the secrecy and third-degree methods of this so-called "trial." But if I am not charged with any specific offense, if as I have reason to believe, this is purely an inquiry into my social and political opinions, then I protest still more vigorously against these proceedings as utterly tyrannical and diametrically opposed to the fundamental guaran-

tees of true democracy. Every human being is entitled to hold
any opinion that appeals to her or him without making herself
or himself liable to persecution. . . :

The free expression of the hopes and aspiration of a free
people is the greatest and the only safety in a sane society. In
truth, it is such free expression and discussion alone that can
point the most beneficial path for human progress and development. But the object of the deportations and of the anti-
anarchist laws, as of all similar repressive measures, is the very
opposite. It is to stifle the voice of the people, to muzzle every
aspiration of labor. That is the real and terrible menace of the
star-chamber proceedings, of the tendency of exiling those who
do not fit into the scheme of things our industrial lords are so
eager to perpetuate. . . .

Miss Goldman's statement was no defense. With Alexander
Berkman, she was ordered to report to Ellis Island on December 5.

As the time for the sailing of the *Buford* drew nearer, the
secretary of labor telegraphed all deportation centers that aliens
with families were not to be included. The secretary's decision
made sense; it was intended to minimize the hardship that would
inevitably be created. The ruling was followed at all deportation
stations except New York where the message either arrived too
late or was disregarded. As a result, many families were sepa-
rated. In one case, a savings account in the husband's name
remained unavailable to his spouse. Neither the wives of the
accused nor their lawyers were informed of the date set for the
sailing. Hence, they were unable to say good-bye. Those interned
on Ellis Island were not told until the night of December 20,
when an announcement was made during dinner. All communication with the mainland was cut off and the deportees were
given two hours to gather their belongings.

The boat on which they were to sail was an ancient vessel,
first used as a troop transport in the Spanish-American War. She
was on loan to the Labor Department to help with the deportations. At two o'clock in the morning, the first of 249 passengers
started boarding. Several congressmen, government officials, and
reporters were watching from the dock. When Emma Goldman
boarded the ship a reporter called out to her, "Merry Christmas,
Emma." Miss Goldman returned the greeting by thumbing her
nose. Berkman followed her; he was wearing his high Russian
boots, khaki pants, and a sombrero or Spanish-type hat. By this

time he had placed himself in charge and was busy issuing orders. But when he saw Bureau Chief Flynn among the crowd of congressmen and reporters on the dock, he paused and shook his fist. "We'll come back," Berkman shouted, "and when we do, we'll get you." Then the *Buford,* or the "Soviet Ark" as the press called it, steamed out of the harbor. The voyage lasted four weeks. After a stop for repairs at the Kiel Canal, it reached Finland on January 16, 1920, and the aliens were soon transferred over the Russian frontier.

Public reaction to the sailing of the *Buford* was generally favorable to the government. In a Christmas message to the people of New York, Mayor John F. Hylan welcomed the deportations as follows:

> These alien fire-brands with their revolutionary doctrines are rapidly being deported and will no longer have an opportunity to pollute the free breezes of America. Though deportation is regarded by many as experimental, its potentialities for good in the interest of the law abiding are immeasurable.

Nicholas Murray Butler agreed: he suggested that other radicals be sent to one of the little islands in the Philippines where they would rapidly solve the radical problem by consuming each other. The *New York Evening Journal* drew a biblical analogy: "Just as the sailing of the Ark that Noah built was a pledge for the preservation of the human race, so the sailing of the Ark of the Soviets is a pledge for the preservation of America."

On the other hand, a few voices registered a resounding "no" to the deportations. The *New York World* maintained that the only real method of meeting unrest was by a greater understanding of its causes and by remedying the wrongs that existed. Algernon Lee was deeply disturbed; he confessed that as a native-born American he felt a certain chagrin that his country was imitating the methods of the Czars. The *New Republic* called on all Americans to repent the deportations as destructive of liberty and due process of law. But these notes of protest were like those of the prophets of old crying out in the wilderness; few were prepared to listen to them.[14]

Once the *Buford* was safely out of the harbor the federal government turned to other matters. It began to close its case against Ludwig Martens. J. Edgar Hoover sent a brief to Palmer defining his status. This brief was the first indictment of the Communist party ever drawn up by the federal government. Hoover contended that the Communist party of Russia was engaged in a conspiracy against the United States and, thus, as a member of this party, Martens was subject to deportation. Martens, it will be recalled, had experienced continuing difficulties with the Lusk Committee. After the raids on the Russian Bureau, he had been called to testify at committee hearings. Then he went to Washington which put him out of reach of the Lusk Committee but involved him with the federal government. In Washington, the Justice Department wanted Martens deported but the Labor Department did not. Deportation had already cleared with the State Department which felt that the foreign relations of the United States would not be hampered by Martens' expulsion. The case ended when Secretary of Labor Wilson allowed Martens to return voluntarily to the Soviet Union. On his arrival in Russia the deportation proceeding was dropped.

Along with the brief on Martens, Hoover prepared similar indictments of the Communist party and the Communist Labor party of America. He also decided to turn to these two organizations as the next targets for raids. To ensure success, Hoover suggested certain changes in the administrative procedure of the Labor Department. The first was a change in Rule 22 which dealt with the right of aliens to consult their lawyers during deportation hearings. Under the revised rule, aliens could still consult their attorneys but only after the "government's interests" were protected. A second change suggested by Hoover allowed the Labor Department to set high bail on all those arrested. Its purpose was to make the release of aliens more difficult.

Hoover then asked the Labor Department for 3,000 warrants for the arrest of the Communists. Palmer assured Wilson that these warrants were necessary to apprehend a large number of people "positively known to be engaged in a conspiracy to subvert our government by physical force." Wilson complied but warned the attorney general that it would be difficult to handle such a large number of cases. But the country was wild for arrests and public pressure ultimately triumphed over prudence. The raids took place on the night of January 2, 1920, in thirty-three cities across the country. Of the 3,000 persons arrested, about 300 to 700 came from New York City.[15] Later, Assistant Attorney General Francis F. Kane was to testify that the total number of arrests was never determined and may have exceeded the figure given in the press. All that was required was "probable . . . membership in the Communist Party." The raids were carefully planned. Field agents of the Justice Department had arranged with their undercover agents to hold meetings on the night of the raid. Many balls and parties were also in progress. The agents were told to gather all available evidence in the form of membership cards or party literature. They were further instructed to prevent the radicals from communicating with outside sources until after their interrogation. If any person claimed American citizenship, he was required to document the claim. The suspects were to be lined up against the wall and searched. Then, they were to be taken to the local Department of Justice headquarters for further questioning.

New York City was again the center of raiding activities. About fifty persons were present at Communist party headquarters on East Tenth Street when agents of the government assisted by the New York police dashed up the stairs of their three-story building and shouted, "Hands up." At the headquarters of the Communist Labor party on East Twelfth Street a meeting was in progress. Agents arrested twenty young men and twelve girls who were brought to the Justice Department building on Park Row for questioning and fingerprinting. While these raids were in progress still others were carried out against a number of radical publications and other Communist centers in the city. The same scene was repeated again and again. For example, in a raid on the Grand Street center, some members tried to trick the police by concealing their membership cards. One man put his card into his shoe while another threw it behind a radiator; but the police were not fooled and the plan was nipped in the bud.

No explosives and only three pistols were discovered in all of the raids conducted throughout the country. In New York, no dangerous weapons were produced. In addition, many pictures and other decorations were stripped from the walls and sent along to Park Row. Among them were portraits of Karl Marx, August Bebel, and Eugene V. Debs. At headquarters the detectives amused themselves by painting Marx's nose red and thrusting a cigarette through his mouth to give him the appearance of smoking. A similar mask was made of the picture of Debs, much to the delight of the office staff.

Benjamin Gitlow, an official of the Communist Labor party,

has recorded an interesting picture of the raid. He was present that evening at the meeting of the executive committee of the party held at the office of a German leftist paper on Spruce Street. Suddenly, a staff member burst into the room to tell the news. He had read of the raids on the news ticker and his first reaction was to tell Ludwig Lore, the editor, to feature the story. After reading the story in detail, the executive committee had its first inkling of the scope of the raids. As Gitlow recalled: "It was uncanny that only a few minutes before I had left our national headquarters on Twelfth Street and now it was already in the hands of federal authorities with all of our records gone."[16] It was decided that the meeting of the executive committee be postponed. Each of its members was assigned to go on a tour of inspection to assess the situation. Then, Gitlow went to the party's Twelfth Street headquarters where he watched agents piling records, files, and literature into a large van. The head-quarters also showed the physical effects of the raid.

Out of 700 people arrested in New York, only 250 were held. If they could prove American citizenship, their names were reported to the state attorney general for prosecution under the criminal anarchy statute. Aliens were sent to Ellis Island for deportation hearings, crowding the facilities still further. The radical organizations produced evidence that people were dying of pneumonia because of poor conditions. While the charges may have been exaggerated, they appeared basically correct, considering the speed and suddenness of the raids.

Charges of violence were also lodged against the government. In a letter to the Justice Department, Charles Recht, a lawyer representing many of the accused, said that federal agents had taken off one man's glasses and punched him in the face. He was unconscious when he arrived at police headquarters. Another man, said Recht, had received a "cruel, inhuman beating." Others had been subjected to the third degree in their preliminary interrogation. When questioned about the violence, Hoover assured the attorney general that it wasn't so. He said that Justice Department agents had been carefully trained and told to avoid violence at all costs. At least one high Justice Department official was skeptical; possibly, he was sensitive to the continued criticism levelled at the department, and sent Hoover to New York to investigate. Hoover reported back that there were clear-cut cases of violence. However, his original denial was probably correct.

Violent acts were not committed by the Department's permanent staff but by the many policemen, special agents and volunteers recruited from the patriotic organizations. Regardless of the source of the violence, the question still remained whether a massive undertaking of such scope should have been attempted in view of the shortage of personnel.

Aside from a few scattered protests appearing in the liberal and radical papers, the press applauded the raids. The *Herald* maintained that the nation owed a "debt of gratitude" to A. Mitchell Palmer and William J. Flynn for the well-planned and well-executed roundup of "reds"; it predicted bigger and better "Soviet Arks" to deport them. The *World* felt that the government need not stand for alien propaganda suggesting that the radicals had no one to blame but themselves.[17]

In Washington, Palmer and Hoover were also well pleased with the raids and with the favorable public response. To guard against public criticism of his methods, Palmer released a letter upholding their legality and necessity. At the same time, he carefully distingushed the Communist parties, which used revolution to secure their goals, from the Socialist party which sought to accomplish its goals by legal means. The *New York Call* was not impressed by this distinction. Fearing that the next raid would be directed against the Socialist party, it predicted that they would not cease until the government ran out of victims.

At least one formidable critic of Attorney General Palmer appeared within the government. He was Louis F. Post, the assistant secretary of labor. Up to this point, Post had cooperated with the Justice Department. But the deportations and the raids on the Communist parties had proved too much for him. Repelled by the many violations of civil liberties which had taken place, he made a number of administrative changes in the policy of the Immigration Service. Due process of law was restored to the hearings. Lawyers were provided at the beginning of the proceedings, and a more reasonable level of bail was ordered. Post also began checking the records of aliens taken in the raids and released many against whom the evidence was insufficient.

Post's liberal policy was approved by the secretary of labor but it opened a wide breach between the Labor and Justice Departments. This antagonism increased after a decision of the Labor Department to deport alien members of the Communist party but not the Communist Labor party.[18] Next, Post went even further and refused to deport members of the Communist party automatically. He differentiated between "conscious" and "unconscious" membership, and declined to deport those aliens who had become party members due to automatic transfers of Socialist locals or foreign language federations from the Socialist party. Post also refused to expel aliens who were truly unfamiliar with the doctrines of communism, whose cases were based on self-incrimination without benefit of counsel, and those whose record of membership had been illegally seized by the government. The liberal policy led to several Congressional investigations of the Labor Department and to an attempt to impeach Post. The impeachment proceeding failed and, in the meantime, the number of deportations decreased.

Still another factor explaining the declining rate of deportations was the substantial effort made by the American Civil Liberties Union to aid those arrested. Isaac Shorr and Walter Nelles were prominent in organizing this defense. Money was raised and the public aroused to the issues. Most of the funds came from public appeals and from the relatives of those aliens being held.

In the final analysis, the raids on the Communist parties accomplished their purpose. Both the Communist party and the Communist Labor party were driven underground and demoralized. So complete was the demoralization that it was impossible to know just how many members were lost. Benjamin Gitlow estimated that both groups dropped from about sixty thousand members in 1919, to a hard core of less than ten thousand a few years later. Furthermore, the raids struck terror into the hearts of those who remained, especially if they were foreign-born. Such simple tasks as communicating with the rank and file through the mails became impossible. To reestablish contact, organizers were sent into the field. Their reports showed that some local centers had been closed permanently and members lost forever. Both the Communist and the Communist Labor parties suffered equally in this respect.

In New York as elsewhere, the Communist movement was in a state of semi-illegality. With many of the leaders in hiding or headed for jail, it was thought best to meet secretly. Local branches were broken up into "cells" based on the Russian model with ten to fifteen comrades in each unit. Meetings took place in private homes and were carefully guarded. All members of the party assumed fictitious names which were used as by-lines in the party press.

Somewhat romantically, the Communists did not seem to mind going underground. They regarded the move as a step towards doctrinal purity and compared themselves to the Russian Bolsheviks who were also driven underground before the Russian Revolution. The Communists attributed the government's attack to fear and speculated that perhaps the revolution was not far away. They felt that the Communist parties, although smaller, were of higher quality now that the "cowards" had withdrawn.

At least one unintended result of the raids was a drastic reduction in the number of native-born Americans who stayed within the Communist parties. At the same time the foreign-speaking group increased in size and became the majority. As a result, the Communist left became even less American than it had ever been. Both Communist parties were soon unified into one body and were subsequently captured by the Third International, or world Communist movement, directed from Moscow. One must conclude, therefore, that had the Palmer raids never taken place, the Communist party would have remained more American and less susceptible to foreign domination.

The Palmer raids continued through January 1920, concentrating mostly on radical activities in the upstate communities of Buffalo, Utica, and Schenectady. Rather surprisingly, even with these raids in progress, the *New York Sun* thought it appropriate to report that no Red Scare existed anywhere in the nation.[19] But the tide was beginning to turn. In increasingly large numbers, liberals, clergymen, and enlightened people began to question the validity of the antiradical crusade. More newspapers began to adopt a more rational view of the supposed leftist threat and of the raids which produced only a handful of deportable aliens.

Apparently, the attorney general was less aware of the shift in public opinion. Writing in *Forum,* a magazine with a national circulation, in February 1920, Palmer continued to justify his actions and plan for the future. But his raids became fewer and his name soon disappeared from the front pages of the press.

Others were more conscious of the fact that public opinion was turning against the attorney general. In April, President Wilson, disabled by sickness during the height of the Palmer raids, held his first cabinet meeting in more than six months. Wilson had something to say to each cabinet member. When it was Palmer's turn, he faced the attorney general and said: "Palmer, do not let this country see red." Later on, when discussing possible candidates for the presidency in 1920, Wilson dismissed Palmer as a "futile" choice.

The Palmer raids widened the scope of the Red Scare from a purely local and state phenomenon to a massive undertaking carried out by the federal government itself. Events were similar to those taking place during the war, but there was a vital difference. During the war the antiradical crusade may well have been justified on the grounds that the nation was under attack. With the left preaching pacifism and resistance to the war effort, a good case might be made for suppression. These arguments were less valid once the war was over.

Why, then, did the federal government cooperate so readily with those forces seeking to expand the drive against the left? Certainly, the public was partly to blame. The bombings of May and June were highly sensational and widely publicized; public passions were whipped into a frenzy by the press. Then, too, the formation of two Communist parties must be noted as a causal factor. Their appearance at this time, as fragments of the Socialist party, highlighted their totalitarian nature. Both of these developments encouraged the federal government to widen the scope of its activities through raids, and later, through deportations. While the government appeared to be providing the leadership, it was actually only responding to a groundswell of public opinion which demanded action.

It must be noted that the government was at a severe disadvantage. The fight against the left had been a relatively easy matter during the war, when the Espionage and Sedition Acts had provided legal weapons. After the war, the Justice Department refused to use this wartime legislation and the Congress tied its hands by not passing a peacetime sedition bill. In the absence of new legislation, the deportation provisions of the Immigration Acts were pressed into service. While these were applicable against alien radicals, they were of no use against those who were native-born. This explains why the Palmer raids often appeared to be more of an attempt to rid the country of undesirable foreigners than to deal with those who were actually supporting revolution.

Palmer's role in the Red Scare was exceedingly complex. He was a man whose actions were usually motivated by lofty idealism and intense patriotism.[20] As a religious man, he was repelled by Soviet atheism and by the stories of violence coming out of Russia. At the same time, he used the Red Scare to further his own political ambitions. Despite his predisposition to antiradicalism and his ambition, Palmer continued the liberal policies of his predecessor after assuming the office of attorney general; for months he hesitated to unleash the full weight of federal suppression. The turning point came in June 1919, when one of the bombs was aimed at him. With calls for suppression mounting, Palmer was unable to delay any longer and ordered the raids.

The November raids netted hundreds of suspects in New York City and in many upstate communities. Other suspects were taken in subsequent raids. But the figures do not reveal the full extent of the suffering involved. For behind each statistic was a real human being. Granted, he was usually an immigrant and did not speak English well; his work was menial and his influence nil. These were, however, insufficient reasons to deprive him of his liberty.

Then, too, the Palmer raids could not have been so successful without the assistance of thousands of people. Justice Department employees throughout the country were of invaluable assistance. Once Frederick C. Howe was removed from the scene, the Labor Department added its cooperation. Even with all this help, the Justice Department left little to chance. Many persons were apprehended on the vaguest of suspicions, and arrests often exceeded the number of warrants.

Again, New York City, with its large concentration of radicals, was the center of raiding activities. In each of the raids, the same charges of brutality, violence, and third degree were heard. The government's denial of violence was a weak one; however, it was probably true that most of the excesses were carried out by temporary employees and not by the department's permanent staff members. Interestingly enough, the mounting criticism seemed not to bother the attorney general who, encouraged by Hoover, considered the raids a success and planned more extensive ones for the future.

The intervention of Louis F. Post helped slow down Palmer's antiradical efforts. Previously, Post had acquiesced in the deportation of many radicals. But, as he became more aware of the excesses of the Justice Department, he decided to slow down the process of deportation by tightening procedures in the alien's favor. Next, the seventy-one-year-old official reopened many cases and reviewed numerous decisions of the Justice Department. This precipitated a power struggle between the two departments and led to the congressional investigation of Post. He was, however, not intimidated. Instead, he literally overwhelmed the house committee with his deep understanding of the issues involved. In this way, he frustrated the attempts made to remove him from the scene and hastened the end of the Red Scare.

The Palmer raids and deportations had a profound influence on all parties involved. The government developed a high degree of skill in this type of operation. Had the tide not turned against the attorney general, there was no doubt that he would have expanded his operations. The public found the raids exciting, a welcome relief from tedium. To many, the raids had a symbolic value as well: they proved that the government was succeeding in its efforts in rooting out the corrupting influences of radicals and foreigners. Perhaps the greatest effect was on the radicals themselves. Many Communists left the movement forever. Lines of communication between the leadership and the rank and file were disrupted. Most probably, many party members who remained behind were frightened into silence out of fear that they were next on the attorney general's list.

It might be argued that the Palmer raids were of some value in awakening the nation to the threat of Russian-style communism, although this was less apparent at the time. On balance, however, his reign of terror failed in a number of significant ways. While he seemed to be giving the people what they wanted, he used his great power to trample over the constitutional liberties of aliens and native-born alike. He made use of the mass raid where individual arrests would have been sufficient and deported aliens without cause. Paradoxically, his very excesses hastened the end of the Red Scare.

NOTES

1. Quoted in Kate Claghorn, *The Immigrant's Day in Court* (New York, 1923), p. 354.
2. Quoted in "Skimming the Melting Pot," *Literary Digest,* March 1, 1919, p. 6.
3. See *New York Times,* June 3, 1919, p. 1. Senator Wilson of Minnesota added: "Ellis Island of all places should be free from any taint of Bolshevism or Socialism, and there should be no

official there who would be willing to give the Bolsheviki . . . a glad hand."

4. Another possible explanation is that Palmer helped Wilson get the Democratic nomination for President in 1912, and was rewarded with this post.
5. A. Mitchell Palmer, "The Case Against the Reds," *Forum,* February 1920, p. 175.
6. *New York World,* June 13, 1919, p. 14.
7. The texts of these laws are in Constantine Panunzio, *Deportation Cases of 1919-1920* (New York, 1921), Appendix I.
8. For a previous raid on the Union, see Chapter III.
9. Claghorn, *Immigrant's Day,* p. 420.
10. Quoted in Louis F. Post, *The Deportation Deliriums of the Nineteen-Twenties* (Chicago, 1923), p. 30.
11. *Buffalo Courier* and *Buffalo Enquirer,* December 20, 1919, clippings in the ACLU Archives, Vol. 52.
12. *New York Call,* July 25, 1920 clipping in the ACLU Archives, Vol. 52.
13. For many more cases see Claghorn, *Immigrant's Day,* pp. 429ff.
14. "Mayor Hylan's Christmas Greeting," December 25, 1919, in the John F. Hylan Papers (Municipal Archives and Reference Center, N.Y.), Box 354; *New York Sun,* January 20, 1920, p. 6, quotes Butler; "The Anarchist Deportations," *New Republic,* December 24, 1919, pp. 96–98; other press opinions in "Shipping Lenin's Friends to Him," *Literary Digest,* January 3, 1920, p. 14.
15. *New York Times,* January 3, 1920, p.1; see also Frederick Lewis Allen. *Only Yesterday* (New York, 1964), p. 47, who puts the figure at 6,000 but this may have included Communists taken in later raids; *Post, Deportation Deliriums,* p. 87, gives a figure of 2,500 but this, too, sounds like an approximation.
16. Gitlow, *I Confess,* p. 64.
17. Press opinion in "Deporting the Communist Party," *Literary Digest,* February 14, 1920, p. 18; *New York World,* January 4, 1920, p. 2.
18. The CLP was found to be more moderate than the CP and not interested in revolution.
19. *New York Sun,* January 8, 1920, p. 12.
20. In addition to the evidence already presented, see Palmer to Woodrow Wilson, February 24, 1913, Wilson Papers (Library of Congress, Washington, D.C.), Box 48, in which Palmer refused appointment as Secretary of War because his duties would have conflicted with his Quaker faith.

Chapter Eight

THE COURTS:
CASES OF
CRIMINAL ANARCHY

Red Scare activities shifted to the courts when a number of cases involving violations of the New York Statute on Criminal Anarchy were tried. For years, all of the defendants had been active in labor and radical circles. All were members of the left wing of the Socialist party and, later, of the Communist party. They were found guilty and sent to jail. While their guilt rested upon a specific violation of a statute, the hysteria generated by the Red Scare was always present in the background.

The disclosures of the Lusk Committee encouraged the State of New York to revive its seventeen-year-old statute to secure convictions against radicals who were American citizens and were, therefore, ineligible for deportation. This law had been passed in 1902 after the assassination of President McKinley. With only one minor exception, it had never been used before.[1]

The law in question defined criminal anarchy as "the doctrine that organized government should be overthrown by force, violence, or any unlawful means." It was a felony to advocate this doctrine by speech or writing, or join any group or society that did. Those found guilty were to be severely punished by not more than ten years in jail, by a maximum fine of $5,000, or both. The New York law was widely imitated across the country. During 1919, twenty-four states adopted criminal anarchy statutes. Two more were added in 1920.[2]

The New York convictions arose out of the publication of the manifesto of the left wing of the Socialist party. The manifesto was conceived at a conference called by dissident Socialists protesting the conservative policies of its parent body. The conference

198

elected a national committee but the pressure of work and the raids of the Lusk Committee prevented it from drafting a manifesto. This was left to the national committee which published it the following month in a magazine called *Revolutionary Age.*

The national manifesto outlined the failures of moderate socialism as pursued by the Socialist party. It pointed out the dangers of capitalist imperialism and called for a complete revision of the tactics and program of the Socialist party. Other provisions were: the establishment of a proletarian dictatorship in the United States, the organization of worker's councils, control over industry by the workers, the repudiation of all national debts, and the expropriation of all banks, railways, and large aggregations of capital.

Prosecutions began after the raids on the Communist parties of November 8, 1919. There was some question as to whether the statute applied to Communists but the state decided to proceed on the theory that the manifesto called for the overthrow of the government of the state of New York by force and violence within the meaning of the law.

The case of Benjamin Gitlow was the first to be tried. The defendant was the child of poor Russian immigrants and was raised in conditions of grim poverty. From his earliest years, Gitlow listened to stories of the Russian Socialist movement told by his parents. By the age of eighteen he was already active in Socialist circles and was soon drawn toward the IWW through the influence of its leader, William Haywood. To support himself Gitlow took a job as a clerk and soon rose to the leadership of the Retail Clerks Union in New York. Then, he spent two years studying law. These varied experiences helped him secure the nomination as a candidate for the state assembly where he served as a member of the Socialist delegation. After the Russian Revolution, Gitlow sided with the left wing of the Socialist party which led to his indictment under the Criminal Anarchy Act.

Gitlow was arrested with his friend and fellow Communist, James Larkin, on November 8, 1919; they spent the weekend in jail. Both men appeared before Judge McAdoo on the morning of November 10 and were charged with publishing the manifesto and other articles in *Revolutionary Age*. The court set bail at $15,000. Charles Recht, their attorney, protested the bail and asked that the amount be reduced. Recht argued that the articles in *Revolutionary Age* were not incitements to violence but peaceful writings containing abstract reasoning. He charged that the state was really trying to make socialism a crime by punishing those who believed in its principles. He summed up by referring to Gitlow and Larkin as "pioneers in a movement for a better day."

These legal arguments in favor of a reduction in bail were opposed by Assistant District Attorney Alexander I. Rorke who argued that Larkin and Gitlow had played a part in the preparation of the manifesto as well as in the printing of it. Rorke repeated the charge that the manifesto called for the overthrow of the government by force and violence. Judge McAdoo refused to reduce the bail, maintaining that, in his opinion, every member of the Communist party in the state of New York was guilty of criminal anarchy. Since the Communist party was still legal at this time, this statement seemed somewhat prejudicial.

As Gitlow's trial date drew nearer, the Communists concentrated their efforts towards securing a good lawyer. They decided to request the services of Clarence Darrow who had earned his reputation defending unpopular clients. A party member was sent to Chicago to persuade Darrow to take the case. Darrow listened patiently but was not enthusiastic. Personally, he thought that Gitlow was innocent but with the Red Scare at its height he did not think he would win. Darrow took the case but he made Gitlow promise not to take the stand in his own defense. Gitlow agreed but reserved the right to address the jury with a summary statement.

The trial began late in January 1920. Assisting Darrow were two civil rights lawyers from New York, Charles Recht and Swinburne Hale. To one radical sitting in the courtroom, Gitlow appeared "big, dark, wholesomely fleshy." He seemed to have been "carved out of a huge granite rock by the sledge hammer of a master." The same man saw Darrow as "a bit bent, a bit scarred, a bit mutilated, not ruined but made nobler by the years."[3] The cause for the prosecution was presented by District Attorney Edward Swann, assisted by Alexander I. Rorke. Rorke shouldered most of the burdens of the trial. Judge Bartow S. Weeks was on the bench. The courtroom was crowded with reporters and interested spectators.

The first few days of the trial were spent in the selection of a jury. As Gitlow was on trial for his ideas and not for his actions, a sympathetic jury was more than an urgent necessity. Darrow subjected each of the prospective jurors to a searching examination on the questions of freedom of speech and communism. District Attorney Rorke questioned each juror on his attitudes toward the war and toward radicalism. At last the jury was selected and the trial could begin.

The trial was a brief one. As evidence, the state introduced the Left Wing Manifesto and other articles written by Gitlow in *Revolutionary Age*. Rorke tried to show that the articles constituted a clear violation of the Criminal Anarchy law. Darrow fought the case on the issue of freedom of speech. He contended that the Left Wing Manifesto did not come under the aforementioned statute. Darrow was careful to oppose the introduction of evidence attacking Gitlow's character rather than his beliefs or actions. At one point in the trial, Swinburne Hale asked whether there was any such thing as criminal anarchy. Judge Weeks was shocked by this statement and reminded Hale that he could be disbarred for questioning "the validity of a statute after it had been passed upon." Hale disagreed and said so in a letter to *The New Republic*. Any lawyer, he maintained, had a perfect right to express himself on any subject. Turning to the New York Criminal Anarchy Statute, Hale said that it could not be criminal to advocate or write about a doctrine in the absence of a "clear and present danger" that the doctrine would be acted upon. As far as the threat of disbarment was concerned, he pointed out that the district attorney himself had spent a considerable amount of time advocating the overthrow of the British government of Ireland by force and violence. After this exchange, the question of disbarment did not come up again.

Darrow's summary for the defense proved to be a highlight of the trial. His stirring remarks included a defense of the right of revolution and an attack on the hysteria of the Red Scare. On the question of revolution, Darrow said: "For a man to be afraid of revolution in America would be equivalent to being ashamed of his own mother. . . . There is not a drop of honest blood in a single man that does not look back to some revolution for which he would thank God that those who revolted won." Rorke said later that he thought that Darrow had won over the jury by his fine speech. Its effect was soon destroyed by Gitlow who delivered his own summary in which he criticized capitalism, attacked the war, and defended the Russian Revolution. He ended by saying that the reasoning of the Left Wing Manifesto was basically correct and predicted the demise of capitalism in the United States.

The case was now ready to go to the jury. In his charge,

Judge Weeks ruled that the issue of free speech was not perti-
nent. The jury left and came back within an hour returning a
verdict of guilty. Charles Recht was on his feet immediately
pleading clemency. Judge Weeks interrupted him saying that
his client had not instructed him to ask for clemency. Weeks
was right, for Gitlow then asked Recht not to make any further
protestations on his behalf. Gitlow was sentenced to five to
ten years in prison. The judge used the occasion to scold him
for his iniquities. He was particularly criticized for his salary
which was only $41 a week, and for the fact that he had not
accumulated any property. Gitlow was sent to the Tombs to
begin his sentence. He was later transferred to Sing Sing, and,
still later, to Dannemora Prison. His case was appealed through
the New York courts and affirmed twice.[4]

In March, the second of the Communist trials took place.
This one involved Harry M. Winitsky, also a leader of the New
York Communists. The entire proceeding was similar to that
already described for Benjamin Gitlow. Winitsky was defended
by William Fallon, "The Great Mouthpiece," one of the greatest
criminal lawyers in the country.

As in the previous case, Rorke attempted to show that the
Communist party through its manifesto advocated the violent
overthrow of the government by unlawful means. Evidence was
presented that Winitsky, although not connected with *Revolutionary Age,* was present at the Chicago convention of September 1919, where the program of the Communist party was
formulated and the manifesto adopted. Charles Donnelly, a
special agent of the Lusk Committee, testified that the manifesto
and other publications could be purchased openly at Communist
party headquarters on East Tenth Street.

In the days that followed, literally thousands of pamphlets were
introduced. Their authenticity was attested to by Detective C. J.
Browne of the New York City bomb squad who had seized most
of them during raids. Another witness was Theodore Brodsky, a
clerk at Communist party headquarters, who had typed three
letters written by Winitsky. One letter called for the celebration
of Red Week honoring the anniversary of the Bolshevik uprising.
An agent for the Justice Department's Bureau of Investigation,
James O. Peyronnin, said that he had been present as an undercover agent at all sessions of the Chicago convention from September 1 to 7, 1919. He gave evidence of the role played by the
defendant.

Fallon defended his client as best he could, but the evidence was against him. The jury was out for only a few hours and returned with a verdict of guilty. On March 29, 1920, Winitsky was sentenced to five to ten years in prison. His appeal to the Appellate Division was refused.

A third indictment was brought against James Larkin, arrested with Gitlow in the November raids. At the time of his arrest, Larkin was described as "one of the most dangerous agitators in the country."[5] He was an extremely interesting and complex person. Early in life, he had worked with the Irish labor movement; in 1914 he came to the United States on a lecture tour, expecting to stay just long enough to complete it. When the war broke out, he decided to remain. In the words of his biographer, "The price he paid was poverty, loneliness, and persecution."[6] His lectures took him to every part of the United States and to Mexico. His speeches were rousing and quite radical in tone. Larkin opposed the war and defended the working class in its desire to improve conditions.

At various times, Larkin expressed sympathy for every radical movement in America and the world. These included not only the Socialist party but the IWW and the radical labor unions as well. He was a good friend of William Haywood and Elizabeth Gurley Flynn. He welcomed and supported the Russian Revolution and shifted easily into the ranks of the left wing of the Socialist party after its creation. Although he was not present at the Chicago convention where the Communist party was founded, he supported its program and attended other meetings where the manifesto was formulated.

One of the most intriguing facets of Larkin's thinking was his belief that there was no conflict between his Catholic faith and Marxist ideology. In one of his first speeches to a radical audience in New York, he unbuttoned his shirt, producing a golden cross. He then went on to explain why Christianity and communism were compatible. To Larkin, communism was a messianic vision of a future, perfect society. This belief pervaded his speeches and was strongly in evidence during his trial.

After his arrest, Larkin had some difficulty raising money to pay for his defense. The necessary funds were finally obtained with the help of the Irish Provisional Government, some local Communists and Socialists, and with an international appeal on his behalf. He was released on November 20, twelve days after his arrest. The following week both Larkin and Benjamin Gitlow

attended a meeting of left wing sympathizers in New York. Larkin
spoke out against his indictment and asked those in attendance
to pledge themselves to fight for Communist principles. In the
course of his speech, he referred to Senator Lusk and his committee as "the microbes of society," as "men with minds of an
amoeba," and as a "body with the vile odor of the skunk in and
about them." These picturesque phrases were reported in the
press and undoubtedly helped prejudice public opinion against
him.

The case came to trial on April 16 before Judge Weeks, the
same judge who had presided in the cases of Gitlow and Winitsky. Sensing that his own trial would follow the familiar pattern,
Larkin was encouraged to dispense with the services of his
lawyer and undertake his own defense. He was not a lawyer but
he had a sound grasp of fundamental principles and an unusual
ability to articulate his thoughts. Decades of speaking from the
public platform had turned him into a formidable debater. Under
the existing conditions of hysteria, he felt that he could do as
well as any trained professional.

Larkin began by protesting the fact that Judge Weeks was
sitting in the court; he said that the judge was prejudiced. Weeks
refused to disqualify himself and maintained that he was not
prejudiced. The state then sought to show that Larkin had tried
to overthrow the government by participating in the writing and
distribution of the left wing manifesto. Larkin did not deny his
connection with the document but insisted that his words and his
deeds were being misinterpreted. He denied having any belief in
violence and avowed his faith in the power of the working class.

The highlight of the trial was Larkin's summary to the jury.
After a few words of introduction, he reminded the jury that he
was not charged with a crime of violence. In his opinion, he was
charged with preaching a doctrine of "order against disorder," of
"brotherhood against brute hatred." He then compared the Socialist movement to a religion. If by religion one meant a reaching
up to a higher order of life, or doing something or learning something that was greater than oneself, then only the Socialists were
practicing their religion. Larkin denied that he advocated force,
violence, or other unlawful methods of overthrowing the government. Quoting Abraham Lincoln as his authority, he said that if
the people of the state of New York grew weary of their government they had the constitutional right to amend it or the revolutionary right to overthrow it. He then went into an abstract

discussion of justice and its relation to economics. The present economic system, he said, could not bring justice; it could only succeed in subverting it. At this point, Larkin related some of his own personal history. He told of the poverty in Liverpool during his youth. These early experiences, he maintained, had led him to adopt socialism. He spoke of his American experiences: how he was influenced by the writings of Whitman, Thoreau, and Mark Twain. Perhaps the greatest influence in his life was Woodrow Wilson who had warned of the dangers of corporations and other special interests seeking to control the government. He told the jury that if they convicted him, they would be free to convict any American with unpopular views. Next, Larkin proceeded to defend the manifesto which could not be properly understood except through a prior study of the works of Karl Marx and Friedrich Engels. Then, he plunged into a discussion of the abstract right of freedom of inquiry. He charged the jury with the responsibility of seeing that justice was done; if in their wisdom they found him guilty, he would accept the verdict. But regardless of the results of the trial, he would continue to defend the rights of the weak, the poor, and the helpless.

The speech was powerful and evoked a favorable response from the jury. Many speculated that it might return a verdict acquitting Larkin. Rorke followed this with his final summary and the jury went out. They returned in less than two hours with a verdict of guilty. Judge Weeks sentenced Larkin to prison on May 3, 1920; he was taken at once to Sing Sing. The entire trial had lasted ten days. An appeal was requested but refused.

The conviction of James Larkin caused a stir on both sides of the Atlantic. In July the dock workers in Dublin went out on strike for him. In October his case was discussed in the British House of Commons. The well-known liberal writer, Agnes Smedley, denounced the conviction in the *New York Call,* while the *Voice of Labor,* the organ of the Communist Labor Party, opposed the "Brutal Sentence on Larkin." Writing in *The Liberator,* a Socialist paper, Louise Bryant said: "They railroaded Jim Larkin to prison as they will railroad every leader they can reach until the tide turns."[7] In Boston some of his friends held a mass meeting on his behalf and demanded his immediate release. Most tragic was the testimony of his wife, who insisted that the American government refused a visa to their eldest son thus preventing the boy from seeing his father after an absence of six years.

Two additional cases came to trial in October when Charles

Ruthenberg and Isaac E. Ferguson, both leaders of the Communist party, were brought before Judge Weeks. Of the two, Ruthenberg was better known; he was born in Cleveland in 1882, the son of German Lutheran parents. As a young man, he observed the poverty of the workers in the city of his birth and joined the Socialist party to protest their plight. Later he trained as an accountant but lost his job when he participated in an organizing campaign conducted by the International Ladies Garment Workers Union. From 1909 to 1919 he was the recording secretary and organizer of the Cleveland City Central Committee of the Socialist party. His organizing abilities were legendary. His dear friend, Elizabeth Gurley Flynn, remembered Ruthenberg during these years as a "tall, slender, blue-eyed young man." He also ran for various public offices in Ohio under the Socialist banner. When the war broke out, Ruthenberg assumed the leadership of the antiwar movement in the Midwest. At St. Louis in April 1917 he led the fight for a strong antiwar resolution and in 1919 assisted in the founding of the Communist party.

Ruthenberg's first conviction came in 1917 when he was arrested for violating the Conscription Act. He was charged with having made a speech in Cleveland against the war thereby encouraging some of his younger listeners not to register for the draft. Found guilty, he served ten months in the Canton workhouse. In 1919 Ruthenberg was arrested again after the May Day riots in the Cleveland public square. In these disturbances, three people, including a child, were killed. This time Ruthenberg was charged with the crime of "assault with intent to kill." He quickly got out a leaflet offering a $500 reward for information leading to the punishment of those who organized the attack. After a hearing, the charge was dropped by the court. Ruthenberg was then indicted under the Ohio Criminal Anarchy Statute. This 1919 law, similar to the one passed by New York, made it a crime to advocate violence "as a means of securing social reform." While the Ohio case was in progress, a suit was started in New York for violation of the New York Statute on Criminal Anarchy. The New York case was given preference and the Ohio suit was quietly dropped.

Ruthenberg was tried along with his friend and colleague, Isaac E. Ferguson, a Chicago lawyer. The charge was the same as that in the previous cases: the publication of the Left Wing

Manifesto. The judge and prosecuting attorneys were also the same. Ruthenberg was defended by Joseph R. Brodsky, an attorney active in labor causes. Ferguson conducted his own defense and assisted Ruthenberg in his.

The first move was made by Ferguson who asked Judge Weeks to disqualify himself because of his conduct in the previous Communist trials. This motion was overruled. Next, a good deal of time went into the selection of a jury. When it finally got under way, the trial resembled a course in the history and principles of left wing socialism. The defendants were asked to explain their beliefs. They readily admitted that they were Communists and believed in revolution. They said further that the workers would take possession of the means of production after the revolution. They would expropriate the present owners and establish the socialized control of industry. Ownership would be transferred from the individual to the state. The expropriation would be accomplished without compensation. Nothing was said about violent revolution but during the "transition to socialism" a dictatorship of the proletariat would become a reality. The right to vote would be denied to those who refused to participate in the new society. Rorke tried to press the defendants into an admission that they advocated violent revolution. Ruthenberg refused to commit himself; in his reply he took refuge behind the standard Marxian dialectic:

> I believe that the workers will capture the power of the state in the following process: that in the development of the capitalist system, its own contradictions bring about a situation in which the machinery of production breaks down. These contradictions are the forces which lead to overproduction, imperialism in the search for markets, international capitalist conflict, and, finally, to war.

As a result of this turmoil, the workers will establish their soviets and their army as competitors to the government. Rorke did not rest but followed with a question. "Then you will have two governments?" "For a period of time there may be, as there was in Russia, two governments, one becoming the government and the other disintegrating and going out of existence," was the reply. "But," Rorke protested, "what would become of the President of the United States who had taken the oath of office to carry on this government under the Constitution? What would become of the Vice President. . . ." The list was a long one continuing on down to mayors and city councils. Ruthenberg's answer was vague: "I am unable to say what would become of them. I would state that the new government would set up new organs for the control and effective administration of society."

At the close of the trial, Ferguson made his own summary to the jury. He stood on his Communist principles and said that he expected to live to see them triumph. He then denounced the capitalist system which, he said, was responsible for his trial. Ferguson predicted that he would be convicted and attributed it to class justice. The trial had lasted nearly four weeks. Both men were found guilty and were sentenced on October 29, 1920, to five years in prison.

By the time Ferguson and Ruthenberg were convicted, the other defendants had already spent some months in jail. Gitlow was the first; he called himself "the first Communist prisoner at Sing Sing." In the spring, he was joined by Harry Winitsky and Jim Larkin. Later, all three were shipped to Dannemora, a maximum security prison, high in the Adirondacks. There they made the acquaintance of Gus Alonen, also convicted for criminal anarchy. The four of them formed a "quartet," became fast friends, and were soon singled out by the authorities who realized that they were quite different from the usual breed of criminals.

To some extent, the effects of the Red Scare were in evidence even behind prison walls. The Communists complained of especially severe treatment, although it should be noted that all of the prisoners, even those whose crimes were nonpolitical, were harshly treated at Dannemora Prison. The *New York Call* thought the situation serious enough to send Agnes Smedley to investigate. Miss Smedley wrote a series of articles for the *Call* which infuriated the state superintendent of prisons. A frightening episode occurred when the prison commissioner took steps to have the "quartet" given psychiatric examinations. If they were judged insane they would have been transferred to a prison for the criminally insane. The Communists held a meeting and decided to seek help from the outside; as a courier they used Rabbi Judelson, an orthodox rabbi from Plattsburg, New York, who acted as an unofficial chaplain and friend to many of the inmates of the prison regardless of their faith. If a prisoner wanted to get a letter out of prison without censorship, he would slip it into the Rabbi's long frock coat. Winitsky was authorized to write for the group and Judelson transported it to New York. Soon help began to arrive in the form of protests to officials and articles in the radical press. It proved effective and instead of being sent to a sanitorium, they were sent back to Sing Sing in November 1920, except for Gus Alonen who went to Comstock Prison.

In Sing Sing the Communists were joined by Isaac E. Ferguson and Charles Ruthenberg. They occupied their time reading, writing, and doing odd jobs about the prison. They appeared to be in good spirits. On one St. Patrick's Day, Jim Larkin was invited to address the prisoners in their annual celebration. He was well received especially by the Irish prisoners and their guards. Ruthenberg kept himself busy by signing up for a correspondence course given by Columbia University. A touching scene took place when Ruthenberg was visited by his twelve-year-old son, Daniel. Little did the boy know that his father was close to death's door when he said: "I saw him pop out of a door over in the corner, just like himself, except for his prison garb, and his prison pallor. Here was someone I knew quite well, and I knew he was all right, and here he was."

The Communists were also busy taking steps to secure their release. Their lawyers were writing the necessary letters and filing the proper papers. Defense Committees collected funds. Benjamin Gitlow was the first to get out of prison. On April 22, 1921, he received a telegram stating that his lawyer's petition for a certificate of "reasonable doubt" had been granted by the courts. Until his final release in 1925 Gitlow was in and out of jail many times. On his first release he was met at the door of the warden's office by his lawyer and by a member of the New York police bomb squad. Gitlow remembered the officer from the 1919 raids.

In July 1922 Judge Benjamin N. Cardozo, then in the New York courts, signed a petition of reasonable doubt for Ferguson and Ruthenberg. This reversed their convictions and granted them new trials. For Isaac E. Ferguson the new trial never took place; he was pardoned by Governor Alfred E. Smith and returned to Chicago where he settled down to the practice of law. Ruthenberg was not so fortunate. Forty days after his release he was arrested by police and agents of the Justice Department in a

raid on a Communist convention at Bridgman, Michigan. This
conclave, held amidst the lonely woods and sand dunes on Lake
Michigan, was an attempt to unify the Communist movement,
split since its creation in 1919. William Z. Foster, already emerg-
ing as the top Communist leader in America, was among those
arrested. All were charged with violating Michigan's Criminal
Anarchy Law.

With the trial of leaders in progress in Michigan, the New
York case was dropped. In Michigan, those accused were defended by a contingent of lawyers sent by the American Civil
Liberties Union. Ruthenberg took the stand for Foster, and then
testified in his own defense. The jury brought in a verdict of
guilty and an immediate appeal was made to the Michigan
Supreme Court which concurred in the decision of the lower
court. The United States Supreme Court agreed to review the
case but Ruthenberg died before it handed down its decision.
His death removed him from the Court's jurisdiction.

Friends of James Larkin were also working to secure his
release from jail. His defense was undertaken by the Larkin
Defense Committee, assisted by the Irish-American Labor League.
In the forefront of this effort was J. J. O'Flaherty, the brother of
the novelist, Liam O'Flaherty. Later, the task was assumed by
Jack Carney, an influential friend, who in the fall of 1922 approached Governor Nathan Miller of New York and asked for
a pardon for Larkin. By this time, Larkin had spent two years
in jail. Miller told Carney to secure the signatures of ten important persons in the community and he would then put through
a pardon. Signatures were secured from many including Father
Duffy, the Chaplain of the Fighting 69th, and from Monsignor
James Powers, a priest prominent in Irish-American affairs.
Cardinal Hayes, the Archbishop of New York, was also approached and although he did not sign, he promised to write a
letter to Governor Miller in Larkin's behalf. Meanwhile, Larkin's
lawyer, Frank P. Walsh, had entered an appeal through the
courts without Larkin's knowledge. This disqualified the petition
and tied the governor's hands. Larkin's lawyers then appealed
to the court for a certificate of reasonable doubt. The certificate
was granted and Larkin was released in July 1922. Shortly
afterwards, the State Court of Appeals upheld his conviction
and he was returned to Sing Sing to finish his sentence.[8]

In November 1922 Alfred E. Smith won the election and

returned to the governor's seat. A few days later, he held a public hearing on an application for a pardon for James Larkin. The hearing was well attended; one speech in Larkin's behalf was made by Mrs. Malcolm Duncan, a representative of the Daughters of the American Revolution, who said: "If the Constitution of the United States were strictly enforced there would be no political prisoners in this country." This favorable publicity did much to secure his release. Larkin was pardoned on January 17, 1923. In his statement granting the pardon, Governor Smith called the conviction a "political case." He said that the state did not seek vengeance and as Larkin had already served two years in prison, he felt that justice had been satisfied. By April 1923 Larkin had decided to return to Ireland and continue his work in the Irish labor movement. To the amazement of the government, he went to Washington and asked to be deported. The government granted his wish and he was returned to Dublin via Ellis Island.

Of all these New York cases involving criminal anarchy, Gitlow's was the only one to reach the United States Supreme Court.[9] The decision was most significant and soon became a landmark in the history of American constitutional law. It came to the Court under the Fourteenth Amendment to the Constitution, which says in part: "nor shall any State deprive any person of life, liberty, or property, without due process of law." In related cases, the court had refrained from deciding whether "liberty" protected freedom of speech as well as liberty of person and contracts. By the time of Gitlow's case, the question was still open, but a few precedents seemed to indicate that the Supreme Court would answer in the affirmative.[10] The defense wanted this question answered. It also attempted to prove that the Statute on Criminal Anarchy was unconstitutional because it sought to punish words and doctrines which did not present a "clear and present danger" to the State.

In his decision, Justice Sanford admitted that nothing of any consequence had taken place as a result of the publication of the manifesto. The only question was whether the Criminal Anarchy Statute violated Gitlow's rights under the due process clause of the Fourteenth Amendment. The Court said it had not. The statute did not penalize changes in government by constitutional or lawful means. It did prohibit the incitement of violence to effect change.

The Court went on to analyze the manifesto and found that it was not a statement of abstract doctrine, as Gitlow's lawyers maintained, or a prediction that industrial disturbances and revolutionary mass strikes would result spontaneously from some inevitable laws of history; rather, it was a call to action using "fervent language" to bring about unlawful changes in the government. The Court agreed that freedom of speech and press was protected by the Fourteenth Amendment; however, these protections were not absolute but relative. By the use of its police power, the state had a perfect right to punish those who incited to violence and revolution, even though the ultimate consequences of the incitement could not be predicted.

Two judges, Holmes and Brandeis, rejected this majority view. The dissenters tried to apply the doctrine of "clear and present danger" stated previously in the Schenck Case. They denied that the words of the manifesto would lead to violence:

It is said that this Manifesto was more than a theory, that it was an incitement. Every idea is an incitement. It offers itself for belief and if believed it is acted on unless some other belief outweighs it or some failure of energy stifles the movement at its birth. The only difference between the expression of an opinion and an incitement in the narrower sense is the speaker's enthusiasm for the result. Eloquence may set fire to reason. But whatever may be thought of the redundant discourse before us, it had no chance of starting a present conflagration.

The case was significant in other respects. In agreeing to pass on the constitutionality of this state law, the Court established the principle that the First Amendment freedoms were "fundamental liberties" protected against encroachment by the word "liberty" in the Fourteenth Amendment. Thus the Court took a step forward towards nationalizing the First Amendment.

Strangely enough, the reaction to the decision was fairly mild; many publications did not comment on it, perhaps an indication that the Red Scare had passed its peak. Some journals did. To the *Christian Century,* the decision in the Gitlow case was a clear example of the "social views" of the judges involved. *The New Republic* wondered how the judges could have found the manifesto, a "tepid rehash" of the doctrines of Marx and Engels, threatening in any way. Such theories were not dangerous but

appeared in the programs of many parties presently holding seats
in various European parliaments.[11]

With the decision of the Supreme Court against him, Benjamin
Gitlow accepted his fate and prepared to surrender to the state
government in order to continue his sentence. However, he did
not return to jail; he was pardoned by Governor Alfred E. Smith.
By this time, Smith had already granted pardons to all of the
other editors.[12] The news was greeted with joy in liberal and
radical circles. "We are delighted," said Forrest Bailey, the director of the ACLU. Meanwhile, in Philadelphia, at a convention of
the ILGWU, the delegates sang the Internationale when the news
was announced.

The pardon of Benjamin Gitlow brought the judicial phase
of the Red Scare to a close. After this time, no further indictments
were begun under the Criminal Anarchy Law.

Each of the cases had followed a similar pattern. It was
admitted that the defendants had not committed any illegal acts.
It was also admitted that they were not engaged in a conspiracy
to subvert the state government. Rather, by the publication of
the manifesto, they were guilty of encouraging others to commit
acts of violence and rebellion. Once this last point was established,
the convictions were a foregone conclusion.

It was strange indeed that the guilt of the defendants rested
upon the publication of a supposedly inflammatory document.
As the defense pointed out, the manifesto was hardly a call to
action. It was merely a summary of Marxist doctrines easily
available to the public through other sources. Furthermore,
written statements of this type circulated freely in Europe where
they were rarely a cause of concern. The publication in which
it was printed, *Revolutionary Age,* was typical of the leftist
journals of the day. Its circulation was small and its influence
meagre. Those who would have been stirred by its message were
persons who were already familiar with radical ideas. Other
readers would not have been influenced. Hence, to properly
understand the trials, we must look elsewhere for an explanation.

Undoubtedly, the hysteria of the Red Scare was always present
and must be considered. It explains why New Yorkers were
encouraged to revive their Statute of Criminal Anarchy, unused
since 1902, and apply it, not to anarchists, but to Communists.
In doing this, New York became the model for similar laws
passed by other states. Antiradical prejudice was also present

when Judge McAdoo set an unusually high bail for those defendants arrested during raids. Had they not been Communists, the amounts would have been much lower. The effects of the Red Scare were also seen in the prejudiced statements made by the judge during the hearing that Communists were automatically guilty by virtue of their membership in the Communist party. This underlying bias was to continue throughout all of the trials. Unquestionably, it influenced the jury. Darrow was aware that it would and he was, therefore, somewhat reluctant to undertake Gitlow's defense. Once the trial began, he used his peremptory challenges carefully, realizing that in this kind of case a sympathetic jury was more than an urgent necessity. Further evidence of antiradical prejudice was seen in the harsh treatment which the defendants received in jail. The threat to transfer them to a prison for the criminally insane was both unconstitutional and inhuman.

In the face of this wall of hostility, the Communists defended themselves as best they could. Assisted by their attorneys, their efforts were brave, intelligent, and forthright. They did not appeal to public sympathy, nor did they hope to become martyrs to their cause. As lifelong rebels against what they conceived to be a repressive society, they explained their position in forceful terms, without resort to emotion or subterfuge. That they often relied too heavily on Marxist doctrine in their arguments can only be explained by their years of participation in leftist causes. On the other hand, Darrow, and Larkin to some extent, tried to Americanize the trial: they showed that the right of protest was well within the American tradition. In addition, Darrow tried to broaden the First Amendment to include statements like those appearing in the manifesto. He argued further that however much one might disagree with the ideas of the defendants, it was their constitutional right to voice them.

It is interesting that the pardons set off more public excitement than the trials did. In Larkin's case, the concern was international. His conviction precipitated strikes in Ireland, and he was the subject of a debate in the House of Commons. In America only the radicals and their press waged any campaign for acquittal. In part this can be explained by the fact that the leftists were not well known outside of their own circles. Then, too, few would risk coming to their defense considering the hysteria of the day. The public participated more openly once the campaign for pardons was under way. This was an encouraging sign but it did not exonerate those who were too timid to speak up earlier.

In a narrow sense, the cases turned on the legal point that the ideas of the manifesto were, in effect, a call to revolution. In a larger sense, however, a more basic question was involved. Could free speech survive during a period of repression? To ask the question is to answer it. Fortunately, the situation was only temporary and it awaited the return of a more tolerant political atmosphere.

Once again, Governor Smith emerges as a humane and decent public official. His opposition to Communist philosophy did not blind him to the necessity of protecting the constitutional rights of the accused. One is also impressed by the courage of those lawyers like Darrow, Fallon, and Walsh who offered their services in the defense of a most unpopular cause.

N O T E S

1. The exception was *Van Gerichten* v. *Seitz,* 94 N.Y. App. Div. 130 (1904) in which an anarchist was accused of slander.
2. McKinney's Consolidated Laws of New York (Brooklyn, 1938), sec. 160; see also Walter Gellhorn, *The States and Subversion* (Ithaca, N.Y., 1952), Appendix B, for a list of other states passing such laws.
3. See Arturo Giovannitti, "Communists on Trial," *The Liberator,* March 1920, p. 7.
4. See *People* v. *Gitlow,* 111 N.Y. Misc. 641 (1920); 195 App. Div. 773 (1921); 234 N.Y. 132 (1922).
5. *New York Times,* November 9, 1919, p. 1.
6. Emmett Larkin, *James Larkin* (Cambridge, Mass., 1965), p. 188.
7. *Ibid.,* p. 243, quotes the *Call* and the *Voice of Labor;* Louise Bryant, "Jim Larkin goes to prison," *The Liberator,* June 1, 1920, p. 1.
8. *People* v. *Larkin,* 234 N.Y. 530 (1922).
9. *Gitlow* v. *New York,* 268 U.S. 652 (1925).
10. The previous cases were *Meyer* v. *Nebraska,* 262 U.S. 390 (1923), and *Pierce* v. *Society of Sisters,* 268 U.S. 510 (1925).
11. "The Supreme Court and the Gitlow Decision," *The Christian Century,* June 25, 1925, p. 818; "The Gitlow Case," *New Republic,* July 1, 1925, p. 142.
12. In addition to the indictments discussed here, four other editors, including John Reed, were never apprehended by the government, so no indictments could be brought against them.

Chapter Nine

THE WANING OF THE RED SCARE: 1920-1924

After 1920 the tide of antiradicalism receded. This waning of the Red Scare coincided with the election of a new Republican administration in Washington. The crusade lasted somewhat longer in New York. In part, this was due to the greater concentration of radicals here, and to the anxiety created by the Wall Street bombing of 1920. Shortly afterwards, there was a lessening of tension even here as stories about the left disappeared from the front pages of the press, and politicians were less inclined to use antiradical themes in their oratory.

However, the vestiges of this crusade could still be found in the work of the patriotic organizations, in the movement to restrict immigration, and, to a lesser extent, in the activities of the American Legion.

The decline of the Red Scare began with the public protest against the excesses of the raids, investigations, and deportations. Many began to realize that these activities included wide violations of civil liberties. Some felt that the nation was losing sight of cherished principles of due process and fair play.

More than any other single event, the trial of the five Socialists in Albany solidified opposition to the Red Scare, and encouraged a return to moderation and political sanity. Even A. Mitchell Palmer, the most celebrated of the antiradicals, was forced to admit that the New York legislature had gone too far, and had treated Socialists as if they were Communists.

In addition to the public protest, the antiradical crusade lost much of its fervor due to a decline in the radical movements themselves. As early as 1919, the Socialist party lost more than half its membership when the left wing withdrew, forming the Communist party. In the election of November 1920, Eugene V. Debs,

216

the Socialist candidate for president, received only 3.5 percent of the total vote. This was well below the 6 percent he had received in the 1912 election. While it was true that the Socialists obtained 131,856 votes for Debs in New York, even this was less than Morris Hillquit's total vote in the mayoralty election of 1917. Furthermore, the Socialist party was losing members throughout the country. Its western wing was largely absorbed by the newly formed Farmer-Labor parties. By 1922, only four states, including New York, had as many as one thousand paid up Socialist members. This was partly caused by the persecution of radicals during the Palmer period. It also reflected, as Abraham Cahan, the editor of the *Forward* pointed out, a growing sense of disillusionment with the Soviet Union.[1] Thus, by 1924, the Socialist party was reduced to a mere shadow of its former self. To David Karsner, the former magazine editor of the *Call,* it was a "political ghost stalking in the graveyard of current events seeking a respectable burial."

The Communists experienced a similar decline. Here, too, the ferocity of the Palmer raids and the deportations depleted the ranks of the faithful and drove the remaining party members underground. The Communists boycotted the elections of 1920 because they refused to "perpetuate the system based on wage slavery." In 1921 they surfaced slightly to form the Worker's party but were only marginally successful. Their strength was further dissipated by battles waged with the Socialists. This inter-radical warfare took an extreme form in New York where Communist attempts to infiltrate the Socialist-dominated needle trades were successfully resisted. The Communists captured a few of the smaller unions like the fur and leather workers, but most of the larger ones remained faithful to the conservative policies of the American Federation of Labor.

The defeat of the new sedition legislation proposed to the Congress after the Palmer raids on the Communist party was another indication of the changing political climate. The first of two measures was the Davey bill which provided for the death penalty, upon recommendation of a jury, for those persons whose subversive activities led to the destruction of life. The bill also sought to close the mails to seditious literature, provided for the continued deportation of aliens, and denied their right to refuse to testify on the grounds of self incrimination. Another measure, the Sterling bill had similar provisions but was slightly less severe.

Press reaction to the proposed sedition bills was hostile. The *New York Globe* deplored the fact that the nation had "lost its nerve," and warned its readers that the country was "backing into reaction." Even *The New York Times,* usually a defender of the drive against dissidents, opposed the peacetime sedition bills; it feared their effect on the freedom of the press.[2] The bills were strongly endorsed by A. Mitchell Palmer and the Justice Department, but with opposition mounting across the nation, they were unable to pass.

The government's inability to secure additional deportations was another indication of the turning of the tide. This occurred as defense attorneys became more proficient in handling cases of this type. Many aliens followed the advice of George F. Vanderveer who told his clients to withhold information concerning citizenship, entrance into the country, and party affiliation until they were adequately represented by counsel.

Still another factor was the Labor Department's own reassessment of its role in deportation proceedings. In January 1920 Secretary of Labor William B. Wilson, under the prodding of his assistant secretary, Louis F. Post, acknowledged that departmental policy in deportation hearings had been too lax in its search for deportable aliens. Wilson learned how the Immigration Bureau had captured control of the Labor Department, ignored his own interpretations of policy, and turned superior department officials into submissive rubber stamps. To reverse this trend, Wilson and Post reestablished due process in deportation cases and reasserted control over their own department. On January 26, 1920, Secretary Wilson, overriding the opposition of his commissioner of immigration, Anthony Caminetti, and of J. Edgar Hoover, revised departmental procedures to give more protection to aliens. These changes included the rights of counsel from the beginning of the hearing and reasonable bail, restrictions on self-incrimination and arrests without warrants, and the creation of a Board of Review to serve under the secretary of labor as a watchdog of immigration affairs. By administrative decision, Wilson also refused to deport members of the Communist Labor party. Post made further restrictions with respect to members of the Communist party, although they continued to be eligible for deportation. These measures reduced the number of deportations drastically. There were 37 deportations in 1919; they rose to 314 in 1920 and to 446 in 1921. Then they fell to 64 in 1922, and to 13 in 1923. Thereafter, they rose and fell until they reached the low figure of 1 in the years from 1928 to 1930. However, even the relatively high figures of 1920 and 1921 might have been still higher without the changes instituted by Wilson and Post.

The new liberal policy of the Department of Labor led to a rupture in its relationships with the Justice Department. In reality, the dispute was more a contest between Hoover, backed by Attorney General Palmer, and Post supported by Secretary Wilson. The Justice Department interpreted this reassertion of control by Wilson and Post as a defense of radicals, rather than mere concern for them.

At this point, the dispute erupted fully, and led to a number of congressional investigations of Post, the Justice Department, and of Palmer. In the first one, the Rules Committee of the House of Representatives spent a good deal of time going over Post's record. J. Edgar Hoover appeared as one of the witnesses. Earlier, in an obvious attempt to undermine Post, he had searched the IWW files in Chicago for some proof that he was the tool of the Wobblies. The search revealed that Post had reviewed a number of deportation cases and released many aliens, who were being held on insufficient evidence. As neither subversion nor dereliction of duty had been proven, the impeachment charge was dropped. The *New York American,* a conservative paper, wrote approvingly that Post had "done his duty as an upright official, an honest man, and as a citizen loyal and faithful to the obligations of citizenship."[3]

Another indication of the waning of the Red Scare took place on June 1, 1920, when Secretary Wilson named Frederick A. Wallis to the post of commissioner of immigration formerly held by Anthony Caminetti. Wallis began an investigation of Ellis Island and other deportation centers and found that they were in a deplorable state. The floors were filthy, the food bad, and disease was rampant. Wallis ordered that conditions be improved and they subsequently were.

All of these changes and reforms took place against a background of continuous agitation from many parts of the country for a cessation in antiradical hysteria. The protestors called for the repeal of the Espionage Law, for amnesty for political prisoners, and for an end to deportations. New York followed the national pattern and even surpassed it to some degree.

The American Civil Liberties Union took the lead. As early

as January 1919 Professor Harry F. Ward was among those contacted by Albert De Silver, the young head of the ACLU, to lend his name as one of the drive's supporters. Rabbi Magnes was also approached; he, too, agreed to help. Professor Albert Parkin Fitch of Amherst College was asked to head the drive in the colleges.

The files of the ACLU indicate that there were many other people around the country who were only too happy to help. These letters suggest that there was a sizable minority which never supported the Red Scare but stood quietly on the sidelines waiting to be mobilized once the political climate improved.

In December, the protestors took to the streets and conducted a "Liberty Walk" down Fifth Avenue. Many ministers and students were among the three hundred marchers. They held placards demanding amnesty for political prisoners and an end to deportations. At Fourteenth Street, the police urged them to "turn back" as they were marching without a permit. Two lawyers in the group stepped forward and informed the policemen that they had a perfectly legal right to march. As the *New York Tribune* reported the scene: "They opened with the rights of man and the old English law, fired sections of the statutes of the State of New York by platoons, and wound up with a constitutional drumfire."[4] Meanwhile, the police were bringing up more reserves. The scene erupted into considerable violence and five arrests were made.

Protests against the alleged police brutality followed the next day. The amnesty committee of the People's Freedom Union, the group that had organized the march, secured affidavits proving that the police had used excessive force. The committee compiled a list of badge numbers of the guilty policemen; they were especially concerned with Officer No. 292, who had followed a number of marchers down Thirty-first Street and urged a soldier and sailor in the crowd to "beat them up."

At the trial of the protestors, the courtroom was filled with many prominent New Yorkers. They included the Reverend Dr. Kenneth Mythen, a clergyman from Baltimore, Mrs. J. A. Hopkins, president of the New York State Suffrage Party, Dr. Josephine Baker, in charge of the Children's Hygiene Department of the Board of Health, Dr. Eleanor Kilham, head of the New York Infirmary for Children, and Ella Riegel, an instructor at Bryn Mawr College.

The trial was reported in the press and came to the attention of the American Civil Liberties Union. Even New York's Mayor John F. Hylan was stirred by the charges of police brutality and ordered an immediate investigation. But Acting Chief Inspector of Police Thomas H. Murphy disagreed:

> The actions of the persons participating was in violation of the law. Their purpose was to create sentiment for the release of prisoners who have been convicted of crimes against the federal government during the late war. . . . It was deliberately unlawful in that they attempted to parade without a permit required by law. . . . The police used necessary force in preserving the peace and in dispersing these unlawful gatherings.

Nevertheless, despite Murphy's opinion, all of the defendants were acquitted.

Three days later additional protests against the Red Scare came from the Socialist members of the Board of Aldermen. Abraham Shiplacoff introduced the first of a series of resolutions which condemned the many raids conducted by the police and the Department of Justice. As expected, Shiplacoff's resolution was tabled.

The following month, a more important sign of the changing political climate came in the form of a petition signed by some of the most eminent clergymen in the country. Among them were five bishops of the Protestant Episcopal Church, and sixteen other prominent clergymen, many from the New York area.

In May the clergymen's petition was followed by still another document called a "Report to the American People." It was drawn up by twelve outstanding constitutional lawyers including Dean Roscoe Pound, Zechariah Chafee, Jr., Felix Frankfurter of the Harvard Law School, and Swinburne Hale and Frank P. Walsh from New York. The report documented the manner in which the Justice Department had violated the constitutional rights of many Americans during the preceding two years. It concluded that punishments had been inflicted, arrests had been made without warrants, searches and seizures had become commonplace, and the Fifth Amendment had been disregarded by forcing witnesses to incriminate themselves. The Department of Justice had relied heavily on undercover agents to secure evidence and information. The report charged that the attorney general had abused his power by using his office to distribute antiradical propaganda. The published report acted as a valuable weapon for those seeking an end to the Red Scare.

However, the tide of the antiradical crusade ebbed and flowed, and as May Day approached, there was a renewal of fear that radical disturbances would take place. From Washington, Attorney General Palmer took the lead, and predicted a national plot in which many American leaders were to be destroyed. In all seriousness, the press reported that the "forces of law and order" were ready to "strike swiftly" at the first sign of a disturbance. In New York, the entire police department of eleven thousand men went on a twenty-four-hour alert. Additional men were assigned to guard the Public Library, Pennsylvania Station, and the General Post Office. Others were sent to the Brownsville section of Brooklyn and to similar hotbeds of radicalism in the Bronx. The national committee of the Socialist party ridiculed the preparations, maintaining that the plot was merely a figment of Palmer's fertile imagination.

The Socialists were vindicated when May Day passed without a single disturbance in any part of the nation. There were, however, important repercussions: infuriated by predictions of violence which had not taken place and disturbed by the criticism of lawyers, clergymen, and liberals, the public began to lose interest in the antiradical crusade. Congress was also up in arms, and invited the attorney general to come before the Rules Committee of the House to defend his policies. Palmer accepted and appeared before the committee on June 1, 1920. In his testimony he denied all of the charges made by the twelve lawyers and by Assistant Secretary of Labor Post. He maintained that his department tried to get as many warrants as possible but admitted that it had been necessary to make some arrests without them. He defended his use of undercover agents as necessary to ferret out underground radical units. Although the department's methods might have appeared arbitrary, he maintained they were necessary to alleviate a real threat to the security of the United States.

Six months later, Palmer was investigated again by the Judiciary Committee of the Senate. Hearings began on January 19, 1921, and lasted until March 3. The attorney general repeated his previous testimony, and defended the raids, the arrests, and the deportations. Senator Walsh, a committee member, was not satisfied and referred to evidence presented by the twelve lawyers which contradicted statements made by the attorney general.

A New York court case added more fuel to the fires that were engulfing the attorney general. Palmer and William J. Flynn, the Justice Department official in charge of the New York raids, were named in a suit brought by Marie Salsedo who complained that the government's antiradical policies had led to her husband's death. The deceased was one of those arrested during the Palmer raids. From March 1 until his death on May 3, 1920, he was kept in solitary confinement at Justice Department headquarters on Park Row. This imprisonment was accompanied by constant questioning, threats, and broken promises that he would soon go free. As a result, the prisoner became "suicidally despondent" and jumped from the window of his cell.

The widow lost her case. The United States Circuit Court of Appeals held that "the suicide was not a result naturally and reasonably to be expected from the acts of misconduct alleged to have been committed by the defendants." One judge disagreed. In his dissenting opinion he said:

> If a man is confined against his will for two months and is continuously and grievously injured and, at the same time, continuously threatened with death, can it be said . . . that the wrongdoer should not have forseen . . . that self destruction might follow?[5]

Amnesty for political prisoners jailed under federal law continued to be an important demand of those seeking to inhibit uncontrolled antiradical hysteria. Here, the record of the attorney general was considerably more liberal. Both Gregory and Palmer had approved of a careful case-by-case review of all the wartime sedition cases arising under the Espionage Act. Some sentences were reduced, others commuted, but the cases involving IWW members were not reviewed. The Justice Department felt that granting of amnesty to Wobblies would have a detrimental effect on industrial and social conditions within the United States.

The amnesty drive continued throughout the year 1920. In November a delegation of labor leaders including Samuel Gompers and Meyer London, representing the United Hebrew Trades, called on Palmer and urged that steps towards total amnesty be taken at once. Meanwhile, the executive council of the AFL reported to its annual convention in favor of amnesty, especially for the convicted Socialist leader, Eugene V. Debs. While the council did not approve of Debs' conduct, it did believe that justice had been served and no further purpose could be achieved by keeping him in jail. Liberals like John P. Gavit, the editor of the *New York Post,* suggested to President Wilson that he could "uplift and electrify the liberal forces in this and other countries" by granting unconditional amnesty "for all persons convicted for expressions of opinion." Even Attorney General Palmer urged Wilson to free Debs, but he refused on the grounds that the aging Socialist violated the law and must pay for his crime.

The amnesty drive continued after the new Republican administration arrived in Washington in March 1921. The Central Labor party, an AFL affiliate, joined with the Socialist party and others to send delegates to Washington. A letter-writing campaign followed. Soon, the files of the pardon attorney of the Justice Department were filled with twenty-two boxes of correspondence urging that the political prisoners be freed.

In New York, the American Civil Liberties Union felt that these efforts were not enough. It planned even more dramatic measures. A special fund of $5,000 was raised. Next, the ACLU opened a special office in Washington, and on Armistice Day, 1921, petitioned President Warren G. Harding for the release of the remaining prisoners. The appeal was signed by many people including veterans holding the Congressional Medal of Honor. Picketing of the Washington Arms Conference followed. Two more delegations went to see President Harding and many congressmen, senators, and other public officials were approached. The *New York World* assisted with a special publicity campaign designed to throw light on the entire situation. The amnesty drive attained partial success on Christmas Day, 1921, when twenty-five political prisoners, including Eugene V. Debs, were released from prisons around the country. In a statement, the White House explained its decision:

> He [Debs] is an old man, and not physically strong. He is a man of much personal charm and impressive personality which qualifications make him a dangerous man calculated to mislead the unthinking and affording excuses for those with

criminal intent. . . . Under the circumstances it was believed that the ends of justice had been sufficiently met and it would be an ungracious act not to release the prisoner.

The release of Debs was opposed by many posts of the American Legion and by the patriotic organizations. *The New York Times* was horrified; it maintained that this step served notice to all persons "that the United States would not seriously punish the most perilous assailant of its safety and life."[6] On the other hand, the American Civil Liberties Union approved of the decision with reservations, as it had expected the release of all the 118 men still left behind prison walls. The Union's approval would have been more guarded had it known Harding's real motivation in freeing Debs. The president acted not only out of altruism but out of desire to deflate the drive for total amnesty by partial concessions. This was admitted by Attorney General Daugherty who felt that partial amnesty was necessary before the movement had "gone too far."[7] If this was the intention of the White House, its calculations were correct for the AFL, one of the main backers of the amnesty drive, soon withdrew its support. However, the ACLU redoubled its efforts, and after Harding's death on August 2, 1923, pressure was directed at Calvin Coolidge who released an additional thirty prisoners in December. All of those remaining were subsequently freed or agreed to accept voluntary deportation.

There were other signs of a change in the government's policy. Earlier, the Harding administration had ended the postal censorship established during the Wilson years. No more periodicals were barred from the mails and all second-class mailing privileges were restored. In 1922, four banned books, including Alexander Berkman's *Prison Memoirs of an Anarchist,* were readmitted to the mails. In addition, the government planned no more raids or investigations.[8] However, the Anti-Radical Division of the Justice Department continued to make information pertaining to radical activities available to state governments and to industry. It also maintained its links with private detective agencies and used its undercover agents to infiltrate leftist and labor groups.

With the appointment of Harlan Fiske Stone as attorney general, the Coolidge administration reversed this trend. Now the Bureau of Investigation ceased its propaganda against organized labor and radicals and assumed its proper role as an investigating arm of the government.

One might have expected that with the Red Scare in decline around the country, New York should have followed the national pattern. Here, however, the crusade lasted somewhat longer. There were a number of factors which explained this. One was the greater concentration of radicals in New York City. Another was the trial of the five Socialists at Albany which kept the cauldron boiling during the winter of 1920. Consequently, police activity continued at a high level. The police estimated that they attended 221 radical meetings and received no less than 698 communications from citizens relating to left wing activities. There were no further raids but the commissioner created elaborate procedures to apprehend persons distributing radical literature.

An important event in prolonging the Red Scare in New York was the Wall Street bombing of 1920. The tragedy began at five minutes before noon on September 16, when an old wagon drawn by an ancient horse went slowly west on Wall Street, coming to a stop in front of the Assay Building. The headquarters of Morgan and Company was directly across the street. The driver alighted and disappeared, as the street began to fill with secretaries, clerks, and businessmen on their lunch hour. All of a sudden the wagon exploded. There was a blinding flash as pieces of metal sailed through the street. People were knocked to the ground; they collapsed in bloody, screaming heaps. When it was all over, thirty persons were dead and over three hundred injured. All of those killed were clerks, typists, or people who happened to be passing by.

Within minutes after the explosion, agents of the bomb squad began arriving at the scene. They were soon joined by A. Mitchell Palmer and William J. Flynn who hurried up from Washington. The bombers failed to destroy any of their intended victims. The famous banker, J. P. Morgan, was in England at the time of the blast, and Thomas W. Lamont and Dwight Morrow, two of his associates, were safe in a conference room at the other end of the building.

Naturally, the newspapers were frantic at this latest outrage. It was immediately assumed that radical elements were responsible. The New York Chamber of Commerce called it an "act of war" and demanded that Governor's Island be improvised with barracks and other facilities to garrison at least a regiment of federal troops to deal with similar incidents.[9] Police forces throughout the nation were alerted and cooperated in the search for assassins. Although many clues were uncovered, the identity of the bomber, or bombers, was never determined.

The publicity given to the Wall Street bombing was sufficient to set off a flurry of radical and antiradical incidents throughout the city. In October, the Lower East Side was flooded with pamphlets blaming the "capitalists who wished to discredit the working class." Several radical groups were visited by Sergeant Geegan. At the Union of Russian Workers about five hundred pamphlets were discovered in the icebox and were promptly confiscated by the police. Still later, in May 1921, Mayor John F. Hylan, addressing the National Police Conference in New York City, found it necessary to suggest a national system to control anarchists and other radicals. But, by 1922, the American Civil Liberties Union could again report that there was "comparatively little police interference" with radical meetings, whether held on public streets or in halls.

In upstate New York there were also a few sporadic incidents but nothing compared to the number which took place earlier. In one of these, Carlo Tresca was prevented from delivering a speech in Buffalo by order of the mayor. The ACLU intervened and the mayor was persuaded to reverse his decision. Other incidents took place in Schenectady, Albany, and Binghamton, where local authorities interfered with the showing of a film, "The Fifth Year," distributed by the Friends of Soviet Russia.

By 1924 government on all levels had withdrawn from the Red Scare. However, the patriotic organizations tried to keep the movement alive. These groups had come into being during the war and continued to flourish throughout the 1920s. In general, they opposed radicalism, favored immigration restriction, and attacked pacifist organizations on the grounds that they were also a part of the bolshevik conspiracy. Their antilabor bias was seen in their support of the open shop.

The many patriotic organizations were structurally dissimilar. Some, like the National Security League, the National Civic Federation, and the American Defense Society were national in scope. From their offices in New York and Washington they lobbied for more laws to curb the various radical organizations. Others, like the Allied Patriotic Societies and the "Keymen of America" were personal enterprises, usually built around the personality of one staunch antiradical. As such, they were not destined to outlive the life of their founder. The Ku Klux Klan and the American Legion were also prominent during this period. While they were not strictly patriotic organizations, they often carried out many of the same functions. Both the Klan and the Legion were organized differently from the patriotic organizations; their memberships were widely distributed throughout the country, and their national headquarters were used chiefly as clearinghouses.

The National Civic Federation was one of the three national patriotic organizations based in New York. It was under the direction of Ralph Easley, and occupied offices in the Metropolitan Tower Building. Easley started his career in Chicago as a civic reformer; he was the head of the Chicago Civic Federation which sought to solve industrial problems by developing a harmonious relationship between capital and labor. By 1914, under Easley's leadership, the Chicago Civic Federation began to widen its scope; it changed its name to the National Civic Federation and started to concentrate more heavily on the menace of socialism and other "foreign threats" to national security. The Federation was one of the first organizations to urge preparedness before World War I. After the Russian Revolution, it began the first of its many campaigns to counteract bolshevism.

In one respect, the National Civic Federation was unique, as it was the only patriotic organization supported by Samuel Gompers and the nonradical labor movement. Gompers joined because he believed that radicalism threatened the conservative labor movement. On the other hand, the Federation drew harsh criticism from left wing spokesmen. To Morris Hillquit, it was an "insidious poison" which robbed the labor movement of its vitality.

All of the patriotic organizations including the National Civic Federation were heavily financed. One estimate placed their total expenditures at two hundred and fifty thousand dollars a year. Only two, the National Security League and the Association for Constitutional Government ever gave a public accounting of their income and expenses. Their contributors included financiers, bankers, and corporation executives.

Structurally, the National Civic Federation was divided into nine departments. They were: Current Economic and Political Movements, Welfare, Immigration, Women's, Workmen's Compensation, Social Insurance, Revolutionary Movements, Public Health, Education, and Industry. These were divided into committees which studied such things as Soviet propaganda in the United States, radicalism in textbooks, and the extent to which "revolutionary forces" had penetrated into the infrastructure of American society.

While Easley's objectives of awakening the country to the bolshevik menace were sincere, his methods left much to be desired. For example, in his attack on disarmament and pacifism, he was once quoted as saying that if he had his way he would "drive every damned Quaker out of America." On another occasion, he referred to Mrs. Willard Straight, an outstanding liberal writer, as "the most dangerous woman in America," and to Mrs. Henry Villard, a philanthropist then eighty years old, as "the most notorious pro-German and leader of the nonresistance forces in this country at a time when they played into Germany's hands." Among others attacked publicly by Easley were Father John A. Ryan of the National Catholic Welfare Conference, the Reverend Gladdings Bell, President of St. Stephen's College, Bishop Charles Brent of Buffalo, the former chaplain of the American Expeditionary Forces, and H. G. Wells whose *Outline of History* was called a "wilful misrepresentation of the teachings of Jesus," and an example of the "unpatriotic Tolstoian psychology of nonresistance."

A second national organization, the National Security League, was similar to the National Civic Federation. Among its many activities, the League sent out speakers to any organization requesting them. It also organized street meetings in New York and debates on college campuses to combat radical influences. Its Educational Bureau was extremely active in sending out material to schools and colleges whose purpose was to instill a knowledge of our form of government, and a "reverence" for the Constitution, in order to "offset ignorance, radical criticism, and apathy." Its efforts were highly successful. For example, it persuaded the New York City Board of Education to revise its economics curriculum in accordance with guidelines suggested by the League.[10]

The League was one of the two organizations which made public its list of contributors. These included, in 1919, Nicholas F. Brady, the president of the New York Edison Company, H. H. Rogers, a director of Standard Oil, William K. Vanderbilt, director of several corporations, T. Coleman Du Pont of Du Pont

Powder Company, Henry C. Frick of the Carnegie Steel Company, George W. Perkins of the United States Steel Corporation, Simon and Daniel Guggenheim of Guggenheim Brothers, and the American Smelting and Refining Company, J. Pierpont Morgan and John D. Rockefeller. Their contributions ranged from $700 to $30,000 each. The League also solicited from smaller contributors in denominations of one dollar and up.

In 1919, the National Security League was the subject of a congressional investigation after it publicly charged some three hundred congressmen with disloyalty. In its report, the investigators found that the League was catering to large economic interests in steel, oil, guns, munitions, and railroads. As such it constituted a "serious menace to the representative government."

The American Defense Society was a third patriotic organization with headquarters in New York. Its chairman was Elon Hooker, the president of the Hooker Electro-Chemical Company. On its staff was a former newspaperman, Richard M. Whitney, the author of a popular antiradical book, *Reds in America*. At least part of this book was compiled through the records of the "red file" of the Justice Department's Bureau of Investigation, which was made available exclusively to Whitney. One of the strangest creations of the American Defense Society was something called the "Spider Web Chart," a joint effort of Richard M. Whitney, assisted by a librarian employed by the Gas and Warfare Service of the government. This was not intended for publication but it was secured by several newspapers and printed. Its major contention was that the pacifist and the Socialist movements were part of the same radical conspiracy. It listed the names of twenty-one Americans who were suspected of radicalism in varying degrees. At the head of this "Socialist-pacifist" plot was Mrs. Maud Wood Park, of the League of Women Voters, and Mrs. Frederick J. Libby, the head of the National Council for the Prevention of War, a "holding company for all of the peace societies in the United States." Also listed were Mrs. William A. White, the wife of the newspaperman, and Mrs. Gifford Pinchot, wife of a former government official.

Generally, the American Defense Society followed the familiar practice of failing to differentiate between types of radicals. To the Society, they all stood for the philosophy of "to hell with the government, to hell with the law, and to hell with the right of any person to be possessed of any property." In its 1924 report, the

Society summarized some of its activities: it had distributed over 90,000 copies of the Constitution of the United States free to school children, published an antipacifist pamphlet entitled "Peace at any Price," and, to inspire even greater patriotism, distributed 100,000 copies of Theodore Roosevelt's picture. Writing in *The Nation,* Will Irwin thought that part of its interest in preparedness was to increase the sale of poison gas manufactured by the Hooker Company, whose president was also chairman of the Society.[11]

The American Legion, a national organization of war veterans, also displayed many of the characteristics of a patriotic organization during these years. In successive conventions, the Legion urged the government to adopt a hard line towards radicals and others preaching "un-American doctrines." At its first convention in 1919, the Legion supported legislation that would enable "our law enforcing officials to rid our country of this scum who hate God, our country, our flag, and who prate of their privileges and refuse to perform their duties." [*sic*] It demanded that the government hurry up and deport all undesirable aliens. In its magazine, *The American Legion Weekly,* it speculated that perhaps execution might be "more merciful."[12]

In its 1921 convention, the Legion attempted to define the term "radical." This was anybody who attempted "to change our form of government through revolution." It also opposed the distribution, sale, or purchase of leftist literature. It urged its members to keep a "watchful eye" on all left wing propagandists and suggested that they be defeated by all "lawful means" to prevent the fulfillment of their plans. Owners of public halls were urged not to rent to radicals and newspapers were asked not to print advertisements announcing their meetings.

As a further antiradical measure, the Legion continued its efforts to Americanize the immigrants. Responsibility for this was placed in the hands of its National Americanism Commission whose stated goal was to "realize in the United States . . . the basic ideal of . . . one hundred per cent Americanism through the planning, establishment, and conduct of a continuous, constructive, educational establishment." To accomplish this, patriotic essay contests were organized and literature distributed in great quantities. However, in its preoccupation with good citizenship, the Legion fell into the common trap of believing that all radicals came from the ranks of the immigrants. Of 4,608 leftists rounded up by the government in the 1920 New Year's Day raids, only ten had good "American-sounding, U.S.A. names." Most of the others were clearly of foreign origin.

The Ku Klux Klan was still another organization which cashed in on the residue of antiforeignism left over from the Red Scare. Founded in Tennessee in 1886, the Klan spread quickly through the Southern states, using methods of terror and actual physical brutality to achieve its stated aim of making the Negro subservient. After a period of inactivity, the Klan was reorganized in 1915. It was strongly nativist and came out boldly against Catholics, Jews, the foreign born, and, of course, the Negro. When the Red Scare was at its height, the Klan followed the lead of the other patriotic organizations, and favored strong measures against bolshevism. In the 1920s it added its voice to those favoring the restriction of immigration, the "Americanization" of school texts, loyalty oaths for teachers, along with other schemes to "purify American life" of its non-Caucasian and foreign elements.

While the base of Klan power was always in the South, it spread rapidly to the West, and into many Northern cities as well. Klan chapters were established in a number of communities in upstate New York, on Long Island, and in New Jersey. In 1921 the Klan began to organize within New York City itself.

Klan efforts to infiltrate the Empire City were actively opposed by Mayor John F. Hylan who instructed his police commissioner to treat Klan members as he had formerly treated "reds and bomb throwers." Hylan wanted them driven out of the city as rapidly as they were discovered. Next, Hylan wrote to President Harding and requested that *Colonel Mayfield's Weekly,* a vicious Klan paper published in Texas and distributed in New York, be suppressed.

Hylan's strong opposition to the Klan was easily explained. In the first place, his own father was a Catholic; also, with so many ethnic, religious, and racial groups in the city it was, undoubtedly, good politics to oppose the KKK. Quite apart from these considerations, the Mayor himself was a decent man and was truly outraged by the Klan's intolerance.

The police department swung into action at once. Sergeant Geegan was ordered to keep the Klan under surveillance. The *World* predicted immediate results, remarking that Geegan and his men had the reputation of always "getting their man." Furthermore, the police commissioner submitted a detailed report of Klan activities in the city to the district attorney. It included the names of eight hundred Klansmen. Some lived in New York City proper, while others resided on Long Island, Jersey City, Newark, Passaic, Paterson, and a number of upstate communities including Buffalo and Troy.

Interestingly enough, the Klan received some unexpected support from the American Civil Liberties Union. While the ACLU hated everything the Klan stood for, it took exception to Hylan's instructions to the police commissioner that the Klansmen be "driven from the city." The Union felt that such statements incited the very lawlessness and violence which characterized the Klan. To Roger Baldwin, the director of the ACLU, it was as necessary to defend the Klan in 1922 as it had been to defend the radicals a few years earlier.

There is no doubt that the patriotic organizations, the Legion, and the Klan wielded great power during these years. As a group they were influential in upholding the torch of intolerance, setting the stage for immigration restriction, and the new surge of bigotry that swept America during the 1920s. It must be remembered, however, that the hatreds of the 'twenties were not created by the Klan or by any other organization. This bigotry served as a replacement for the Red Scare, as that had replaced the anti-German feelings of the war years. In this new form of prejudice all minority groups were suspect: the Catholics were questioned because their religious practices diverged from those of the majority of Protestant sects. The Jews were feared as competitors in the business world, and as symbols of all that was wrong with America's overcrowded cities. The Negroes were hated on racial grounds, and at least as far as the working classes were concerned, for their potential competition for jobs and housing. These manifold fears, suspicions, and hatreds resulted in the creation of a variety of discrimination devices, designed to keep the minority groups from rising too high on the socioeconomic ladder. For Catholics, outright discrimination was less severe; their large numbers and their remarkable ability to achieve success in business, politics, education, and the civil service helped soften the blow. For Jews, discrimination took the form of quotas on admission to educational institutions, to places of employment, and housing. For the Negro, discrimination was most devastating and extended into virtually every area of his life. Nevertheless, each minority group met this hostility in its own way and with varying degrees of success was able to surmount the obstacles.

The antiradical crusade also reappeared in the controversy surrounding the immigration legislation of the 1920s. The movement to control the flow of immigrants was a complex one, but the antiforeign attitudes generated by the Red Scare were much in evidence. Immigration restriction was a fairly recent development. It was conceived at the time that the "new immigrants," or those from Southern and Eastern Europe, began to enter the country in great numbers. In time, many people came to support the idea, often for contradictory reasons. Some people with frankly racist views hoped to preserve the racial and ethnic homogeneity of the American people. As one member of this group explained it, they hoped to prevent the "mongrelization of the Nordic races."[13] Others sought to bar immigrants in the belief that many of them were radicals, while still others favored restriction because they thought the new immigrants were overly conservative and, therefore, a possible hindrance to social progress. Owners of large companies favored immigration as a source of cheap labor; on the other hand, some employers opposed the flow on the grounds that it would strengthen the trade union movement. Labor unions supported restriction to lessen the threat to their members' jobs. Some advanced thinkers favored restriction as a method of population control, and as a necessary step towards a more ordered society. Regardless of the motivation, the movement began to assume an importance which could not be denied.

The first steps were taken in 1921, when President Harding signed the Emergency Quota, or Johnson Act. This new law provided that Congress could restrict the number of immigrants entering the country to 350,000 per year. Each European country was assigned a fixed quota based on the proportion of its nationals in the country according to the census of 1910. In effect, this discriminated against immigrants from Southern and Eastern Europe. The 1921 measure was made permanent in 1924, when the quota system based on national origins became a permanent feature of the immigration law. It was not repealed until the 1960s.

In New York reactions to the immigration legislation followed the national pattern. The New York Chamber of Commerce heartily endorsed the proposals and suggested that the federal government go even further in stopping the flow. Other business spokesmen saw unrestricted immigration as the creator of "deleterious social and economic conditions." They felt that the stream of immigrants was approaching the saturation point and might, in time, lead to an exhaustion of natural resources. William F. Kehoe, the secretary of the Trades and Labor Council of New York (AFL), agreed with the businessmen but for different reasons. Kehoe urged a complete embargo on all immigration as a method of keeping wage levels high. *The New York Times* put the case for restriction this way: "It is both natural and wise that the American race wishes to preserve its unity, and does not care to see the present blend greatly changed."[14] The views of New York's mayor, John F. Hylan, were interesting. In 1922 Hylan opposed restriction but qualified his opposition by saying that a larger number of immigrants from Northern Europe would be "highly desirable." By 1924, possibly in response to the escalating hostility to restriction based on discriminatory quotas, Hylan altered his views. He now said that immigrants from various parts of Europe were equally desirable as they would all help to build the country.

On the other hand, immigrant groups and liberal politicians spoke out as forcefully on this issue as they had against the nativist aspects of the antiradical crusade. For instance, when the National Origins Act of 1924 was being considered, Congressman Fiorello H. LaGuardia of New York opposed its quotas as discriminatory:

> The discrimination against immigrants of the Jewish faith and against Italians is so apparent that its true purpose cannot be disguised, and the majority party cannot escape the responsibility if it permits such narrow-minded religious and racial prejudice to be enacted into law.

Essentially the same point was made by Rabbi Nathan Krass, a liberal, who wondered what would have happened if "a committee of Indian immigration officers had stood on Pilgrim Rock and, after admitting ten Pilgrim Fathers, had said, 'Your quota is full. The rest of you go back to England.'" Finally, the *New York American* addressed itself to the charge that the new immigrants made poor Americans: "Not our immigrants, but our lawmakers are in need of Americanization and rededication to the ideals of the Republic."[15]

Thus, by 1924 the curtain came down on the antiradical crusade. The radical movements were in eclipse and the public had little interest in pursuing the question any further.

The return of good times was partly the cause. An antiradical crusade demands an intense commitment. The public must be kept in a state of heightened, almost revolutionary fervor. As many public figures have since discovered, it is difficult to maintain this for any length of time. Barring the most extreme provocation, normalcy soon returns to capture the public mood. The patriotic organizations utilized the momentum generated by the Red Scare. But their accomplishments were nil as were those of the Klan which never made the inroads in New York that its supporters had hoped it would. Even the American Legion, always in the forefront of antiradicalism, soon muted its more extreme utterances.

Still another aspect explaining the waning of the Red Scare was a change in the status of the immigrants. As fewer immigrants came into the country after 1924, the problem of the unassimilable foreigner began to solve itself. Those who were already here began to find a place for themselves in the American mainstream; their children were little interested in the radical movements which sustained their parents. Thus, as the natural victim of the Red Scare began to disappear, so too did the movement.

Developments in the Soviet Union were also a cause. During the 1920s, Russia began its long descent into bureaucracy and totalitarianism. Many American radicals observed these events with increasing dismay. Their effect was to deplete the leftist ranks still further.

NOTES

1. In a speech to the 1920 Convention of the Socialist party, Cahan said: "We have been flirting with Soviet Russia long enough. Somehow, at first, we all felt there was a man, Lenin, who was willing to make a great trial of Communism. We thought it worthwhile to give the revolutionists a chance, and see how they would work it out. . . . We have given them their chance, but they have failed." Quoted in *New York Times,* May 20, 1923, II, 1.
2. For press opinion, see "Drastic Sedition Laws," *Literary Digest,* January 24, 1920, p. 18; *New York Times,* January 7, 1920, p. 20.
3. Quoted in "Justice for Alien Reds: Policy of Louis F. Post," *Literary Digest,* May 22, 1920, p. 25.
4. *New York Tribune,* December 26, 1919, in ACLU Archives, Vol. 66.
5. Decision in the Case of Marie Salsedo v. A. Mitchell Palmer, *et al.,* typewritten, in the Department of Justice Files, No. 213479-19, National Archives.
6. *New York Times,* December 26, 1921, p. 12.

7. For a different interpretation, see Department of Labor Research, *American Labor Yearbook* (New York, 1923–24), pp. 209–10, whose editor believed that Harding backtracked after freeing Debs "probably" due to the "large industrial strikes then in progress"; in *Incredible Era: The Life and Times of Warren Gamaliel Harding* (Boston, 1939), pp. 254–55, Samuel Hopkins Adams stressed Harding's humane feelings as his reason for freeing Debs.

8. Albert D. Silver, then head of the ACLU, wrote: "They are getting some sense down in Washington, too. The new administration . . . is an administration of practical politicians, and while the Republican boys can certainly not lay claim to any taint of intellectuality . . . they have . . . more practical horse sense than the Democrats had. The new Attorney General [Daugherty] is a nice fat man with a big cigar in his face and instead of getting excited as Palmer used to do, he groans when somebody talks about revolution and says well, he thinks it is probably best 'not to agitate too much.' " Quoted in Harold Hyman, *To Try Men's Souls: Loyalty Oaths in American History* (Berkeley, 1960), p. 322.

9. "New York Chamber of Commerce Describes the Wall Street Explosion as an Act of War," *Commercial and Financial Chronicle,* October 16, 1920, p. 1526.

10. The revision incorporated concepts of classical economics in an apparent effort to offset any ideas which might threaten free enterprise.

11. Will Irwin, "Patriotism That Pays," *The Nation,* November 12, 1924, p. 513.

12. *American Legion Weekly,* January 9, 1920, p. 10.

13. He was Rear Admiral Caspar F. Goodrich, U.S. Navy.

14. *New York Times,* April 5, 1924, clippings in the John F. Hylan Papers (Municipal Archives and Reference Center, N.Y.), Box 349. Six months earlier the *Times* had supported restriction on the grounds that all of the free land was gone and the period of expansion was over. In addition, it pointed out the danger of "foreign colonies taking permanent form within our territories." *Ibid.,* October 20, 1923, p. 14.

15. *New York American,* December 17, 1923, in the Hylan Papers, Box 349.

Chapter Ten

CONCLUSIONS

This history of the antiradical crusade in New York has led to the following conclusions. In general, events here conformed to the national pattern. Both were characterized by many public raids, investigations, and convictions of leftists. In each case, press coverage tended to heighten fears of leftist subversion. This sensationalism increased the prevailing hysteria and encouraged politicians to plan even greater antiradical moves. In New York, as elsewhere, the scope of the Red Scare soon widened to include, not only leftists, but liberals and some labor leaders as well.

In terms of causation, our study substantiates the findings of Stanley Coben and other scholars. These historians have explained the Red Scare as a movement of national regeneration dedicated to the removal of the twin cancers of foreignism and radicalism from the American body politic. According to this interpretation, American values were felt to be threatened by a variety of factors including foreign ideologies, immigrants, and leftists. Hence, the Red Scare was a necessary device to remove these unwholesome, "un-American" influences. Once this was accomplished, the nation could return to a preexisting "Golden Age."[1]

There were, however, a number of factors which made the New York experience somewhat unique. The large concentration of leftists and immigrants, the success of the Socialist party in electing its people to public office, and the immediate tensions produced by the postwar demobilization combined to heighten public fears even further. Then, too, the Red Scare in New York was better organized. In addition to occasional mobs and the more formal patriotic organizations, it involved governments on all levels, state and municipal. This superior organization was best illustrated by the work of the Lusk Committee, and by the efforts of the Judiciary Committee in the expulsion of its five

Socialist members. It was further in evidence during the trials of the New York Communists convicted of violating the Statute on Criminal Anarchy. Furthermore, in New York, the Red Scare lasted longer than it did in most other states. This was traced to the length of the trial of the five Socialists and to the fears stirred up by the Wall Street bombing of 1920. Eventually, the Red Scare lost its momentum even here as New Yorkers turned their attention to issues of a more pressing nature.

As we have seen, the elements for a Red Scare in New York existed as far back as 1914. New York City, the most populous city in the state, took the lead. At this time, antiradical feelings were related to leftist attempts to agitate on behalf of the urban unemployed and the striking Colorado miners. Still, city officials acted with moderation, and there were no wholesale efforts to interfere with the "legal" aspects of organized radicalism. This situation changed drastically once the nation went to war. Responding to intense public pressure, Mayor Hylan ordered a ban on all displays of the red flag. The police disrupted radical meetings and made it all but impossible for them to rent halls. Meanwhile, public school officials in various cities carried out a witch hunt against "unpatriotic" teachers and students. This official policy tended to unleash other rightist elements whose own vigilante efforts were legitimized and added to the harassment of the left.

The postwar Red Scare intensified feelings developed during the war. With the foreign enemy defeated, the full weight of the prevailing hysteria fell heavily on the left. Again, New York City, with its history of bombings and bomb scares, became the focal point of the antiradical crusade. The virus spread to a score of upstate communities, all of which had considerable past experience with radicals and with aggressive trade unions, some under leftist leadership. At this point, the Republican-dominated state legislature responded to the leftist "threat." Its response was motivated by two considerations. Many legislators were sincerely convinced that the forces on the left were growing and needed to be controlled. In addition, they used the opportunity presented to strike a blow against the Democrat-controlled cities, with their large concentrations of reformers, progressives, immigrants, and Socialists. This urban-rural, or liberal-conservative, confrontation was an important ingredient of the New York Red Scare.

It was always beneath the surface but it appeared prominently on several occasions.

The career of the Lusk Committee was a case in point. It provided a clear illustration of antiradical hysteria and of the urban-rural clash. It also showed that the Red Scare benefited by the involvement of the government. Financed by an appropriation of thousands of dollars, the Lusk Committee embarked on one of the most thorough investigations of New York radicalism ever attempted. If its results were meagre, and they most certainly were, it can only be attributed to the committee's misdirected efforts in investigating a conspiracy which did not exist.

Urban-rural conflict was also in evidence during the trial of the five Socialists. While the trial appeared to be simply another manifestation of antiradicalism, it was, in a deeper sense, part of the drive to restore those traditional values which many thought were challenged by foreign-radical groups in the cities. In reality, the trial was a success; the Socialists were expelled. But the expulsion had a further result which the Judiciary Committee had not anticipated. Once its real meaning became known, it helped set in motion those forces working towards an end to antiradical hysteria. In this way, too, the New York Red Scare was exceptional.

The study has also explored attitudes held by the public towards the left. We have seen how the radicals excited strong negative feelings on the part of the business community, the labor unions, the churches, and others in the public at large. In general, the left was opposed because of the popular belief that it sought, not merely the rectification of certain economic and political problems, but the replacement of the entire system by a competing one based on a foreign ideology. Related to this was the view that the left was conspiratorial in nature; this conspiracy, it was thought, threatened the very existence of the American way of life. While many of these fears were excessive, even irrational, there was, considering the totalitarian nature of communism in later years, some degree of justification to them. Unfortunately, those who carried out the Red Scare were highly unselective, and tended to include the Socialist party and the other democratic elements on the left, in the same category as the totalitarian Communist party. As a consequence of this decision, the immigrant and the alien radical became the unfortunate and defenseless scapegoats of the hysteria of the times, as did those liberals who merely supported the right of leftists to be protected by normal constitutional safeguards. These were some of the mistakes which were committed during the antiradical crusade in New York. But there were others.

The advocates of the Red Scare, it would appear, were in error in never bothering to define with any degree of precision exactly what constituted subversion. In a calmer period, one distinguished writer, Walter Gellhorn, had attempted to do this.[2] In Gellhorn's view, subversion included the use of violent or otherwise unconstitutional means to change a nation's political or economic institutions; the commission of espionage or other crimes in behalf of foreign enemies or domestic groups; the bearing of arms against the United States or carrying out other acts in favor of foreign powers; entering into a conspiracy to do any of these acts or attempting to carry them out. All of these were definitely subversive, and if they had taken place would have justified punishment. But none of these occurred during the Red Scare. Instead, individuals were convicted or otherwise harassed for mere membership in organizations which allegedly taught or advocated revolution and not for the commission of the acts themselves. Thus, if any lesson can be learned from the period, it must be that governments should be wary of prosecuting beliefs or teachings in the absence of acts.

Still another error committed by the leaders of the Red Scare was their erroneous definition of loyalty. During these years, there was a strong tendency to define loyalty as a fixed quantity, as conformity to existing political and economic institutions, and to the mandated policies of the government. Under this definition loyalty could be proven in a number of ways. For example, service in the army was an act of loyalty. Loyalty could also be proven by membership in a patriotic organization, by advocating militarism, or by such ritualistic signs of loyalty as saluting the flag, or marching in a parade. Conversely, anyone who questioned the status quo, whether it was the institution of capitalism, the two-party system, or the righteousness of war was, by definition, disloyal or un-American. This definition of loyalty was and still is too narrow; for loyalty as conformity negates the concept of progress. It considers institutions as static entities, whereas they are, in reality, dynamic and must be subject to constant scrutiny. The long-range view of American history bears this out; all of our institutions have undergone modifications as conditions war-

ranted. The Constitution itself, through the use of the elastic
clause and the amending process, makes provision for change.
Thus, to inhibit the right of radicals to question the war, the
economic system, and even the moral fabric of the nation was
to deny them a basic right, and, in the long run to do violence
to the real meaning of American democracy.

A final but related error committed during the period was
narrowing the range of permissible dissent. One can well understand how the public reacted with horror when the left opposed
the war. Perhaps a restriction of the bounds of dissent might
have been justified during this period of national emergency.
It was more difficult to justify it during the following two years.
These were years of peace but the same intolerance of dissenting opinions reappeared. As we have seen, many felt that the
leftist threat was sufficient to justify a constriction of the limits
of dissent. This, too, was unfortunate. For if a society is strong,
if economic wants are provided for, if avenues for the expression
of protest are available, it is unlikely that the vast majority of
citizens will follow the few malcontents who hope to destroy the
society by violent revolution. The Red Scare might have been
avoided by the implementation of more liberal economic reforms,
and then by dealing with those who practiced subversion *as individuals* and not as members of a group. To attempt to meet
problems by the use of the mass raid and deportations was not
a satisfactory substitute.

NOTES

1. See Stanley Coben, "A Study in Nativism: The American Red Scare
   of 1919–20," *Political Science Quarterly*, LXXIX (March, 1964),
   pp. 55–75.
2. Walter Gellhorn, *The States and Subversion* (Ithaca, 1952), p. 359.

BIBLIOGRAPHY

Manuscripts and Archives

Archives of the American Civil Liberties Union. New York Public Library.

August Claessens Papers. Tamiment Library, New York.

Department of Justice Files. National Archives.

Department of Labor Files. National Archives.

Emma Goldman Papers. New York Public Library.

Warren G. Harding Papers. Library of Congress.

John F. Hylan Papers. Municipal Archives and Records Center. New York.

David F. Karsner Papers. New York Public Library.

Algernon Lee Papers. Tamiment Library, New York.

Papers of the National Civic Federation. New York Public Library.

A. Mitchell Palmer Papers. Library of Congress.

Charles Solomon Papers. Tamiment Library, New York.

William Sulzer Papers. New York Public Library.

B. Charney Vladeck Papers. Tamiment Library, New York.

Frank P. Walsh Papers. New York Public Library.

Woodrow Wilson Papers. Library of Congress.

Public Documents

McKinney's *Consolidated Laws of New York*. Brooklyn, New York: Edward Thompson Co., 1938. Sec. 160.

New York, *Constitution,* Art. 13, sec. 1.

New York State. *Annual Reports of the Attorney General.* Albany: J. Lyons Co., 1914–1924.

————. *Journal of the Assembly of the State of New York.* 143 Session, 1920.

————. *Proceedings of the Judiciary Committee of the Assem-*

bly in the Matter of the Qualifications of Its Socialist Members. Leg. Doc. No. 35. Albany: J. Lyons Co., 1920. 3 Vols.

Proceedings of the Board of Aldermen of the City of New York. New York: The Board, 1919. Vol. I.

Senate of the State of New York. *Revolutionary Radicalism.* Report of the Joint Legislative Committee Investigating Radical Activities, filed April 24, 1920. Albany: J. Lyons Co., 1920. 4 Vols.

U.S. Department of Commerce. *Historical Statistics of the United States.* Washington, D.C.: Government Printing Office, 1960.

U.S. Department of Justice. *Reports of the Attorney General.* Washington, D.C.: Government Printing Office, 1914–1924.

U.S. House of Representatives. Committee on Rules, *Hearings, Attorney General Palmer on Charges Made Against the Department of Justice by Louis F. Post and Others.* 66 Cong., 2d Sess., 1920.

————. Committee on Rules, *Investigation of the Administration of Louis F. Post, Assistant Secretary of Labor in Matter of Deportation of Aliens.* 66 Cong., 2d Sess., 1920.

————. *Investigation of the National Security League.* Report No. 1173. 65 Cong., 3d Sess., 1919.

U.S. Senate. Committee on the Judiciary. *Hearings, Charges of Illegal Practices of the Department of Justice.* 66 Cong., 3d Sess., 1921.

Cases

Van Gerichten v. *Seitz,* 94 N.Y. App. Div. 130 (1904).

Goldman v. *United States,* 245 U.S. 474 (1918).

Kramer et al. v. *United States,* 245 U.S. 478 (1918).

Masses Publishing Co. v. *Patten,* 244 Fed. Rep. 535, 245 Fed. Rep. 102, 246 Fed. Rep. 24 (1918).

United States v. *Binder,* 253 Fed. 978 (1918).

Abrams v. *United States,* 250 U.S. 616 (1919).

Debs v. *United States,* 249 U.S. 216 (1919).

Schenck v. *United States,* 249 U.S. 47 (1919).

Colyer et al. v. *Skeffington,* 265 Fed. 17 (1920).

Pierce et al. v. *United States,* 252 U.S. 239 (1920).

People v. *Gitlow,* 111 N.Y. Misc. 641 (1920), 195 App. Div. 773 (1921), 234 N.Y. 132 (1922).

People v. *Ferguson and Ruthenberg,* 234 N.Y. 159 (1922).
People v. *American Socialist Society,* 202 N.Y. App. Div. 640 (1922).
People v. *Larkin,* 234 N.Y. 530 (1922).
Skeffington v. *Katzeff,* 277 Fed. 129 (1922).
Meyer v. *Nebraska,* 262 U.S. 390 (1923).
Gitlow v. *New York,* 268 U.S. 652 (1925).
Pierce v. *Society of Sisters,* 268 U.S. 510 (1925).

Pamphlets, Minutes, Speeches, etc.

"The A B C of Hylanism," a pamphlet, n.d., n.p., in the New York Public Library.
Address of Richard E. Enright, Police Commissioner at a Dinner at the Waldorf Astoria, October 6, 1920, in the New York Public Library.
American Civil Liberties Union. *Annual Reports, 1921–1924.* New York: American Civil Liberties Union, 1921–1924.
———. "Fight for Free Speech," *Report for 1920–1921.* New York: American Civil Liberties Union, 1921.
———. *State Political Prisoners.* New York: American Civil Liberties Union, 1924.
American Jewish Committee. *File on Jews and Communism.* In the Library of the American Jewish Committee, New York.
———. *The Protocols, Bolshevism, and the Jews.* New York: The Committee, 1921.
American Legion. *Summary of the Proceedings of the National Conventions, 1919–1924.* Locations vary: The Legion, 1919–24.
Association of the Bar of the City of New York. *Brief of the Special Committee Appointed by the Bar of the City of New York in the Matter of L. Waldman, A. Claessens, S. DeWitt, S. Orr, C. Solomon,* January 20, 1920. Reports, XXI, Leg. Doc. 219. New York: The Association, 1920.
———. *Resolution Adopted January 13, 1920, Respecting the Suspended Socialists.* Reports, XXI, Leg. Doc. 217. New York: The Association, 1920.
———. *Statement by the Special Committee Appointed by the Association of the Bar of the City of New York.* Reports, XXI. New York: The Association, 1920.

Biographical Materials on Samuel Orr. Tamiment Library, New York.

Central Conference of American Rabbis. *Justice and Peace.* Resolutions passed 1917–1956. New York: The Conference, 1956.

———. *Twenty-Sixth Annual Convention* (Michigan, 1915). Yearbook No. 25. Michigan: The Central Conference, 1915.

———. *Thirty-Fifth Annual Convention* (Ohio, 1924). Ohio: The Central Conference, 1924.

Claessens, August. *Didn't We Have Fun.* New York: The Rand School, 1953.

———. *The Socialists in the New York Assembly: Work of the Ten Socialist Members During the Legislative Session of 1918.* New York: The Rand School, 1918.

A Collection of Trials Involving Allegiance to the Communist Party. *Gitlow, Ferguson and Ruthenberg.* New York Public Library (Microfilm).

Handlin, Oscar. *American Jews: Their History.* New York: Anti-Defamation League, n.d.

Linville, Henry R. *The Gag on Teaching.* New York: American Civil Liberties Union, 1931.

Marvin, Fred R. *Are These Your Friends?* Denver: Americanization Press Service, 1922.

Methodist Church. *Minutes of the New York Conference of the Methodist Church.* Report of the Committee on the State of the Country. New York, 1919.

Methodist Federation of Social Service. *The Social Service Bulletin.* 1918–1923.

National Civic Federation. *The Social Problem as Seen From the View Point of Trade Unionism, Capital, and Socialism.* New York: The Federation, 1914.

National Civil Liberties Bureau. *War Time Prosecutions and Mob Violence.* New York City: The Bureau, 1919.

National Defense Committee: *A Communist Trial: Excerpts from the Testimony of Charles E. Ruthenberg and the Closing Address to the Jury by Isaac E. Ferguson.* New York: National Defense Committee, n.d.

National Popular Government League. *Report on the Illegal Practices of the United States Department of Justice by Twelve Lawyers.* Washington, D.C.: National Popular Government League, 1920.

National Republican Club. *The Spread of Socialistic Doctrine in New York City*. Report of a Special Committee appointed by the Honorable Charles D. Hilles, September 16, 1919. New York, 1919.

Nelles, Walter. *Seeing Red: Civil Liberties and Law in the Period Following the War*. New York: American Civil Liberties Union, 1920.

New York City, Board of Education. *Annual Report of the President of the Board of Education to the Mayor of the City of New York*. Submitted September, 1920. New York, 1920.

New York City, Office of the Police Commissioner. *General Orders for 1919–1921*. New York: The Department of Police, 1919–21.

New York City, Police Department of the City of New York. *Annual Report for 1919*. New York: Bureau of Printing, 1919.

O'Brian, John L. *Civil Liberties in Wartime*. New York: Bar Association of the City of New York, 1919.

Platform of the Socialist Party of the State of New York. New York: The Socialist Party, 1911.

Program of a Testimonial Dinner to Judge Samuel Orr. Hotel Shelburne, April 14, 1951. Tamiment Library, New York.

Riley, John L. *Administration and Organization of Immigrant Education in the State of New York*. University of the State of New York Bulletin No. 765. New York: University of the State of New York, 1922.

Russell, Charles Edward. *What the Socialist Candidate for Governor of New York Has to Say in Accepting Nomination*. New York: The Socialist Party, 1919.

Schenectady Socialist Party Campaign Book. Schenectady: Campaign Committee, Socialist Party, 1913.

Socialist Aldermen's Delegation to the New York City Board of Aldermen. Minutes of Meetings. 1917–1919. (Typewritten) Tamiment Library, New York.

Socialist Aldermen's Scrapbook. 1917–1920. Tamiment Library, New York.

Socialist Party of New York. *Platform of the Socialist Party in New York*, 1911.

Socialist Party of the United States. Minutes of Meetings of the Central Committee of the New York Local of the Socialist

Party. 1916–1920. (Typewritten) Tamiment Library, New York.

———. Minutes of Meetings of the Executive Committee of the New York Local of the Socialist Party. 1916–1920. (Typewritten) Tamiment Library, New York.

Smith, Alfred E. *Progressive Democracy: Addresses and State Papers of Alfred E. Smith.* New York: Harcourt Brace and Co., 1928.

———. *Public Papers of Alfred E. Smith.* Albany: J. B. Lyons Co., 1924.

Books, Encyclopedias, Theses

Abbott, Edith. *Immigration: Select Documents and Case Records.* Chicago: University of Chicago Press, 1924.

Adams, Samuel Hopkins. *Incredible Era: Life and Times of Warren Gamaliel Harding.* Boston: Houghton Mifflin, 1939.

Allen, Frederick L. *Only Yesterday: An Informal History of the Nineteen-Twenties.* New York: Harper and Row, 1964 ed.

Anderson, Paul H. *The Attitude of American Leftist Leaders Towards the Russian Revolution, 1917–1923.* Indiana: Notre Dame, 1942.

Barth, Alan. *The Loyalty of Free Men.* New York: Viking Press, 1952.

Beale, Howard K. *Are American Teachers Free?* New York: Scribner's, 1936.

Bell, Daniel. "Background of Marxian Socialism in the United States." *Socialism in American Life,* ed. Donald Egbert and Stow Persons. 2 vols. Princeton: Princeton University Press, 1952.

Berkman, Alexander. *The Bolshevik Myth: Diary, 1920–1922.* New York: Boni and Liveright, 1925.

Bestor, Arthur. *Backwards Utopias.* Philadelphia: University of Pennsylvania Press, 1950.

Brissenden, Paul. *The IWW: Study in American Syndicalism.* New York: Russell and Russell, 1957.

———. "Industrial Workers of the World." *Encyclopedia of the Social Sciences,* ed. Edwin R. A. Seligman. Vol. 8. New York: Macmillan, 1932.

Broderick, Francis L. *Right Reverend New Dealer: John A. Ryan.* New York: Macmillan, 1963.

Chafee, Zechariah. *Free Speech in the United States*. Cambridge: Harvard University Press, 1941.

Chamberlain, Lawrence. *Loyalty and Legislative Action: A Survey of Activity by the New York State Legislature, 1919–1949*. Ithaca: Cornell University Press, 1951.

Claghorn, Kate. *Immigrant's Day in Court*. New York: Harpers, 1923.

Coben, Stanley A. *A. Mitchell Palmer: Politician*. New York: Columbia University Press, 1963.

Commager, Henry S. *The American Mind*. New Haven: Yale University Press, 1950.

Commons, John R. "The American Federation of Labor." *Encyclopedia of the Social Sciences*, ed. Edwin R. A. Seligman. Vol. II. New York: Macmillan, 1932.

————. *History of Labor in the United States*. 4 Vols. New York: Macmillan, 1935.

Corwin, Edward J. *The President: Office and Powers*. New York: New York University Press, 1940.

Davis, Jerome. *The Russian Immigrant*. New York: Macmillan, 1926.

Department of Labor Research. *The American Labor Yearbook. 1916–1925*. New York: Rand School, 1916–26.

Dombrowski, James. *The Early Days of Christian Socialism in America*. New York: Columbia University Press, 1936.

Draper, Theodore. *The Roots of American Communism*. New York: Viking, 1957.

Dubofsky, Melvyn. *We Shall Be All: A History of the IWW*. Chicago: Quadrangle Books, 1969.

Dulles, Foster R. *Labor in America*. New York: Crowell, 1960.

Fine, Nathan. *Labor and Farmer Parties in the United States. 1828–1928*. New York: Russell and Russell, 1961.

Fleischman, Harry. *Norman Thomas: A Biography*. New York: W. W. Norton and Co., 1964.

Flynn, Elizabeth Gurley. *Debs, Haywood, and Ruthenberg*. New York: Workers Library Publishers, 1939.

————. *I Speak My Own Piece*. New York: Masses and Mainstream, 1955.

Foner, Philip S. *The Bolshevik Revolution, Its Impact on American Radicals, Liberals, and Labor*. New York: International Publishers, 1967.

———. *History of the Labor Movement in the United States.* 4 Vols. New York: International Publishers, 1965.

Fosdick, Raymond B. *John D. Rockefeller, Jr.: A Portrait.* New York: Harper, 1956.

Foster, William Z. *The History of the Communist Party in the United States.* New York: International Publishers, 1952.

Gambs, John. *The Decline of the IWW.* New York: Columbia University Press, 1932.

Gellhorn, Walter (ed.). *The States and Subversion.* Ithaca: Cornell University Press, 1952.

George, Henry. *Progress and Poverty.* New York: Robert Schalkenbach Foundation, 1940.

Ghent, William T. *The Reds Bring Reaction.* Princeton, N.J.: The Princeton University Press, 1923.

Gitlow, Benjamin. *I Confess: The Truth About American Communism.* New York: Dutton, 1940.

———. *The Whole of Their Lives.* New York: Scribner's, 1948.

Glazer, Nathan. *The Social Basis of American Communism.* New York: Harcourt Brace, 1961.

Goldman, Emma. *Living My Life.* 2 Vols. New York: Knopf, 1931.

Goldman, Eric F. *Rendezvous With Destiny.* New York: Vintage, 1952.

Goldsmith, Margaret. *Seven Against the World.* London: Methuen and Co., 1935.

Gompers, Samuel. *Seventy Years of Life and Labour: An Autobiography.* 2 Vols. New York: Dutton, 1925.

Handlin, Oscar. *Al Smith and His America.* Boston: Little, Brown, 1958.

———. *The American People in the Twentieth Century.* Cambridge: Harvard University Press, 1954.

———. *The Uprooted.* Boston: Little, Brown, 1951.

Hapgood, Norman. *Professional Patriots.* New York: Boni, 1927.

Haywood, William D. *Bill Haywood's Book.* New York: International, 1929.

Higham, John. *Strangers in the Land: Patterns of American Nativism (1860–1925).* New Brunswick, N.J.: Rutgers University Press, 1955.

Hillquit, Morris. *From Marx to Lenin.* New York: Hanford Press, 1921.

————. *History of Socialism in the United States*. New York: Funk and Wagnalls, 1903.

————. *Loose Leaves From a Busy Life*. New York: Macmillan, 1934.

———— and John A. Ryan. *Socialism: Promise or Menace*. New York: Macmillan, 1920.

————. *Socialism in Theory and Practice*. New York: Macmillan, 1910.

Howe, Frederick. *The Confessions of a Reformer*. New York: Scribner's, 1926.

Hylan, John F. *Mayor of New York: An Autobiography*. New York: Rotary Press, 1922.

Hyman, Harold M. *To Try Men's Souls: Loyalty Tests in American History*. Berkeley: University of California Press, 1960.

Jackson, Kenneth T. *The Ku Klux Klan in the City, 1915–1930*. New York: Oxford University Press, 1967.

Jessup, Philip C. *Elihu Root*. 2 Vols. New York: Dodd, Mead and Co., 1938.

Johnson, Donald. *The Challenge to American Freedoms: World War I and the Rise of the American Civil Liberties Union*. Lexington: University of Kentucky Press, 1963.

Johnson, Oakley C. *The Day Is Coming: The Life and Work of Charles E. Ruthenberg*. New York: International Publishers, 1927.

Johnson, Walter. *William Allen White's America*. New York: Henry Holt, 1947.

Jones, Maldwyn Allen. *American Immigration*. Chicago: University of Chicago Press, 1960.

Josephson, Matthew. *Sidney Hillman: Statesman of American Labor*. New York: Doubleday and Co., 1952.

Kelly, Alfred H. and Harbison, Winfred A. *The American Constitution: Its Origins and Development*. New York: W. W. Norton and Co., 1955.

Key, V. O. *Politics, Parties, and Pressure Groups*. 5th ed. New York: Crowell, 1964.

Kipnis, Ira. *American Socialist Movement, 1897–1912*. New York: Columbia University Press, 1952.

Konvitz, Milton R. *Civil Rights in Immigration*. Ithaca: Cornell University Press, 1953.

LaFollette, Bella Case and LaFollette, Fola. *Robert M. LaFollette*. New York: Macmillan, 1953.

Larkin, Emmett. *James Larkin: 1876–1947.* Cambridge: The MIT Press, 1965.

Link, Arthur S. *American Epoch.* New York: Knopf, 1956.

———. *Woodrow Wilson and the Progressive Era.* New York: Harper and Row, 1963.

Mann, Arthur. *La Guardia: A Fighter Against His Times, 1882–1937.* New York: J. B. Lippincott, 1959.

Marx, Karl and Engels, Friedrich. "The Communist Manifesto." In *The Essential Works of Marxism.* Edited by Arthur P. Mendel. New York: Bantam Books, 1961.

———. *Selected Correspondence: 1846–1895.* New York: International Publishers, 1942.

Mason, Alpheus Thomas. *Brandeis: A Free Man's Life.* New York: Viking Press, 1946.

———. *William Howard Taft: Chief Justice.* New York: Simon and Schuster, 1965.

McCoy, Donald R. *Calvin Coolidge: The Quiet President.* New York: Macmillan Co., 1967.

Menes, Abraham. "The Jewish Labor Movement." In *The Jewish People: Past and Present.* Vol. IV. New York: Jewish Encyclopedia Handbooks, 1955.

Mereto, Joseph J. *The Red Conspiracy.* New York: National Historical Society, 1920.

Meyer, Donald B. *The Protestant Search for Political Realism (1919–1941).* Los Angeles: University of California Press, 1960.

Miller, Robert M. *American Protestantism and Social Issues (1919–1939).* Chapel Hill, N.C.: Chapel Hill Press, 1958.

Mock, James R. *Censorship, 1917.* New Jersey: Princeton University Press, 1941.

Murray, Robert K. *The Red Scare: A Study in National Hysteria, 1919–1920.* Minneapolis: University of Minnesota Press, 1955.

Myers, Gustavus. *The History of Bigotry in the United States.* New York: Random House, 1960.

Nelles, Walter. *A Liberal in Wartime.* New York: W. W. Norton Co., 1940.

Nevins, Allen. *John D. Rockefeller.* New York: Charles Scribner's Sons, 1940.

Panunzio, Constantine. *Deportation Cases of 1919–1920*. New York: Federal Council of Churches of Christ in America, 1921.

Paxson, Frederic L. *America At War: 1917–1918*. Boston: Houghton Mifflin, 1939.

Peterson, Horace S. and Fite, Gilbert C. *Opponents of War: 1917–1918*. Madison, Wisconsin: University of Wisconsin Press, 1957.

Petix, Joseph R. "An Account of the Investigation of Radical Activities in New York Following World War I, Chiefly As Reported in the New York Times." Unpublished Master's dissertation. Department of History, New York University, 1951.

Pierce, Bessie L. *Public Opinion and the Teaching of History in the United States*. New York: Knopf, 1926.

Post, Louis F. *The Deportation Deliriums of the Nineteen-Twenties*. Chicago: Charles Kerr, 1923.

Preston, William. *Aliens and Dissenters: 1903–1933*. Cambridge: Harvard University Press, 1963.

Pringle, Henry F. *Theodore Roosevelt: A Biography*. New York: Harcourt, Brace, 1931.

————. *The Life and Times of William H. Taft*. New York: Farrar and Rinehart, 1939.

Pusey, Merlo J. *Charles Evans Hughes*. 2 Vols. New York: Macmillan, 1951.

Quint, Howard H. *The Forging of American Socialism*. Columbia, S.C.: University of South Carolina Press, 1953.

Reznikoff, Charles. *Selected Papers and Addresses of Louis Marshall*. Philadelphia: Jewish Publication Society, 1957.

Rich, J. C. "The Jewish Labor Movement in the United States." In *The Jewish People: Past and Present*. Vol. II. New York: Jewish Encyclopedia Handbooks, 1955.

Roche, John P. *The Quest for the Dream*. New York: Macmillan, 1963.

Root, Elihu. *Addresses on Government and Citizenship*. Cambridge: Harvard University Press, 1916.

Roy, Ralph Lord. *Apostles of Discord*. Boston: Beacon Press, 1953.

————. *Communism and the Churches*. New York: Harcourt, Brace, 1960.

Russell, Charles Edward. *Bare Hands and Stone Walls: Some*

Reflections of a Side Line Reformer. New York: Charles Scribner's Sons, 1933.

Savage, Marion D. *Industrial Unionism in America*. New York: Ronald Press, 1922.

Seidman, Joel. *The Needle Trades*. New York: Farrar and Rinehart, 1942.

Shannon, David A. *Between the Wars: America, 1919–1941*. Boston: Houghton Mifflin, 1965.

———. *The Socialist Party of America*. New York: Macmillan Co., 1955.

Sinclair, Andrew. *Prohibition: Era of Excess*. Boston: Little, Brown, 1962.

Slosson, Preston W. *The Great Crusade and After: 1914–1928*. New York: Macmillan Co., 1930.

Smith, Alfred E. *Let's Look at the Record*. New York: Thistle Press, n.d.

———. *Up To Now: An Autobiography*. New York: Viking, 1929.

Soule, George. *Prosperity Decade: From War to Depression, 1917–1929*. New York: Rinehart, 1947.

Stephenson, George M. *History of American Immigration, 1820–1924*. Boston: Ginn and Co., 1926.

Stone, Irving. *Clarence Darrow for the Defense*. New York: Doubleday, 1941.

Sullivan, Mark. *The Twenties*. Vol. VI of *Our Times: The United States, 1900–1925*. New York: Scribner's, 1935.

Sward, Keith. *The Legend of Henry Ford*. New York: Russell and Russell, 1968.

Voss, Carl Herman. *Rabbi and Minister: Friendship of Stephen S. Wise and John Haynes Holmes*. New York: World Publishing Co., 1934.

Waldman, Louis. *Albany: The Crisis in Government*. New York: Boni and Liveright, 1920.

———. *Labor Lawyer*. New York: Dutton, 1944.

Walworth, Arthur. *Woodrow Wilson*. 2nd ed. revised. Boston: Houghton Mifflin, 1965.

Weinstein, James K. *The Decline of Socialism in America: 1912–1925*. New York: Monthly Review Press, 1967.

Whitehead, Don. *The FBI Story: A Report to the People*. New York: Random House, 1956.

Whitney, Richard M. *Reds in America*. New York: Berkwith Press, 1924.

Articles and Periodicals

Advance. 1917–1920.

"A.F.L. Denounces the Communist Philosophy." *Commercial and Financial Chronicle,* October 24, 1925, p. 1997.

A.J.T. "Socialism A Benevolent Despotism." *The Outlook,* October 29, 1910, p. 517.

"Albany's Ousted Socialists." *The Literary Digest,* January 24, 1920, pp. 19–20.

"Alien and Sedition Bills of the 1920's." *The Literary Digest,* February 7, 1920, pp. 11–13.

"American Federation of Labor Denounces the Communist Philosophy." *Commercial and Financial Chronicle,* October 24, 1925, pp. 1997–98.

The American Federationist. 1914–1924.

"American Labor and Bolshevism." *The Literary Digest,* June 21, 1919, pp. 9–11.

"American Labor Unshaken." *American Federationist,* XXIX (August, 1922), 573–80.

The American Legion Weekly. 1920–1924.

"Americanism in New York." *Journal of Education,* LXXXIX (April 23, 1919), 382–83.

"Americanism and Socialism." *The Outlook,* June 13, 1917, pp. 245–46.

"The Anarchist Deportations." *The New Republic,* December 24, 1919, pp. 96–98.

"Anarchist Terrorism and the Need for Firmness in Dealing With It." *Commercial and Financial Chronicle,* June 7, 1919, pp. 2279–80.

"Are the Reds to Blame?" *Magazine of Wall Street,* October 16, 1920, pp. 839–40.

"Bishop Quigley's Attack on Socialism." *The Literary Digest,* January 12, 1902, p. 508.

Bloodgood, W. P. "After the War Problems Can be Solved by Cooperation." *American Federationist,* XXVI (January, 1919), 52–53.

"A Blue Day for the Reds." *The Literary Digest,* May 19, 1923. p. 12.

Blum, John M. "Nativism, Anti Radicalism, and the Foreign Scare, 1917–1920." *Midwest Journal,* III (Winter, 1950–51), 46–53.

"Bolshevism in New York and Russian Schools." *The Literary Digest,* July 5, 1919, pp. 40–41.

"Bombs." *The New Republic,* May 10, 1919, pp. 37–38.

The Brooklyn Eagle, 1914–1924, *passim.*

Brooklyn Standard-Union, 1914–1924, *passim.*

Brown, Rome G. "The Disloyalty of Socialism." *American Law Review,* LIII (September, 1919), 681 ff.

Bruere, Robert. "Industrial Workers of the World." *Harper's,* July, 1918, pp. 250–52.

Bryant, Louise. "Jim Larkin Goes to Prison." *The Liberator,* June 1, 1920, p. 1.

Buffalo Evening-News, 1914–1924, *passim.*

"Burleson and the Call." *The New Republic,* January 7, 1920, p. 158.

"By Stevenson Out of Lusk." *The New Republic,* June 15, 1921, pp. 64–66.

"Capitalism, Progressivism, Socialism." *Outlook,* September 7, 1912, pp. 15–17.

"Catholic Campaign Against Socialism." *The Literary Digest,* June 9, 1906, p. 875.

"The Church and Socialism." *The Arena,* September, 1908, p. 243.

Cline, Leonard. "The War on the Peace Seekers." *The New Republic,* July 2, 1924, pp. 149–50, and July 9, 1924, pp. 184–85.

Coben, Stanley. "A Study in Nativism: The American Red Scare of 1919–1920." *Political Science Quarterly,* LXXIX (March, 1964), 55–75.

Colonel Mayfield's Weekly. Houston, Texas, July 15, 1922.

Commager, Henry Steele. "Who is Loyal to America." *Harper's,* September, 1947, pp. 193–99.

The Communist, 1919–1924.

The Crisis, 1919–1920, *passim.*

"Current Topics and Notes." *American Law Review,* LIII (September, 1919), 429–32.

"Demoralized Schools: Extra Judicial Trial of Teachers in New York." *New Republic,* May 31, 1922, pp. 8–9.

"The Deportations." *Survey,* February 22, 1919, p. 722.

"Deporting the Communist Party." *The Literary Digest,* February 14, 1920, pp. 18–19.

"Deporting a Political Party." *New Republic,* January 14, 1920, p. 186.

"The Despotism of Organized Labor—The Tide has Turned." *Commercial and Financial Chronicle,* October 9, 1920, p. 1415.

"The Dismissal of Communist Teachers in New York City Schools." *School and Society,* X (November 22, 1919), pp. 605–606.

"Drastic Sedition Laws." *The Literary Digest,* January 24, 1920, p. 18.

Duker, Abraham G. "Socio-Psychological Trends in the American Jewish Community Since 1900." *Studies in American Jewish History and Culture,* IX. New York: Yiddish Scientific Institute, 1954.

Edgerton, Alice. "Individual Liberty in America." *The Nation,* October 11, 1919, pp. 494–95.

"Education from Albany." *The Nation,* May 8, 1920, p. 613.

Einziz, Paul. "Bolshevism and Banks." *Bankers Magazine,* October, 1920, pp. 580–84.

Eisenstein, Ira. "Should Jews Be Socialists." *The Reconstructionist,* I (May 3, 1935), 8–10.

"Ellis Island Gates Ajar." *The Literary Digest,* December 13, 1919, pp. 17–18.

"Extent of Bolshevism Here." *The Literary Digest,* January 17, 1920, pp. 13–15.

Ford, Lynn. "The Growing Menace of the IWW." *Forum,* January 1, 1919, pp. 62–70.

"Freedom of Opinion and the Clergy." *New Republic,* February 11, 1920, pp. 303–305.

"Freedom of Speech in the New York City Schools." *School and Society,* IX (February 8, 1919), 178.

Gannett, Louis S. "The Socialist Trial at Albany: A Summary." *The Nation,* March 20, 1920, pp. 361–63.

Giovanitti, Arturo. "Communists on Trial." *The Liberator,* March, 1920, pp. 1–8.

"The Gitlow Case." *New Republic,* July 1, 1925, pp. 141–42.

Goldstein, Max. "Outlook for Russian Bonds." *Magazine of Wall Street,* July, 1919, pp. 568–70.

Gompers, Samuel. "Labor's Protest Against Rampant Tragedy." *American Federationist,* XXVII (June, 1920), 521–32.

Griffin, Henry Farrand. "The Rising Tide of Socialism." *The Outlook,* February 24, 1912, pp. 438–48.

Guggenheim, S. R. "Peace Will Bring Great Industrial Activity." *The Magazine of Wall Street,* March 15, 1919, pp. 1064–66.

Hale, Swinburne. Letter to the Editor. *The New Republic,* January 28, 1920, p. 270.

Hapgood, Norman. "Liberal or Reactionary." *American Federationist,* XXVII (November, 1920), 1003.

Herrick, Robert. Letter to the Editor. *The New Republic,* February 8, 1920, p. 355.

Howard, Sidney. "Baiting the Bolshevist." *Collier's,* January 10, 1920, p. 15.

————. "Our Professional Patriots." *The New Republic,* August 20, September 3, 10, 17, 24, October 15, 1924, *passim.*

"Immigration and Labor Problems." *Magazine of Wall Street,* February 7, 1920, pp. 441–42.

Industry. 1918–1920.

Irwin, Will. "Patriotism That Pays." *The Nation,* November 12, 1924, pp. 513–16.

Johnston, Frank. "Religious and Racial Prejudices in the United States." *Current History,* XX (July, 1924), 573–78.

Jones, George D. "Why I Am Not A Socialist." *The Arena,* January, 1907, pp. 274–75.

"Justice for Alien Reds: Policy of Louis F. Post." *The Literary Digest,* May 22, 1920, p. 25.

Karsner, David. "The Passing of the Socialist Party." *Current History,* XX (June, 1924), 402–407.

Keir, Malcolm. "Scientific Management and Socialism." *Scientific Monthly,* V (October, 1917), 359–67.

Knoles, T. C. "Labor and Radicalism." *Commercial and Financial Chronicle,* October 29, 1921, pp. 146–49.

"Labor's Attitude Toward Red Agitators." *The Literary Digest,* March 20, 1920, pp. 21–23.

Levine, Louis. "Development of Syndicalism in America." *Political Science Quarterly,* XXVIII, No. 3 (1913), 451–79.

The Liberator. 1919–1921.

Lockwood, W. S. "Can Advertising Stop Bomb Outrages?" *Printers Ink,* September 30, 1920, pp. 73–76.

London, Meyer. "The Promise of Great Russia." *The Ladies Garment Worker,* February, 1918, pp. 11–12.

Lusk, Clayton R. "Radicalism Under Inquiry." *Review of Reviews,* February, 1920, pp. 167–71.

Maurer, James H. "Produce More—What For?" *Printers Ink,* August 26, 1920, pp. 129–30.

"Meeting Radical Propaganda With Reason." *Printers Ink,* August 26, 1920, p. 129 ff.

The Messenger, 1919.

Miller, C. R. "Why Socialism Is Impractical." *Century,* April, 1910, pp. 903–908.

Mitchell, John B. "Reds in the New York Slums." *Forum and Century,* April, 1919, pp. 442–55.

"The Mob in High Places." *The New Republic,* February 4, 1920, pp. 279–81.

"Mooney Trial." *The New Republic,* May 19, 1919, p. 52.

"Mr. Gompers and His Doctrines—Where They Lead To?" *Commercial and Financial Chronicle,* October 23, 1920, p. 1608.

The Nation. 1914–1924, *passim.*

National Civic Federation. *Declaration Against the Recognition of Soviet Russia,* March 29, 1920. New York: By the Federation, 1920.

The New Age. 1917–1923, *passim.*

The New Republic. 1914–1924, *passim.*

New York Call. 1914–1924, *passim.*

"New York Chamber of Commerce Describes the Wall Street Explosion as an Act of War." *Commercial and Financial Chronicle,* October 16, 1920, p. 1526.

New York Communist. 1919–20.

New York Herald. 1914–1924, *passim.*

New York Sun. 1914–1924, *passim.*

New York Times. 1914–1924.

New York World. 1914–1924, *passim.*

"New York's Disloyal Teachers." *The Literary Digest,* December 8, 1917, p. 733.

O'Neal, James. "The Changing Fortunes of American Socialism." *Current History,* XX (April, 1924), 92–97.

Oppenheimer, Francis J. "Immigration: Dark Horse or White Elephant." *Wall Street Magazine,* May 1, 1920, pp. 957 ff.

Palmer, A. Mitchell. "The Case Against the Reds." *Forum,* February, 1920, pp. 173–85.

Persons, Frank. "The Truth at the Heart of Capitalism and Socialism." *Arena,* January, 1907, pp. 7–10.

Poole, Ernest. "Abraham Cahan—Socialist Journalist: Friend of the Ghetto." *The Outlook,* October 28, 1911, pp. 467–78.

Powers, F. P. "Feminism and Socialism." *Unpopular Review,* January 1915, pp. 118–33.

"The Progress of the World." *Review of Reviews,* February, 1920, p. 128.

"Promoters of Agitation and Unrest." *Industry,* June 15, 1919, p. 3.

Putnam, Emily Hames. Letter to the Editor. *The New Republic,* February 4, 1920, p. 294.

"Putting the Three R's to Work." *The American Legion Weekly,* January 16, 1920, p. 5.

"Radicalism in the Churches." *Industry,* June 15, 1919, pp. 10–11.

The Rebel Worker. 1918–1919.

"The Resuscitation of Liberty." *The Nation,* October 25, 1919, p. 539.

Rittenberg, Louis. "Exploding Another Myth." *American Hebrew and Jewish Tribune,* August 17, 1934, p. 2.

Seligman, Herbert J. "The Press Abets the Mob." *The Nation,* October 4, 1919, pp. 460–61.

"Shipping Lenin's Friends to Him." *The Literary Digest,* January 3, 1920, pp. 14–15.

"Skimming the Melting Pot." *The Literary Digest,* March 1, 1919, p. 16.

"Social Unrest." *Magazine of Wall Street,* March 19, 1921, p. 694.

"Socialism in the New York Campaign." *The Outlook,* November 3, 1906, pp. 541–42.

"Socialism on Trial at Albany." *The Literary Digest,* February 7, 1920, pp. 14–15.

"The Socialist as Patriot." *The Literary Digest,* June 16, 1917, pp. 1836–37.

Solomon, Charles, *et al.* "The Unforgettable Meyer London." *The Workmen's Circle Call,* July, 1951, pp. 4–5.

"The State Constabulary: Why Is It Opposed?" *Industry,* August 15, 1919, pp. 12–13.

"The Supreme Court and the Gitlow Decision." *The Christian Century,* June 25, 1925, p. 818.

Sutherland, Sidney. "The Mystery of the Wall Street Explosion."
    Liberty, April 26, 1930, pp. 48–56.
Swisher, Carl B. "Civil Liberties in Wartime." *Political Science
    Quarterly,* LV (September, 1940), pp. 321–47.
Syracuse Post-Standard. 1914–1924, *passim.*
The Tablet. 1919–1922.
Taylor, Graham. "The Bolshevism of Professor Ward." *Survey,*
    March 29, 1919, pp. 920–21.
"Teaching Disloyalty in American Colleges." *Industry,* March 15,
    1919, pp. 10–11.
Tipper, H. "How to Check the Radical in Labor Circles." *Auto-
    motive Industries,* XLI (October 9, 1919), 736–37.
"Trial of New York City Teachers." *School and Society,* VI
    (December 8, 1917), 674–75.
"The Truth About Soviet Russia and Bolshevism." *American
    Federationist,* XXVII (March, 1920), 254.
"Un-Americanism in Public Schools." *Industry,* April 15, 1919,
    pp. 12–14.
Vadney, Thomas E. "The Politics of Repression: A Case Study
    of the Red Scare in New York." *New York History,* IL
    (January, 1968), 56–75.
Veblen, Thorstein. "Bolshevism: A Menace to Whom?" *The
    Dial,* February 22, 1919, pp. 174–79.
Wall Street Journal. 1914–1924, *passim.*
"The Way to Unconstitute Authority." *The New Republic,*
    February 11, 1920, pp. 306–309.
"What is Americanism." *American Journal of Sociology,* XX,
    No. 4 (January, 1915), 433–86.
"What is Back of the Bombs?" *The Literary Digest,* June 14,
    1919, pp. 9–11.
"What Thinking Men Are Saying." *Wall Street Magazine,* Feb-
    ruary 7, 1920, p. 445.
Whittlesey, W. L. "Where Do the Reds Come From." *American
    Legion Weekly,* January 30, 1920, pp. 12–13.
"William Z. Foster." *The New Republic,* January 7, 1920, pp.
    163–66.
Woll, Matthew. "The Thing Called Bolshevism." *American
    Federationist,* XXVI (March, 1919), 236.

INDEX

262

264

INDEX

Lunn, George R., 20, 22, 23, 27
Lusk Committee, 31, 106, 119-141, 204

Magnes, Judah L., 90, 127, 135, 220
Malone, Dudley Field, 90, 127
Marshall, Louis, 152, 174
Martens, Ludwig, 123, 187-188
Masses, 14, 58, 62
Merrill, Herbert, 23
Messenger, 95
Methodist Federation for Social Service, 92
Mitchell, John Purroy, 39, 44, 70
Mooney, Tom, 81
Morgan, J. P., 88, 226, 230
Murray, Robert K., 4
Muzzey, David S., 16, 105

National Civic Federation, 228-229
National Civil Liberties Bureau, *see* American Civil Liberties Union
National Security League, 1, 229-230
Nearing, Scott, 57, 83, 114
Nelles, Walter, 55, 153, 170, 192
New Age, 63
New Republic, 62
New York Call, 11, 14, 62, 90
Norris, George W., 48

O'Hare, Kate Richards, 68
O'Reilly, Leonora, 51
Orr, Samuel, 58, 144-167
Overman Committee, 119, 172-174
Owens, Chandler, 83, 95

Palmer, A. Mitchell, 88, 93, 174-196, 216, 222, 226
Panken, Jacob, 24, 71, 83
Pearson's Magazine, 47
Perkins, George W., 230
Pierce, Clinton H., 59

Poole, Ernest, 11
Post, Louis F., 218
Preston, William, 36

Quinlan, Patrick L., 28

Rand, Carrie D., 15
Rand School, 15, 31; raided by mob, 91; Lusk Committee, 127-130
Randolph, A. Philip, 83, 95
Rebel Voice, 66
Red flag, 80-82
Reed, John, 14, 52, 58, 101, 115
Revolutionary Age, 199
Rockefeller, John D., 88, 230
Rockefeller, John D., Jr., 40-41
Roe, Gilbert, 110, 127, 153
Roosevelt, Franklin D., 91-92
Roosevelt, Theodore, 24, 48, 105
Russell, Charles Edward, 11, 14, 19, 46, 47
Russell, Bertrand, 58
Ruthenberg, Charles, 101, 205-208
Ryan, John A., 229

St. John, Vincent, 25, 66
St. Louis Declaration, 2, 47
Salsedo, Marie, 223
Schlossberg, Joseph, 29-30, 64, 83
Sedition Act, 2, 54
Seidel, Emil, 19
Shiplacoff, Abraham L., 50, 58, 221
Simons, A. M., 47, 114
Sinclair, Upton, 14, 16, 42, 43, 47, 61
Slobodkin, Henry, 18
Smith, Alfred E., 73, 82, 174, 209, 210-211; vetoes Lusk bills, 137-139; pardons Communists, 213
Socialist Party, 1-2, 8-24, 99-101
Solomon, Charles, 83, 121, 144-167